for She ... with love, [signature] *(handwritten inscription)*

Turn My Head to the Caucasus
The Biography of Osman Ferid Pasha

AYDIN OSMAN ERKAN

© Çitlembik / Nettleberry Publications, 2009
© Aydın Osman Erkan's inheritors, 2009
Visual materials on the cover and in the book
© Kim Joan Erkan, 2009

Library of Congress Cataloging-in-Publication Data

Erkan, Aydın Osman 1932-1998
     Turn my head to the Caucasus/Aydın Osman Erkan
İstanbul: Çitlembik Publications, 2009.
288 p.; 14x21 cm

ISBN: 978-9944-424-64-6

1.Caucasus–History. 2.Caucasus–Biography.
3.Caucasus–Description and travel. 4.Circassians–Biography.
I. Title.

LC: DK509.E75 2009   DC: 947.9

Editor: Nancy Öztürk
Layout: Çiğdem Dilbaz

Printed at Mart Matbaacılık Sanatları
Mart Plaza, Merkez Mah. Ceylan Sok.
No: 24 Nurtepe, Istanbul

In Turkey:
Şehbender Sokak 18/4
Asmalımescit - Tünel
34430 Istanbul
www.citlembik.com.tr

In the USA:
Nettleberry LLC
44030 123rd St.
Eden, South Dakota 57232
www.nettleberry.com

Turn My Head to the Caucasus

The Biography of Osman Ferid Pasha

AYDIN OSMAN ERKAN

Çitlembik Publications 155

OSMAN FERID PASHA:
1st. FERIK SHEIKH-UL-HARAM
GUARDIAN OF THE HOLY SHRINE OF MEDINA,
PROTECTOR AND KEEPER OF THE PROPHET'S TOMB,
AIDE-DE-CAMP TO SULTAN ABDÜLAZIZ,
GENERAL OF THE IMPERIAL OTTOMAN ARMY.

For my daughters Ceylan and Rana
And grandchildren, Alican, Emrecan and Selina...

Contents

INTRODUCTION

The Caucasus has been a region of romance and mystery from the earliest times. Its inhabitants existed as a nation, scattered into tribes split by deep ravines and high snow-peaked mountains. When they were exiled by the Russians, Circassians never lost their uniquely rich and variegated inheritance, with its traditions and characteristics which set them apart from other nations. Their story survived in tales and legends of their forefathers and their famed leader, Imam Shamil, whose long struggle against the might of Imperial Russia was one of the most romantic episodes in the history of the world.

These stories were handed down from one generation to another. I grew up in a Caucasian family proud to share the glories and tragedies of their ancestors with its younger generation. As children we were told stories and anecdotes of our family and the Caucasus by our aunts and uncles and Osman Ferid's wife, Nefiset, my grandmother. I am indebted to them for relating the adventures and events of my Caucasian ancestors, perhaps romanticized, perhaps exaggerated but with such imagination, patience and enthusiasm it left a deep imprint in my mind and heart.

Most weekends were spent at the Beşiktaş Konak [mansion], visiting my father's mother, Nefiset Hanım, his brothers and sisters. I remember her as small, slim, and rather severe-looking but exceptionally kind and gentle. After lunch, while the grown-ups drank coffee in the sitting-room, we raced upstairs, waiting for grandma to open her treasure chest and bring out a precious heirloom, a sets of photographs, an ivory kinjal, a dagger or sword or a medal encrusted with precious stones or some old papers, each one with a story which Grandma told in her quiet, dramatic voice. Hood Lala, big and ebony black, sat on a wooden chair in front of the konak door in the summer when he was not attending Grandma. He told me he had been a poor Nubian slave until Ghazi Pasha bought him and his mother from a slave market in Arabia and treated them as part of the family. He was devoted to Nefiset hanım and was never far from her side.

My dear Uncle Şamil was everyone's favourite; he was extremely polite and elegant, the perfect gentleman admired for his English taste in fashion. A wonderful story-teller, his description of Shamil's battles and life with his father and grandfather were so vivid and compelling that we adored him. He taught us to fence in the large games room and to use a bow and arrow. In the summer he set up shooting targets in the garden and built a tennis court.

Uncle Şamil never married, but loved children and was more than happy to spend time with us. Uncle Bekir was the handsome debonair man-about-town, shocking us with stories of romantic escapades with exiled princesses in Paris and Geneva, which I learned later were true!

My father was serious and authoritative. He entertained his Caucasian friends at our summer house in Büyükdere on the Bosphorus, allowing us to join them on condition we were well-behaved. He recorded tapes of his life in Arabia and Mytilene. He was proud of his Caucasian background and set the same high standards of honesty and loyalty within his own family. On my birthday I received small family heirloom, a dagger, pocket-knife, book or medal from my aunts, Saadet, Habibe, Safiye and Zübeyde, elegant, educated ladies of the new Republic.

Saadet, her son, Inal, Habibe and Safiye, Bekir, his wife,

Fatma and daughter Bedia continued to live at the *Konak* until it was sold. Inal and I spent our childhood playing among the broken, dusty relics of the past grandeur of the konak at Beşiktaş.

Later I realized the family's private letters, personal papers and faded photographs, part of which I inherited, were not just a jumble of memoirs and mementoes, but the story of a family caught in the upheaval and exodus of the North-Caucasus war and the last critical period as the Ottoman Empire passed into history and emerged as the state of Turkey. I decided to write a biographic novel of my grandfather, Osman Ferid Pasha.

I wish to thank the late Rosemary Baldwin for her encouragement and sincere interest in my family history. Finally to my wife Kim, I am deeply grateful for her tireless effort, contribution and outstanding help.

I make no claim to historical correctness or scholarship, but have attempted, whenever possible, to check my sources to ensure that what I have written is factually correct. I have kept the names of places most frequently used by the family; they referred to the country, at that time, as Ottoman rather than Turkey, Constantinople rather than Istanbul or Stambul and Scutari for Kadikoy.*

My grandfather's papers were partly destroyed by flooding in the basement of the Beşiktaş konak. When Aunt Zübeyde married an Egyptian ambassador she also took many of her father's personal belongings, books, papers to Egypt. This is the story of my grandfather as I remember him from photographs and conversations we enjoyed at the crumbling Beşiktaş konak with my parents, aunts and uncles, all members of an exceptional family.

Aydın Osman Erkan. Beşiktaş, March, 1989

---

* Although during this period place names were used interchangebly, "Istanbul" has been used throughout.

ACKNOWLEDGEMENTS

Aydın wrote this book in English. I would like to thank Laurence and Linda Kelly for the friendship and encouragement they showed to my late husband. Linda was the first to read and discuss the manuscript with him. In Aydın's large collection of valuable titles on the Caucasus, most of the books contain letters carefully folded and preserved from his dear friend, Laurence. Many friends have generously given their time and support. I am profoundly grateful to Steven Richmond for sharing his historical knowledge, to Murat Papşu for correcting Caucasian names, spellings and events, to Janita Şadalak and Can Zulfikar, to Güniz Büyüktür for her sensitive translation of the Turkish volume and special thanks to my publishers Nancy and Zarife Öztürk at Çitlembik for their enthusiasm and helpful suggestions.

That the book is finally published is due to my daughter Rana and her husband Erol Tabanca. Above all, I wish to express my profound appreciation for their unfailing support, encouragement and love without which Aydın's manuscript would not have been realized. I owe them both a debt of gratitude.

Kim Erkan

Part One
Circassia (1844-1864)

Oh the wild people who live in these countries,
Whose God is freedom and whose law is warfare,
Where friendship is strong and revenge is stronger
These feelings are inflicted on them by their Lords in the sky.
They answer goodness with good and evil with equal evil,
And for them hatred is as eternal as love.

–Lermontov from his book Ismael Bey

Chapter 1

A Warrior is Born

The autumn of 1844 in the Caucasus was remembered as mild and pleasant by the mountaineers who inhabited its remote, unspoiled domain wreathed in clouds and mist, a land of harsh, forbidding winters with gales and thunderstorms, its mountain peaks hidden by eternal snows. That autumn the wind softened the air allowing the sun to burst through its mist and floating caps of clouds to reveal glittering white, snowy peaks holding up the sky. Far, far below the rocky cliffs, thundering waterfalls, primeval forests and valleys, the waves of the Black Sea spilled softly over the golden sands of Sochi Bay. Weather-wise and superstitious, old highlanders scattered in aouls and villages under the mountain's shadow believed Thae, the great god of the mountains, had commanded the elements to be kind.

A lone figure on a grey stallion rode slowly through the long, meadow grasses into the forest at the foothills of the mountains. He bent low as his horse made its way through the dense undergrowth, painfully brushing aside the branches and foliage with his bloodied arm. Tall and lean, a black, unkempt beard shadowed his lined face, he strained his eyes for signs of the bridle path that would lead him to the camp nestled deep in the forest. Every movement sent a searing pain through his right side; his body ached after hours in the saddle yet he still appeared ferocious and defiant in his papakha wool hat and Tcherkesska bourka, a black, hairy cape with pointed shoulders fastened at the neck hanging tent-like over the knees. Under the bourka he carried a double-edged dagger, a silver-sheathed ivory kinjal, and a sword attached to his belt; a loaded rifle was slung carelessly over his shoulder. It was the dress of a Caucasian warrior.

Shapli Bereketuko Hasan was an Ubykh chieftain returning home from a bloody skirmish against the Russians. This time casualties had been high with many badly wounded. He had lost eight of his most stalwart warriors, including his closest companion and friend, Osman.

He had ordered his men to rest and care for the wounded before beginning the arduous journey back to camp while he, although exhausted and in pain, rode ahead praying, he would be in time for the birth of his second child.

Sighting the narrow opening hidden behind a bush of thick brambles, he reined his horse to a halt. Far below in the distance valley he recognized the deserted village nestling amongst the vivid, rolling green hills. It was the Shapli aoul, home to the Shapli tribe for decades. Now a scene of destruction, it had been torched into a shambles of smouldering wood and stone under collapsed roofs, with the doors of the emptied outbuildings and barns swinging on broken hinges.

Since the beginning of time, life amongst the towering Caucasus Mountains had been a struggle for survival against assailants and aggressors hostile to the Caucasian traditional homogeneous culture and way of life. The mountaineers, cursed by decades of guerrilla warfare, touched with a bitter taste for revenge, had kept invaders at bay by fiercely defending their territory through freezing blizzards, storms and gales, in forests, highlands and lowlands.

Fired by a gallant spirit and superb mountain strategy, Caucasian mountaineers, for whom danger was a spur to courage, for the first time faced the possibility of defeat against the powerful aggression and persecution of the Russian Empire.

Hasan dismounted wearily, leaning against a rock as he gazed at the wreckage of his beloved aoul. He remembered the sweet smell of the juniper trees, orchards of fruit and flowering trees, and filling baskets of luscious grapes from the vineyards that covered the hills, as children played and climbed trees. His head and body ached. He was tired, fatigued from fighting, from seeing his men and loved ones killed mercilessly. He gave a deep sigh; his face grimaced. It was fate, the fate of Circassia, he thought, recalling a proverb learned at school and often repeated by teachers:

"When shall blood cease to flow in the mountains of the Caucasus?"

"When sugar canes grow in the snow," shouted the children.

Tarry a while my impatient horse
Let me look back again
Let me look again at my native aoul
For my heart is full of pain.

Fly onward, my horse, and never look back
For surely this isn't the end;
Many aouls await us ahead
Where we will find both brother and friend.

(*My Daghestan* by Rasul Gamzatov)

As chief of the Ubykh tribe, Hasan's duty was to lead and safeguard his people in their freedom fight against persistent Russian threats, a commitment, in honour bound, handed down from father to son. Circassians revered, even elevated the heroic bravery of thousands of warriors who had charged, sword in hand, against the might and power of the Russian army. Hasan held the same respect and sang their praises, but he longed for peace for his people and family. He realized the futility of war and wanted it to end, but he knew it was not to be; it was not his decision. His destiny was to fight for the cause, hopeless though it might be. The only solace in his anguished heart was the burning hatred every Caucasian bore for their eternal enemy, Russia.

The Caucasus is an extraordinary world of mountains, of extremes, as breathtakingly beautiful as it is cruel. With a history of vengeance and violence, it is peopled with brave, sometimes ruthless, tribesmen. As much as they fought, they loved, for they were wild romantics at heart, poets who wrote love songs and poems to their women, daggers, swords and horses. Their unique, ethnic diversity was formed by the environment: a landscape of forbidding mountains, steppes and deep ravines where life and death was a daily diet of extremes. Caucasian mountaineers were an exceptional race, handsome, resilient and wildly courageous. They reflected qualities evolved over centuries of survival in a harsh, unbending environment where glory, honour and family traditions formed the foundation of their very existence.

Ubykhs, who inhabited land around the Black Sea coast from the Shakhe River to the Khosta Khamysh River and inland as far as the Caucasus mountain chain in the east, were a large tribe numbering forty to fifty thousand. Except for minor territorial skirmishes and tribal attacks, it was not until 1830 that the Ubykhs were drawn into the greater conflict with the Russians. The Adrianople Treaty, signed by the Ottoman government in 1829, ceded all rights of the Black Sea coastal area of the Caucasus to Tsar Nicholas I of Russia. The Tsar, who firmly believed the Caucasus should be an integral part of the Russian Empire, viewed this treaty as an invitation for the Russian conquest of the Western Caucasus. He lost no time in ordering a force of two thousand infantry and cavalry called 'The Abkhazian Expedition' to occupy the Abkhazian coast, establishing direct land communications between Sukhum and

Anapo. From Sukhum, a mission set sail by sea for a landing operation in Gagry while patrolling the coast from Sukhum to Anapo. The Ubykhs were left with no choice but to join the rest of the country in full-scale battle against the Russian army.

Despite being severely wounded three times, Chief Hasan led his men in a series of raids; most were successful but at times he and his men were forced to make a hasty withdrawal. These continual onslaughts, unexpected ambushes and raids forced Russian commanders to postpone their plans to expand with the steady movement of troops into the interior and then to regroup so as to defend garrisons and fortifications in Golovinskae, Navsginskar and Svyatoidukh along the coast.

The Shapli family occupied a large aoul in the lush Sochi valley in the Ubykhb province. Surrounded by rolling hills, sealed by a barrier of dense jungle forest and thick undergrowth, it was protected by high mountains in the north. A river meandered through the valley, watering its rich meadows and orchards of fruit trees, apples, pears, and walnut. Chestnut and oak trees grew to gigantic heights. The western side of the hill was covered with vineyards whose succulent grapes were enjoyed by the inhabitants of the hillside hamlets.

Hasan feared the entrance to the aoul would be discovered by Russian convoys. Lacking sufficient arms or heavy weapons to defend the village, he decided to move the tribe deeper into the forest to a safe camp. The sites of these safe camps were predetermined for maximum security; they were usually well-equipped, stocked with dried foods, waterholes, clothing and weapons, allowing women, children and the aged to survive in safety from the Russian offensives, which after the erection of beachhead strongholds and military forts at Sochi Bay had become more threatening.

By the time Hasan reached camp, darkness had fallen. A man crouching near the camp entrance rose peering into the darkness at the sound of horse's hooves. It must be Chief Hasan, he thought, running to meet him.

"Welcome Sire, good news, you have a son, a healthy boy, Sire."

It was Akhmet, Hasan's faithful servant who guarded the Shapli family with his life. He grabbed the reins of the sweating horse as Hasan dismounted.

"Thank God, thank Thae. Take my horse, Akhmet, feed him well and brush him down.

"Yes, Sire, congratulations Sire and Thae bless you."

Akhmet's lined face broke into a wide grin as he led the horse to the stables. Hasan removed his bourka, clenched his teeth, willing himself to overcome the throbbing pain in his side before walking towards a cottage lit by a dim light from an oil lamp swinging from the porch. His sister, holding his two-year old daughter, Zissi, in her arms, rose to greet him.

"Congratulations, Brother, you have a son," she beamed with delight.

After embracing and kissing, he entered his wife's bedroom. Kudenet lay with the baby by her side. She opened her eyes, smiling when she saw her husband.

"Shapli Berektuko Hasan, you have a healthy son."

As he sat on the bed next to her, he suddenly felt weak. Overcome by emotion, he cupped her face in his hands, gently kissing her forehead, cheeks and lips, choking back tears of joy and relief. For weeks he had been consumed with fear and had prayed for her safety and well-being in this make-shift camp. Gently he stroked his son's head. Kudenet had suffered a difficult pregnancy; alone with her sister-in-law and small daughter, she had supervised the move into the forest, bringing a semblance of normality into the lives of the villagers in her care. Rough cottages were repaired; a safe study and play area was cleaned for the children and look-out posts for guards who patrolled the compound day and night on the alert for strangers or Russians were built and reinforced. In the case of an attack, an escape route further up the mountain had been cleared. Caucasian women were as courageous and resilient as their menfolk. Hasan leaned over to kiss his wife; she smelt warm and soft. He hungered to hold her in his arms, hungered for her gentle touch and sweet words.

Caucasian women are famed for their dark, mysterious beauty.

"So moved on earth Circassia's daughter,
The lovliest bird of Franguestan."

(from *The Giaour* by Lord Byron)

Kudenet was no exception. Her thick, black hair—usually plaited and hung with braids of gold and silver coins under a silk kerchief wound around her head—now hung loose over her shoulders, framing her delicate, white face with its high cheek bones, straight nose and large brown eyes. Women played an important role in this patriarchal society. Never overshadowed by their men folk, they were proud and courageous, prepared to fight side by side with their brothers and husbands. According to an old Circassian custom, boys were given their first taste of solid food on the tip of a sword with a prayer for long life, but should death befall them, the mother prayed it be by the sword in battle, fighting for his country.

Young men of Circassia rush forth to the battle
For brave youths always love war
If ye fall, ye become martyrs
And if ye survive ye have half that glory.

—19th century Circassian war song

Mothers were responsible for the care for their sons until the age of ten when they were supervised by warrior guardians, while they and their daughters turned their attention to the aoul, worked in the fields and prepared their husbands for war. They were active, independent and respected in society. Caucasian women were slim and tall; they moved with the smooth grace of a gazelle. Their narrow waists were shaped by a tight corset worn from the age of ten until their marriage, usually at fifteen. The prerogative of cutting the strings of the bride's corset was given to the groom. Women delighted in displaying their slim silhouette in attractive, loose, flowered silk trousers under a full skirted, tight-waisted robe with silver braided fastenings and wide flowing sleeves. Proud of their beauty, they took pains to prepare for important tribal occasions such as presentations, weddings, funerals and gatherings. While the colour and intricate details of a costume signified the rank of the woman within the community, every woman wore a belt of ivory or gold niello with a decorated dagger around her waist, a dagger she would not hesitate to use.

"I know how to use a dagger; I was born in the Caucasus," wrote Pushkin, the Russian writer, about Circassian women.

Kudenet was a confident, lively woman, deeply in love with her husband and devoted to her family. She and Hasan had been inseparable since childhood. Their wedding celebration had lasted three days and three nights, attended by princes, nobles and tribal chiefs from far and wide. They spent their time galloping out of the aoul towards the mountains, laughing, urging the horses faster, drunk with love and youthful energy. Kudenet was radiant, her cheeks pink and her hair hanging loose under a thin veil. She was his wife, lover, friend and confidant.

Had she not been pregnant, she would have followed Hasan and his warriors; instead she had taken charge of the move to the camp. Each day, as she went about her chores, she too had prayed for the birth of a healthy son and her husband's safe return.

Hasan's sister dressed his wounds with poultices of herbs and balms before he fell into an exhausted sleep. In the morning, refreshed and bathed, he rushed to his wife's room. Taking the baby in his arms, his handsome face creased with smiles of joy and happiness for the first time in weeks, he announced,

"I thank Thae for my son. He shall be called Osman Ferid after my bravest and closest comrades in arms, Osman and Ferid, who died in battle fighting so that my son and all the sons in the Caucasus might live in freedom. I name you, Shapli Osman Ferid."

In the distance the sound of Russian cannons bombarding Circassian posts could be heard echoing through the valley, a seemly gun salute for the birth of the tiny Uybhk warrior.

The Caucusus has no frontiers; its ice-capped mountains are woven into a chain that separates west from east, stretching for 1,100 miles. This is a land of steep slopes and ice-caped mountain barriers, losing height to rainy plains as it stretches from the Black Sea in the northwest to the Apsheron peninsula in the Caspian Sea in the southeast. On the south side is Transcaucasus, in the north, the North Caucasus. The immense height and wilderness of its great snowy mountain ranges, valleys, furious rivers that cut gorges thousands of feet deep and its vast forests made the Caucasus a refuge for man long before recorded history.

The splendour and magnificence of the snow-capped mountain ranges often called Allah's Mountains, coupled with the romantic, brave exploits of its inhabitants, inspired poets and writers such as Pushkin, Lermontov, Tolstoy and Gorky to write about its beauty and legends. According to one Caucasian legend, God, after creating the world, decided it was too flat, so he made snow-capped mountains and green hills, put them into a large sack to scatter over the earth. Seeing this, the devil became jealous. Not wanting man to possess such beauty, he seized the first opportunity to slit the sack with a knife. At that moment the Creator was passing between the Black Sea and the Caspian Sea. The mountains and hills tumbled out of the sky to form the magnificent chain stretching from shore to shore making the Caucasus the most beautiful land in the world.

In *Letters from the Caucasus and Georgia*, a travelogue written by Mr and Mrs W. F. von Freygan, Mrs. von Freygeng wrote in a letter from Wladi-Caucasus on Nov 8, 1811:

"It is almost impossible to ascertain with accuracy the height of these mountains their tops being for most part hidden in the clouds; while torrents, precipices, and avalanches render them frequently inaccessible. The principal mountains contain everlasting glaciers; and, in other places, their granite crags stand quite bare. Some of the hills have, as one may say, several storeys; the basement being clothed with forests, the centre destitute of all vegetation, and their summits generally covered with ice and snow. Upon the hills of less elevation, which are of slate, vegetation shows itself already; and one notices some birch, pine and juniper trees and other Alpine plants...

"According to accurate estimates, it is said that the Caucasus is inhabited by nearly a million of men fit to bear arms; making an immense population, when you add the aged, the women and children. These people form many tribes, speaking diverse languages and their manners are distinct; but their general character is bravery, a spirit of independence, independent in heart as in mind, a passion for arms the necessity of being constantly on their guard has confirmed their natural inclination for warfare."

The Caucasus, a vast tangle of mountains and valleys bordering Persia, Turkey and Russia, was home to many indigenous tribes. The people of North Caucasus, Daghestan, Chechnya and Circassia came from different ethnic backgrounds and spoke different languages; any cultural similarities were the result of occupying the same land. The Shapsugh, Ubykhs and Abhaz of the south were ethnically related and shared a similar language. Since the nineteenth century it was known that Ubykhs spoke at least two languages— Ubykh and Abzeh, and many were also fluent in Abazaca. They lived in independent city states like the ancient Greek 'polis,' preserving their own customs and languages. Arabs call the Caucasus "the mountain of languages." Pliny, the famous Greek writer, wrote:

"We conducted our affairs there with the aid of one hundred and thirty interpreters."

Caucasian mountaineers were fiercely attached, and spiritually bound to the land of their ancestors. The spell of its haunting magnificence was shared by travellers who crossed its wild, desolate ranges. They too felt the same personal desire to preserve its breathtaking, utterly unspoiled beauty.

The highlanders were known to be superstitious with animistic beliefs. They believed mountains possessed guardian spirits and powers, whose voices and omens were expressed in fast flowing rivers, clear streams, shooting stars or wind as it whistled through the leaves of gigantic trees, horses' hooves in the night, in the jabbering of the village idiot or the natural elements, stormy winds, rain and thunder, waterfalls and cloud formations. For centuries, Caucasians protected their inheritance with pride, believing the mountains to be sacred, never to be forsaken. Their strong sense of identity, culture and tradition made them as intuitive, mystical, melancholy and impulsive as their surroundings. Cloaked in the myths and mystery of the mountains, Caucasians thrived on haunting tales of wondrous sagas and poetic love.

Circassians lived in the Caucasus long before classical antiquity. It is said their heredity goes back to the ancient Cimmerians – ancestors of the Celts. Ancient Greek and Roman writers wrote about Ceretae, Heniochae, Maeotae, Sindi Zichi or Zighi, ancestors of Circassian tribes.

German writer, F M von Bodenstedt, wrote in 1848,

"The origins of the Circassian lie in the most distant times, their knightly sentiments, their manners of patriarchal purity, their strikingly comely traits place them indisputably in the first rank of the free peoples of Caucasia."

Besides their remarkable physical beauty, Circassians practised a uniquely chivalrous lifestyle. As a race surviving in one of the remotest corners of the world, their civic sense was quite remarkable. They were talented artisans, expert horsemen, and skilful warriors; morality and loyalty to family and tribal structure were above question. Their social structure was extraordinary for a community divided into tribal states. Known for their high moral standards and good manners, elders and womenfolk were afforded great respect. Crime was rare, punishment severe. Strangers were welcomed with kind, simple hospitality; they were the mountaineers' life-line to the outside world. A visitor was part of the brotherhood of Muslims, where all were equal under Allah. In the mountains a guest became part of the family for the duration of their stay, pampered and protected.

Circassia was a land of contrasts with the appearance of a democratic state populated by a race of handsome, wild warriors.

They had fought against the Russian Empire since 1760, now more than a century later it was, a noble struggle of a mere two million people against the imperial power of one of the strongest countries in the world. Never in the history of mankind has such an unequal struggle lasted for such a length of time.

In his will, Tsar Peter Alexandrovich, Peter the Great, wrote of his ambition to expand Russia's boundaries north and south by the conquest of Circassia towards the vast Baltic and Black Sea coasts. Russia needed these coveted harbours to strengthen its sea power, build shipyards and ships for the execution of its grand plan, a waterway to the Mediterranean, Istanbul and India.

At first International foreign powers were indifferent to Russia's conquest of Kazan and Astrakhan and its claim over the right banks of the Kuban river comfirmed by the 1791 Peace Treaty, but as the mighty Russian army marched towards Northern Caucasus, European political leaders, aware of its strategic position, realized the implications of a powerful Russia in confrontation with a weakening Ottoman Empire. As the army moved southward it established military lines and built fortifications joined by chains of forts criss-crossing the land like a black spider's web. The first fortress, erected by Catherine the Great in the Kabardian town of Mazdok, was forcibly populated with Cossacks and connected to the military lines of Kizliar and Azove. As the Russian military machine moved through the country, the Russian town of Ekatinodar was built as a connection fort-town to the Chernovski Cordon line until, by 1800, the aggressors had systematically incorporated areas of North Caucasus within its borders, sealing off the territories under their control with inter-linked fortresses inhabited by Cossack villages (stanitsas), fortified passages and defences. Chains of fortresses and posts sprung up along the Don and Terek river connected to the Caucasian and Sunja defence lines. The success of this military invasion would place Russia in a position where it would be strong enough to confront the diminishing powers south of the Caucasus, the Ottoman Empire and lands beyond.

Russia made ready to set its sights on North Western Caucasus, the territory of Circassia. As the army moved forward, strongholds with chains of ten or more fortresses to house the Russian garrisons were erected at Grozni and Nalchik and along a line of foothills on the rivers Cherek, Chegem, Baksan and the upper reaches of the Malka River. The land on the right banks of the Kuban river was granted to the Chernomorski (Black Sea) Cossacks. During the conflict, Tsar Nicholas I ordered the construction of fortresses at every point of the captured land on the coastline. After much fighting against the Circassian during the months of April and May, 1838, strong Russian detachments landed at Sochi and Tuapse to construct forts at Gobvinsk and along the coast from Gelenjik to Adler. As the menacing chain spread its strangling hold on the Black Sea coast line, the Russian army encounted unexpected adversity, frustration and heavy losses. A mass counter offensive on enemy positions led to the fall of several forts. The Russian army soon realized that building a fort was far easier than maintaining it against cunning guerilla attacks and the extraordinary courage and devotion for freedom and country that inspired the fiercely defiant, brave Circassian warrior tribes.

In the 19th century, Circassia was an independent country governed by a democratic confederacy, the United Princes and Chiefs, of which Shapli Bereketuko Hasan was one. It consisted of three tribes, the Adyghe, Abhaz and Ubyhk.

When, in 1830, the Russians aligned one hundred thousand men in arms along its frontiers, the tribes united under one national standard, the Sandjak-i Sherif of the United Princes of Circassia. All Circassian males over the age of twelve were conscripted to fight. Desperate for aid they appealed to their spiritual leader, the Caliph, Sultan of the Ottoman Empire, Sultan Mahmud II, but by 1840 the Ottomans were fast becoming a spent force, able to offer little support.

In March, 1836 an appeal known as 'The Declaration for Circassian Independence' was addressed to the courts of Europe. This declaration was debated in Britain at the House of Commons. Its authenticity was approved by Her Majesty's secretary of foreign affairs. In 1837, British Prime Minister, Lord Palmerston, wrote a declaration in which Great Britain officially recognised the independence of Circassia. This was delivered to the Caucasus by J. A. Longworth, British envoy and Caucasian sympathiser.

A written appeal addressed to Queen Victoria in 1839 by the United Princes of Circassia requested active British support in their fight against Russia. The cause was embraced by politicians and a group of supporters in England and Scotland who, as well as being inspired by the romance and tragedy played out in the Caucasus, responded to the international political reality that competition between British and Russian Empires, at that very moment, was becoming more and more furious. David Urquhart, James S. Bell, J. A. Longworth, Edmund Spencer and Lord Ponsonby sided with the brave mountaineers and financed shipments of arms and ammunition to Circassia. It became fashionable for aristocratic Victorian ladies at court to knit warm garments for the brave warriors fighting in the Caucasus.

Shapli Bereketuko Hasan had fought side by side with his father, Mirzauko Bereket, from the age of thirteen and was at his side when he was killed at the battle of Sochi on April 25, 1838. Sochi had been bombarded with incessant cannon fire and heavy artillery by a Russian fleet of thirty ships for days, until they secured a landing base to set up a beachhead at the mouth of the river.

His father had divided the cavalry unit of 250 men into small groups. Stealthily they crept through the forest towards the beach. Surprise and mobility were potent weapons of the guerrillas. The deadly silence between cannon blasts was broken as they sprang from behind every tree, every bush, sabre in hand, sword waving, charging with the swiftness of mountain panthers. As suddenly as they appeared, they disappeared; a group from the south would spring in a counter-raid and so it continued until their force was spent. This hide-and-seek warfare made it all but impossible for an organised army to wager a face-on battle or to gain ground. This guerrilla fighting approach frustrated the Russian advancement, forcing them to defend their positions time and time again. The dense, brush-choked forest neutralised the strength of Russian's greater numbers while weakening the force of its superior artillery. But each charge cost the Caucasians precious lives and ammunition they could not afford. Battered and outnumbered, this desperate attack fought on defiantly.

"More desperate fighting has never been witnessed in these mountains," said one Russian general.

Finally the Russians regained the lost terrain, but not before they had suffered serious losses: 150 men, three cannons and twenty prisoners of war. Most of the Circassian cavalry was killed, including Shapli Mirzauko Bereket. Hasan, wounded and unnerved by fear and grief, lifted his father's bloody, torn body across the saddle of his horse for the nightmare journey back to their aoul.

Princes, nobles and warriors, from all over the Caucasus, came to attend the funeral of Shapli Mirzauka Bereket, to honour and respect a brave warrior, comrade-in-arms, son of the famous leader, Berko Mirza Han of the Shaplis, whose deeds were sung in songs and ballads around camp-fires.

The ceremony was long and full of angst with songs and funeral oration recalling the dead man's bravery, the wars he fought and the Caucasian tribulations.

As the burial rites drew to an end Hasan, now chief of the tribe, stared at the grieving, war-worn faces of his family, friends and the Caucasian noblemen. He made a silent oath to *Shibley*, ancient god of war and thunder, to revenge the death of his father and the misery of his people with his life. He would lead his warriors into battle as the Shapli family had for five generations, from Kubilaiko Mahomet to his beloved father.

Hasan led his men into raid after raid with the strength and courage of a mountain lion but his heart was weary and heavy. During the precious intimate hours he lay with Kudenet in his arms, he talked of his longing for peace for his family and country, of his wish to gratify her dream to visit and settle in Istanbul. But even to his beloved wife, he could not express his growing fear that their cause was already lost.

Chapter 2

Childhood in Circassia

Osman Ferid was a quiet, obedient child, with his father's aristocratic features, brown hair and his mother's expressive, dark eyes. Hasan called him "my little shadow,' for the moment he was out of school, he jumped on his pony to follow his father around the aoul or fields. He sat quietly by his father's side at meetings with princes, chieftains and imams. He was healthily competitive, carrying off prizes at the sports and equestrian competitions regularly held between boys from nearby aouls.

Constantly under guard, children were allowed to play within restricted areas. It was their war ground; like little monkeys they climbed trees and jumped on ponies, charging one another with wooden swords or daggers. Imitating their warrior fathers they crawled on their stomachs attacking in make-believe skirmishes and war games while girls watched, cheering the winners, urging them to perform even more dangerous feats. Kudenet had given birth to two more boys, Mehmet now six and Ahmet three years old. One of Osman Ferid's duties was to care for his brothers and see they came to no harm in the forest.

Although the younger children were told to sit quietly while their brothers played, they often scampered off to climb trees or hide behind thick bushes. These escapades usually ended in tears when they fell off broken branches, injured themselves fighting and squabbling over a wooden sword, slipped into a pot-hole or got caught in animal traps. Osman Ferid wiped away their tears, cleaned their wounds and scratches showing them how to play without getting hurt. But when their mother saw their bruises and torn clothes, Osman Ferid received a sharp scolding for not caring for his young brothers properly. Much to their relief, he stood, head bent, listening to his mother, muttering apologies and promising to be more vigilant next time. Fearing the constant threat of Russian or Cossack patrols and the safety of the children, Kudenet imposed strict rules of behaviour in the playground and forest and expected her children to set good examples. Mehmet and Ahmet knew they would be punished and banned from playing with their friends if their misdemeanors were discovered; their brother was their saviour.

Failing to subdue the mountaineers or break their defence lines, Russian forces were unable to control or penetrate deeper into the forest. As the deadly raids continued they could not continue their advance but were forced into defensive combat to maintain their positions over the strongholds and fortresses on the beachheads and along the coast. Fighting raged from one province to another. Circassians, born to the rattle of guns and clash of sabres, were steeled against conflict. News of battles echoed through the mountains carried by messengers galloping through the night from one aoul to another.

Tsar Nicholas's patience was sorely tested as the situation in the Caucasus against "those rebellious mountaineers" continued to deteriorate. He was infuriated by the ability of "a band of religious, wild rebels" to sustain victorious campaigns and manoeuvres against his army. The "Ruler of all Russia" thought the war was being mismanaged so he decided to take matters into his own hands and called a meeting of military strategists, government ministers and advisors to discuss the problems and weaknesses of the Caucasian campaign. After intense discussion it was unanimously decided that a change of military strategy was imperative. A treatise was agreed which as General Vorontsov pointed out would, "in due time improve our situation here in a more certain, albeit in less spectacular fashion."

The "System of the Axe" was to replace the system of the bayonet. Thousands of troops and woodcutters were deployed into the area to fell trees and clear the tangled vegetation, repair pot-holes and rid the paths of Circassian traps along treacherous mountainous roads. Wide highways were laid to transport troops, military vehicles and weapons. The construction of these roads through the mountains would allow the Russian army to mobilise its equipment and forces so as to strengthen existing fortifications and barracks. Clearing the area would provide the ability to move the armed forces in safety on wider roads; at the same time it would seriously undermine the capability of guerrilla warfare, whose defence and strategy depended on its natural bastion - dense forest camouflage for surprise attacks and raids.

As fast as woodcutters chopped down trees and removed bushes and undergrowth, the forest, sheltered by mountain barriers, grew thicker, the trees taller. This was nature's way perhaps to protect its inhabitants but for how long? Would the new strategy, "power of the mighty axe, accompanied with economic demographic and psychological warfare" prove too powerful a force for the mountain guerrilla fighters?

The conquest of the Caucasus played an imperative part in Tsar Nicholas's plan for the Russian colonial expansion eastward with an overland route to India. Unfortunately for the Tsar, the plan coincided with a fearsome religious revival known as Muridism, after the Muridi, holy warriors who roamed the land, preaching national liberation and resistance to the oppressor as a condition for religious revival and reform. The leader of this mountain resistance was Shamil, the Aver, the Lion of Daghestan, Prophet and Warrior. This inspired, powerful leader from the wild mountains of Daghestan in Eastern

Caucasus was able to rally and unite the Chechens and Daghestanis with cries of nationalism and religion in a holy war of resistance against the "Infidels". Chechenia and Daghestan had been converted to Islam in the seventh or eighth century by the Arabs and the Islamic Şafidir, Nakşibendi and Kadiri religious sects were widespread.

In 1834, Shamil succeeded as 3rd Imam of Daghestan and was elected leader of the Muslim tribes of northeast Caucasus. Born into a noble family in Gimry, he had been prepared for priesthood by Mollah Jamulu'din, a descendant of the Prophet, and sent to study Sufism at Yaragll, the centre of Muridism. According to Sufi mystics and Muridism, Islam consists of three separate but interwoven parts: *Sharia*, the Law, *Tarikat*, the Path and *Hakikat*, the Truth. The religious revival began peacefully enough; Mollah Jamulu'din was a pious man of learning opposed to violence and never fought himself, but the time for peace had long passed in the Caucasus. The mountaineers were ready for war, and as it gained momentum the revival developed into a religious political- military movement synonymous with the war for independence against Russia, the Infidel. Soon it developed into a Holy War, led first by Ghazi Mollah, his successor, Hamzad Beg and finally Imam Shamil. Shamil was a man of profound religious fervour with an unshakeable belief that his mission in life was to gain independence for his country from the infidels by uniting the tribes in the Caucasus into one powerful force to fight a holy war under the banner of Islam. His vision was to unite the dissenting tribes under his violent, powerful personality and leadership. His religious zeal fired emotions of loyalty and obedience with its potent cocktail of hope: a mixture of religion, nationalism and liberty. Once in power, Shamil imposed strict Islamic Sharia law throughout North Caucasus.

In one of his speeches he preached,

"Once you have gone to war, be cautious and patient during the horror of conflict; you must survive until the end. Victory to him who upholds the faith; defeat to the unbelievers! May God forgive your past and future sins. May His love carry you on the straight path. May God help and protect you Allah, Allah, Allah!"

It was said that one of his Daghestani Murids, Djigit, could match one hundred Tsarist troops.

On June 1, 1840, Shamil defeated a campaign led by Count Grabbe, a Russian general of great repute in Chechnya. Following this embarrassment, Count Grabbe requested to be released from his command. He was replaced by General Neidhardt, former military governor of Moscow and a commander with years of military and administrative experience. The change in military policy was to be initiated under his command. Neidhardst was personally briefed by Tsar Nicholas I, who continued to voice his exasperation at the incompetence of the Russian army in quelling the rebels.

The Tsar chose to initiate the political tactics so successfully used by the British in India, tactics based on consolidating their power, preserving their forces while gaining time to subdue the country. The Russians saw this new policy as a way to "sow disunity amongst the mountaineers by all the means at our disposal." The Tsar commanded:

"Do not spare money in order to draw to us some of Shamil's brothers in arms."

The government imposed a two-year ceasefire on the Russian campaign to allow commanders and generals time to set up spy rings for espionage and to relocate military forces.

Shamil welcomed the ceasefire; it allowed him time to recruit and persuade other Muslim tribes, with valued warriors, to join the cause, time to improve the artillery corps and harass his foes with occasional attacks on under-guarded fortifications.

Shamil was a brilliant strategist.

With the rallying cry, "Find your enemy, strike as hard as you can and keep moving," he led his Murid warriors with the disciplined precision of a military general and the cunning skills of a mountaineer, changing tactics according to the territory or strength of his opponents. His raids were fanatical and quite ruthless; any show of mercy was considered weakness. He planned daring precise attacks, but like a mountain panther he knew the wisdom of retreat; if it was humanly possible, he never allowed his men to be endangered or overpowered. Shamil was a stern but just autocrat, a handsome, larger-than-life leader who held a powerful mystic influence over his followers, the country and everyone with whom he came into contact. He imbued his warriors with loyalty and a religious fervour, at times leading as many as ten thousand Caucasians into battle.

Shamil's military tactics and surprise assaults led General Neidhart, the Supreme Commander, into a series of disasters and further confusion. Although he had initiated the new "policy of politics over warfare," and proclaimed a reward—the weight of Shamil's head in gold for Shamil's capture—the general proved no match against Shamil's cunning, energy and lightening force.

A rare document quoted in *Muslim Resistance to the Tsar* by the Israeli historian Moshe Gammer gives Shamil's official version of his attack on Ghazı- Ghumuq on April 2, 1842 as promulgated at that time:

"With trust in God (His) slave Shamyl to the valiant Chechen people peace and God's blessing be upon you, Amen!

"I congratulate you with an event which Providence has allowed me to accomplish in Ghazı-Ghumuq.

"With God's help I took with no difficulty at all the town of Ghazı-Ghumuq- the mother of all settlements (umm al-qura). Five hundred prisoners both infidels and (Muslim) renegades, the khan's treasure, and the most precious local treasures are the trophies of my victory.

"The entire Khanate (wilaya) of Ghazı-Ghumuq and the neighbouring communities up to Derbend itself submitted to my rule without resistance.

"The people of Aquusha have entered an agreement with me

and sent their qadı and honourable elders with bowed and guilty heads to negotiate. In one word, this campaign is over-filled with such miraculous events that the believers have a rea-son to rejoice while the infidels- to torment themselves in annoyance.

"I have taken 35 hostages from the rulers of Ghazi-Ghumuq.

"Everything told here is as true as the words you speak."

(Shamil's Proclamation to the Chechen People following the Capture of Ghazı-Ghumuq.)

In 1843, General Niedhardt received orders from Tsar Nicholas "to enter the mountains of Daghestan and defeat and scatter all Shamil's hordes, and take possession of all the most important points in the mountains."

The Tsar emphasized his expectation of an end to the war by December 1844. When Neidhardt failed to execute the Tsar's plan, he was recalled; Shamil escaped after killing a large num-ber of Russian troops.

Neidhardt was succeeded by Field Marshal Prince Micheal Vorontsov, Russian Viceroy of the Caucasus, a sixty-three year old, outspoken, independent veteran of the Napoleonic War. In June 1845, Vorontsov decided to attack the pass between Salatau and Goumbet which led to Dargo, Imam Shamil's head-quarters in Daghestan.

Shamil faced Vorontsov's forces of two columns, 10,000 infantry and Cossacks, with a force of 5,000 tenacious warriors, who made up in courage what they lacked in numbers and artillery. Shamil and his Muridis stood fast, holding their ground against assault after assault, pouring streams of fire into the enemy for as long as possible, until— faced by the superior incessant bombardment and battery of artillery— Shamil sig-nalled a retreat into the forest. Vorontsov was confused and angered; he had foreseen a bloody, but victorious siege. With half his forces, he followed Shamil into the dense forest across the wild mountain passes of Andikoysu into the district of Dargo, only to be, once again, frustrated for they marched into the aoul without any resistance. Had a battle ever been so perverse, so contrary? Vorontsov's hopes of a frontal assault had yet again been thwarted. Glowering with rage and frustration, he ordered his weary troops to return to base in Grozny. With daylight fading, they were making their way slowly through the shadowy beech forest when Shamil attacked. A warrior lay in wait behind every tree. Chaos broke out as the enemy fought in the night darkness pierced only by flashes of light from muskets, as bullets came buzzing from every direction. Shamil's tactics were evasive; his men vanished only to re-appear.

"We have not yet begun to fight the Russians. Let them go where they will; we know where to attack them.

"Would that I could anoint the forests of the Caucasus with holy oil and pour libations of honey on its mud and mire, for these are the best protectors of its independence."

Muzzle blasts set leaves ablaze and the dry underbrush flamed into forest fires, sending the battered Russian army fleeing without horse, supplies or artillery. It took Vorontsov seven days to cover the thirty mile track through the forest to Grozny. Four thousand men, including three generals and 200 officers had died. Voronzov escaped with the remnants of his exhausted army to Gherzel. It was a disaster, an unimaginable, deeply embarrassing defeat for the beleaguered Russian army.

Shamil's fame was heralded throughout the land. His meticulous leadership and warcraft against such superior forces mobilised tribes to arms from regions far and wide under his black banner. With Daghestan and Chechnya in the central Caucasus firmly under his rule, Shamil turned his sights west to Kabardia to rally the Kabardan Circassians and the Black Sea tribes.

Imam Shamil had appointed Muhammed Emin as *Naib* (deputy) Viceroy, to Circassia, with power to rule by Sharia law over the Circassian noblemen and chiefs. Caucasians were prepared to fight and die for the freedom of their country and to join Shamil in his victorious stand against the Russians. Although they appreciated the fact that the revival of Islam with its strict Sharia laws had inspired warring tribes to unite as one force against the Russians, Circassians were not religiously inclined; they preferred the more moderate, traditional, archaic laws of the mountains, the Adat. Muhammed Emin's choice as viceroy aroused strong opposition. He was an unpopular, cruel man who exercised his authority with unnecessary autocratic severity.

Circassians did not convert to Sunni Islam until the mid-17th century. The religion became widespread during the 18th century, influenced by the Murid movement in Daghestan and by the visiting Muslim emissaries sent abroad for religious and political purposes from the Ottoman Empire. Before their conversion, Circassian worshipped pagan gods similar to those of ancient Greece and Rome. Sacred rocks, gigantic trees, and groves were glorified and worshipped as powerful gods of nature to appease the spirits of their ancestors with ancient offerings. The Ubykh tribes were amongst those least affected by the surge of Islam.

"There are certain places that are rarely ever seen, and in those you will find a special sort of magic."

Magic in the Caucasus was seen in the mist and wind, the snow and sun. The mountains, sacred since antiquity, were called the Mountains of Happiness by the Circassians, the Mountains of the Great Spirits by the Abkhazians and the Mountains of the Stars by the Tartars. Ancient beliefs and traditions survived throughout the ages. Circassians lived in a close-knit tribal system; the ruling class, princes, nobles and chieftains were powerful but just rulers who ruled by example and were highly respected. At community gatherings every Caucasian had the right to voice an opinion or state his complaint no matter how trivial, confident he would receive a fair hearing.

The naib's arrogance and unapproachability led to a deepening hostility among the tribes against his religious extremities and vicious misuse of power. His behaviour aroused such acrimony and resentment that a secret meeting was called to discuss the issue and decide whether a delegation should be sent to Imam Shamil informing him of the naib's conduct. After serious deliberation, they decided to bide their time. The unity of the tribes, achieved by the revival of the Sharia under Shamil's banner, was too precious and fragile to be jeopardised simply by the misrule of one man, the viceroy, the naib.

Shamil, with his fierce Daghestani and Chechen-Ingush mountaineers, fought the Russians with splendid success as they moved eastward. His battles and victories were sung across the mountains from aoul to aoul, inspiring hope and renewed energy in the fight for independence against the infidels.

In October 1846, the *Times* in London reported, "Shamyl, Imam of Daghestan is believed to be still holding out in the hills north of Khounzak. A force of 4,000 Russian regulars and Cossack cavalry under the command of General Gourko are closing in but rebel reinforcements led by the Chiefs, Tenguz the Wolf and the Lion of Shepsuk, are flocking down from the mountains to harass the Russian lines. The campaign is likely to continue throughout the coming winter, in the most severe conditions..."

Blake wrote in the 18th century, "Great things happen when men and mountains meet, that is not done by jostling in the street."

Princes and chieftains from neighbouring tribes in the region met to share information, discuss strategies for future attacks, choose appropriate hideouts and escape routes. There were regular meetings with Turkish merchants for the purchase and distribution of guns and ammunition. It was an opportunity to conscript warriors for campaigns, settle disputes and update the news spread by a large network of galloping messengers.

Besides attending to her five children, Zissi, Osman Ferid, Mehmet, Ahmet and Ismael, Kudenet's main occupation was to oversee the daily running of the Shapli aoul. As well as mundane chores, preparing meals, and looking after children and the elders, a woman's main duty was to ensure the chief and his warriors were equipped to leave for war at a moment's notice. Soldiers had to be well-fed, clothed, with weapons on hand; horses were brushed, fed and ready to ride. Elders were asked to oil and clean the arms and ammunition; wagons of dried foods and warm clothes were regularly checked. Each day Kudenet checked and rechecked her husband's forces, well aware that their lives and the lives of every family in the aoul depended on quick, effective action in the face of an attack or emergency. It was an 'on alert' existence, warriors ready to fight; their loved ones ready to flee. Chief Hasan and his warriors set off on regular patrols around the Sochi plains.

The stone and wooden houses grouped together on the southern slopes for defence, light and warmth, usually included a large storeroom and guest room with a hearth. The harsh landscape, treacherous winters, mountains and craggy barrier paths made travelling extremely precarious. Distances between aouls were far; it could take weeks to cover a short distance. Travellers and visitors played an important part in the social life of an aoul and were warmly welcomed. Regular visitors included brave, sturdy messengers galloping in and out, imams, and traders from Turkey who sometimes spent months at the aouls setting up trading centres to exchange goods and arrange new deals for weapons, ammunition and guns. They traded from Anapa, travelling the length and breath of the Caucasus, making friends, renewing business contacts and often returning to Turkey with beautiful, young Caucasian brides.

To overcome the isolation imposed by topography of pathless ravines and high mountains, tribes had adopted a system of "fostering." Sons of noble families were sent at the age of ten to live for one or two years with host families from related tribes, a practice that strengthened relationships between families and tribes. These extended families "bonded," becoming a close-knit group which in times of war could gather into a strong force. Known as the "Atalık" family, the object was to prepare boys at a young age to be self-sufficient and acquire lifelong friends who would become comrades-in-arms in the future.

Osman Ferid was sent to stay with the famous Berzek family, who lived in a large comfortable aoul. The Berzeks were a well-known military and political family who had been involved in the leadership of the first stages of the Ubykh resistance and were frequently chosen to lead military raids. Khadzhi- Berzek hailed from this family; he had enjoyed great authority, not only among the Ubykhs but throughout western Caucasus. In 1839, the Tsarist government placed a substantial price on his head.

Osman Ferid was polite, well-behaved and soon became a favourite, especially with the Berzek boys who, like himself, preferred to roam the mountains than study. They taught him to swim in fast flowing rivers, to jump from swinging ropes tied to a tree into the cold swirling waters below and how to manoeuvre a horse through rivers and flowing rapids. Osman Ferid spent two years with his Atalık family, and, except for occasional pangs of homesickness, especially for his mother, he was content until one day a messenger rode into the aoul with the sad news of Chief Berzek's death in a cannon blast in battle. Osman Ferid returned to his aoul.

Happy to be home with his family, he went from cottage to cottage greeting his elders, hugging old friends. He had grown tall, healthy and strong, toughened by his time with the Berzak family. To Osman Ferid's dismay, Kudenet sent him off to the mosque-school to be taught by the old Hodja. He was not a good student. He hated sitting still in the dark, confined space, listening to the monotonous teachings and prayers of the Hodja. He longed to be riding his horse in the forest or playing war games. Each morning his mother would call,

"Osman Ferid, Osman Ferid, you'll be late for school again."

Obedient, but despondent, he set off to the mosque. He found the Hodja's lessons a bore, but when his father's friends visited, Osman Ferid sat enthralled, listening to the exploits of Shamil and his Murid warriors.

At the age of thirteen, young boys from tribes far and wide in the region gathered for the "Presentation Ceremony" at the Shapli aoul. It was the most important moment in their young lives, "a coming of age" ceremony when they were presented to the leaders and community as young warriors. Trained from childhood for this illustrious day, boys were taught to respect the traditions and rules of their society but above all to defend the freedom of tribe and country. In times of war, the need for fighters was greater than ever.

Young Caucasian girls were taught not only to be a good wife but also companion-in-arms to her men folk. "I was born in the Caucasus. I know how to use a dagger" were not empty words. Women enjoyed greater freedom and a higher status in society than in other Muslim countries. Their faces were uncovered and they mingled freely with the opposite sex. Unveiled, but modest and feminine, unmarried girls danced with their male partners in the traditional Caucasian folk dances.

Nurtured to be future warriors, young boys were fed on stories and lullabies of heroes and heroic deeds, the magnificence of their land and the power of mountain spirits. The welfare and protection of family and tribe were indoctrinated as a matter of life and death. Discipline was strict. The boys were encouraged to develop physical skills and to grow strong and fearless. They listened to tales of the mystic power of the mountains, how to respect, befriend its peaks, gorges and valleys and survive its changeable climate, the harsh, bitterly cold winters, biting winds, downpours of rain and cool pleasant summers. At a very young age boys learned the skills necessary for a highlander in the magnificent, Caucasian mountains.

Janbolat, his father's standard-bearer, was Osman Ferid's

favourite warrior. He carried the Shapli coat-of-arms and was tall and muscular, dark-skinned with cold steel-grey eyes and the movements of a mountain panther. Rarely did a smile soften his fierce features. His father had instructed Janbolat to take charge of Osman Ferid's military training.

Whenever Janbolat was at camp, he and Osman Ferid rode into the woods. "In war, in the mountains, your life depends on your horse. He is your best friend. To ride like an Ubykh warrior you have to understand his spirit and character as your own." Janbolat would throw his kalpak on the forest floor, jump on his horse, ride a fair distance and then, like a flash of lightening, turn at full gallop, bending low over the horse's belly to retrieve the kalpak, then gallop off. Caucasians rode either Kabardin horses, the local North Caucasian breed, or Karabakh mountain horses. These animals were famed for their ability to cope sure-footedly over rough terrain and for their remarkable feats of endurance as they negotiated the steep mountain passes, crossed rivers and plodded through deep snow. They possessed an unerring sense of direction that enabled them to find their way in the dark and through heavy mountain mists.

Janbolat used trees and shrubs to practise shooting and sword thrusts; his sword could penetrate the bark of the walnut tree from thirty feet.

"To shoot you need a steady hand, nerves of steel, a straight aim, and never to take your eye from the target. Your sword is the extension of your hand." He spoke slowly, his voice deep and low emphasising every word as though it held a special meaning.

"Listen to the sounds of the forest. That is your safety zone, camouflage and war zone; it will protect you, hide you, warn you of danger. You can hear the sound of an approaching friend or enemy by the soft thud of horse's hooves or the crackling of dried leaves, twigs moving in the wind or a splash in the stream. You may hear a person approaching if you are alert and aware of the signs: the forest will guide and protect you."

The Sangiac Sheriff of the
Confederated Princes of Circassia.

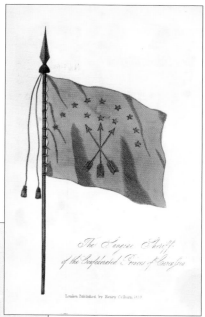

Circassian 1815.

Shapli Osman Ferid.

شیخ الحرم حضرتلری ومدینهٔ منوّره محافظی باودرنخری هنایه شهریاری
برنجی فریق

عثمان فرید

Osman Ferid Pasha's visiting card.

Shamil, 3rd Imam of Daghestan.
(1797-1871)

Warriors crossing the mountains.

Shamil, Imam of Daghestan (1797-1871).
Ruler of North Caucasia Daghestan-Circassia-Cherchenia. With his sons.
Ghazi Mohammed Pasha, Gal. Muhammed Şefi.

Emine Nefiset's father,
Şamilzade Ghazi
Mohammed Pasha and
mother, Habibet Hanım.
(Kuluça, 1865)

Emine Nefiset
As a child in Russia.

Leader of the Ubykh tribe.
(1770-1880)

Prince Circassien,
(Pşı Hacı Berzek Kalenduko)

Meeting of the Caucasian
Simali tribe.

Preparing for war.

Shapli Bereketuko Hasan, Chieftain of the
Ubykh tribe, Osman Ferid's father.
(Circassia 1850)

A painting of the Caucasian battle at Dargo, July 1845.

Circassian on horseback.

Osman Ferid yearned for the life of a warrior, but obedient and wishing to please his mother, he would sit in the dark corners of the mosque listening to the old imam.

To Circassians, the Russian Cossack tribes who roamed the steppes were as hateful as the Russians. The Cossacks were wild, nomadic groups in the pay of the Russian army. The government at St Petersburg had had the foresight to manipulate their destructive pursuits into military communities. They were skilled horsemen, but wasted their skills by galloping through aouls and hamlets to rob, rape and cause chaos. Cossacks were mean and disreputable. They imitated the Circasians' dress-style and weapons, but that is where the similarity ended. Cossack horsemen of the Black Sea lacked the discipline to fight against Circassian raids. After many bitter encounters with the Circassian swordsmen, they accepted that Circassians were superior warriors, more agile and swifter. A face-to-face combat meant sure defeat. They were prepared to fight side-by-side with the Russian army against their enemy, but would retreat at a gallop rather than face them alone. They sought revenge by plundering and raping Caucasian villagers in unprotected hamlets.

Occasionally Osman Ferid was allowed to join Janbolat and his comrades around an open fire where they ate and drank *shuat*, a potent national drink made from fermented millet, flour, honey and water. They narrated stories of legendary epic heroes from North Caucasia, the Narts, mythical figures similar to the knights of the round table who fought to preserve similar values: honour before life, discipline before pleasure, moderation rather than lust, and weapons before gold. Osman Ferid's favourite was the exploits of Savsorouko, the greatest of all the Narts.

When Chief Hasan and Janbolat were at home, time passed quickly. Sports and competitions were organised to test strength and physical prowess, along with the speed and horsemanship skills of the boys. Shooting ranges were set up. Competition was fierce, but Osman Ferid had developed extraordinary stamina and agility which gave him a head's start. His father, younger brothers and Janbolat watched him compete, shouting and cheering him on. At the end of the competition, his father presented silver kinjals as prizes; when Osman Ferid came forward to receive his, Hasan, with rueful formality, shook his hand with an approving nod.

Many a time, as dusk fell, a messenger would gallop into the aoul carrying news of an imminent, nearby attack. Prepared, Chief Hasan and his warriors rode off into the night. Silence fell over the village. Guards increased their watch around the hills. Worried mothers did not allow the children to play far from the house, scolding them for the slightest misdemeanor, as they prayed for the safety of their husbands and sons. At such times boys, including Osman Ferid, listened to the Imam with respectful attention. To play war-games was frowned upon when their fathers were fighting for their lives. For centuries the hodja (teacher) had preached the law of the Adat, a religion followed by most Caucasian tribes such as the Abkhazians in the south, until Shamil imposed the laws of the Sharia.

The viceroy, Naib Muhammed Emin, forbade the teaching of the Adat in mosques but, a traditionalist at heart, the old hodja at the Shapli aoul chose not to change his habits; he continued to teach Adat principles and traditions much to the delight of student and parent.

Two weeks passed without word from Chief Hasan and his men, until early one morning at dawn, a guard shouted,

"They're coming; they're coming."

Kudenet ran to the balcony to see a cloud of dust in the distance rising through the mist.

"Come let's meet them; let's meet them," she shouted, pushing the children out of the house, clasping their hands as she ran up the slopes. Osman Ferid was the first to reach the opening in the forest; he jumped up and down, waving his arms, but the horsemen were too far away. By the time they reached the entrance, most of the elders, women and children had gathered to greet them happy but apprehensive, their eyes searching for loved ones.

Chief Hasan led his men through the opening followed by Janbolat carrying the Shapli standard. Warriors, with the wounded stretched across their saddles, rode in line, weary and dirty after days of skirmishes, but surprisingly in good spirits as they greeted family and friends with smiles. Chief Hasan rode in front of the crowd, raised his hand for silence, and in a loud voice:

"We return with good news. The raid against the infidels was successful without any loss of life but that is not all. God, Thae, has answered our prayers. The great powers of Europe, Britain, France and Turkey have declared war on Russia. The forces of the foreign powers will join Imam Shamil's warriors to fight for our independence. Thank Thae, Thank God."

The crowd could not believe their chief's words. "It's true, it's true," Hasan shouted laughingly as everyone began cheering, dancing and hugging each other; the boys galloped up the slopes to the aoul, shooting into the air. It was April 10, 1854.

That night Osman Ferid crept out of the house to Janbolat's quarters. He found him lying on the grass outside his hut gazing at the sky. When Janbolat saw Osman Ferid he beckoned him to join him.

"I am too tired, too excited to bathe, or sleep," he said.

"I have waited for this moment for so long I cannot believe its true. It's hard to grasp that after all these years of fighting and suffering alone, Britain and France have declared war against our enemy, Russia." Janbolat laughed, shaking his head and waving his hands. Osman Ferid had never seen him so happy.

"When I was young, I met Englishmen from Britain who came to visit the Caucasus. They were polite and eager to be friends.

"Some travelled throughout the Caucasus, spending the night at aouls eager to learn our ways and habits, some even spoke a few Circassian words. They sympathized with our fight for independence. I remember David Urquhart. We called him Daud Bey, another was Yakub Bey. James S. Bell spent two years at my father's aoul. He spoke our dialect quite well. I taught him to shoot and ride without a saddle. He hero-worshipped Imam Shamil and his Muridis and followed them to Daghestan. Before he left for Britain, he promised to use his influence and power to gain recognition for the Caucasian cause. They were true friends and kept their promise; we received British aid and weapons but in small quantities. We have suffered so many disappointments but this time is different, Osman Ferid, this time the forces of the British, French and Ottoman armies will join us in our fight against the Russians. Thank Thae."

Janbolat laughed hugging Osman Ferid in a rare show of emotion.

CHAPTER 3

Boy Warrior

In *Britain in World Affairs* Lord Strang wrote:
"The Crimean War broke out because the concert of Europe had ceased to function. It was primarily a Turkish, secondarily French and only on the last count a British war against Russia. Austria, who did not enter the war, played an important part in bringing it to an end. The main causes of the war were first Russia's forward policy in Turkey, her determination to reassert her influence, which had declined since the settlement in 1841, and in particular her claim to protect the Greek Orthodox Christian subjects of the sultan and so exercise a kind of suzerainty over Turkey; secondly, Turkey's stiff resistance to these claims, based on the confident expectation of European support; and thirdly the split amongst the four other powers at crucial moments, Austria and Prussia tending to the Russian side and Great Britain and France to the Turkish."

The Crimean War will be remembered most for the heroic feats of thousands and thousands of men whose lives were lost in a power struggle between Russia and the West, a war initiated by conflicting interests, misunderstandings, diplomatic errors, even personal grudges between lead players in the game for power. The consequences of the war failed to help the Caucasian cause; in fact it ultimately brought down the final curtain on the tragedy of the Caucasus.

An editorial in *The Times* wrote, "The English people are resolved that Russia shall not dictate conditions to Europe, or convert the Black Sea with all the various interests encompassing its shores, into a Russian lake."

The *Morning Chronicle* wrote, "To stop the aggressor with a blow was as plain a duty towards humanity as to send succour to Sinope."

The declining state of the Ottoman Empire led to serious international complications which caused deep concern amongst the western powers. Affairs of the Porte had, over the years, been drawn into the western diplomatic system through a series of debates called the "Eastern Question," in which issues concerning the troubled empire were discussed. These debates often caused disruptions in peace agreements between countries within the western bloc. At the London Straits Convention in 1841, France, Austria, Great Britain, Prussia and Russia agreed with the Porte that no single power was to seek exclusive influence in Ottoman affairs. Vessels of war belonging to foreign powers were forbidden to enter the Dardanelles or the Bosphorus in times of peace. Even so, the dire state of the Ottoman Empire threatened by internal disruption remained of great concern.

Tsar Nicholas I remarked, "We have a sick man on our hands."

For decades, western powers had played a cat and mouse game with the Ottoman Empire. Politicians negotiated, threatened and courted Ottoman sultans to gain their favour and confidence and a large slice of the financial spoils from the largest and most powerful empire in the world, an empire whose territories spread from the Balkans to the Mediterranean and the Middle East. With the empire on the brink of collapse, political intrigue deepened. Each country was eager to stake their claim. Tsar Nicholas I, in 1853, told Sir Hamilton Seymour, British Ambassador to St Petersburg:

"It will be a grave misfortune if one of these days, he (the sultan of the Ottoman Empire) slips through our hands, especially before the necessary arrangements are made."

Napoleon III, protector of the Roman Catholic Church and Tsar Nicholas I, protector of the Greek Orthodox Church, caused major diplomatic conflict by their interference into the right of travel and safety of the Christian population residing in the Ottoman Empire.

The newly-crowned Emperor of France was young, ambitious and restless with a great army at his disposal. Napoleon III hoped, by imposing his own will, to settle affairs in Europe and find a solution for the "Eastern Question." One of his objectives was to upset the settlement of 1815. He challenged the principles implied in the Straits Convention concerning the question of Christian pilgrims not being permitted to visit the holy lands freely. The Russian ambassador, in no uncertain terms, reminded members of the Convention that Catherine the Great, under the Treaty of Kuchuk Kainardji, had been given the right to protect all Christians, especially those in the Danubian principalities, Moldavia and Wallachia. Emperor Napoleon III argued that France had the right to protect the Catholic Christians and held the guardianship of the holy places in Palestine through earlier treaties signed between France and the Porte. Abdülmecid, the Ottoman Sultan, feared these growing disputes would threaten his sovereignty, until France found an ally in Britain. The sultan realised that should a crisis arise between Russia and the Ottoman Empire, the Ottomans could depend on the support of the British and French.

The Porte refused Russia's demands. In 1853, the Russian Army occupied the Danubian principalities but Austria interceded with an ultimatum to pressure the Russians into evacuating the areas. Russia, fearing Austria's involvement might lead them to join the French and British camp, agreed to evacuate the principalities. But fate had played her hand. It was too late. Britain and France invaded Crimea. In autumn 1853, Turkey declared war on Russia. On March 12, 1854, Great Britain and France concluded a military alliance with Turkey and declared war on Russia on March 27.

In this theatre of political intrigue, news of the world powers gathering against Russia was, to the weary warriors in the rugged mountains of the Caucasus, an answer to their prayers.

Russian troops evacuated posts in the Caucasus to march towards Crimea where the impending allied landing was expected. British and French warships filled the Black Sea and the Russian blockade was lifted. An imperial edict carrying the seal of Sultan Abdülmecid appointed Pshi (Prince) Zanko Sefer, a Caucasian general of great repute exiled in Turkey, as supreme commander of the Circassian forces over Shamil's envoy, Naib Muhammed Emin. The naib was outraged. His reaction almost led to strife among the national forces. Pshi Zanko Sefer, a hardened militarist oblivious of the friction his appointment caused, hoisted the 'Sandjak- I Sheriff of United Circassia' above the fortress at Anapa with pride and military fanfare. At the same time, a Circassian army under the command of Pshi Hatuko Thughuz liberated the port of Sohum-Kaleh in Abhazia.

Shamil, with a large army, moved southward towards Georgia to meet Field Marshal Abdi Pasha, commander of the Turkish army waiting at Kars in eastern Turkey. The plan was to move towards Georgia to besiege the Russian army. Shamil penetrated the Russian defences but was unable to support the attack due to the delay and defeat of Abdi Pasha's offensive on Tiflis from Kars. With Abdi Pasha's forces defeated, the Russians sent heavy reinforcements to strengthen the army in Georgia. Shamil realized he could not possibly maintain a full scale attack against such forces. After brave resistance, his forces retreated to Dargi Vedeno, his mountain stronghold.

The lands of the Caucasus were ravaged by war. The incessant sound of artillery cannons echoed through the mountains and valleys as messengers rode throughout the night spreading the word and news of events as they unfolded. War in the Caucasus was the curse of their turbulent and violent history. Its people had no choice. They made no compromises but simply checked their weapons, fastened their swords, and bade farewell to loved ones before galloping off into the hills at first light of day.

War! War! War! War!
It has blazed up and scorched us sore.
The highlands are filled with its roar.

A Pre-Islamic Poet

In autumn 1857, Chief Hasan announced the long awaited date for the Shapli Presentation, the most important day in the life of a young Circassian boy, a "coming of age" celebration from childhood to manhood.

According to their status within the clan, boys were meticulously trained for the event by "brother warriors." When he was not on duty, Janbolat supervised the boys training; otherwise it was left in the capable hands of Akhmet. The boys preferred Janbolat. He rode, shot, climbed and hid with them as though it was a game, but Akhmet was a disciplinarian and stood no tomfoolery. He had ridden with Mirzanko Bereket and was loyal to his son, Chief Hasan. Akhmet's expectations were high; training began at sunrise and lasted until sunset. Warrior skills and prowess were developed; endurance and stamina tested. Fencing bouts and shooting practice were especially popular. The boys were taken into the forest with only dried meat in their sacks: horses were trained to stay close to their rider without being tied. They hunted for food in the woods, collected berries and fruits, shot and cooked the catch of the day perhaps a wild boar, rabbit or brace of birds; they drank the fresh, cool water from streams and slept under the stars with their kinjals and guns at their sides.

They climbed trees, hid in the dense undergrowth, and camouflaged before surprise attacks. Bruised and scratched, dirty and cold at the end of the day, they gathered around the camp fire, cooking and eating while Akhmet explained the healing properties of specific leaves, flowers, sap, or the bark of trees, which to use for wounds, bleeding, snake-bites and fevers. On a clear night they lay under the star-filled sky wrapped in their bourkas against the mountain cold listening to Akhmet's tales of battles fought with their fathers until, exhausted, they fell asleep, only to dream of the brave warriors heroic deeds. One morning they rode throughout the day to the highest peak of the mountain; climbing the last heights, the boys were amazed at Akhmet's stamina.

He whispered: "Listen, listen to the silence of the mountain then you will hear the voice of Allah."

As a race, Caucasians were renowned for their handsomeness; they took pleasure in their physical beauty and wore their traditional costumes with grace and pride. Days before the event costumes and gowns were brought out of chests to air; jewels and weapons were waxed and polished until they shone like mirrors, and the horses were groomed to perfection. Preparations for the feast had begun weeks in advance; even so, a last minute flurry and hysteria pervaded as elders checked the seating arrangements and women fussed over their sons, while the menfolk prepared to meet the guests. Nothing was left to chance. The Circassian costume, the Tcherkesska, is an ideal garment for a horseman. Comfortable and practical, it looked elegantly dramatic and flattering on the tall, slim Caucasians. It consists of a long shirt with buttoned sleeves and collar and narrow trousers worn under a knee-length black jacket with wide sleeves. The jacket with inside pockets is belted at the waist to hold weapons, a gun holster, two-foot double edged fluted kinjal and the *shashka*, a heavy, slightly curved, sabre. Two rows of silver cartridge cases, in rows of fourteen or twenty-eight, form decorative pockets on the front of the jacket. Each holds a stick of gunpowder for the pistols. The jacket is designed to carry everything a horseman might need as he gallops in the lonely mountains. The black fez-like headgear filled with grass makes a comfortable pillow at night while the bourka acts as a protective cloak for rider and his weapons in cold, rainy weather and doubles as a warm rug on cold winter nights in the mountains.

Osman Ferid checked his Tcherkesska, polished his kinjal, cleaned his guns and spent hours brushing and whispering into his horse's ear. His father had given him a superb, black stallion to ride in the competitions that followed the presentation with the promise that if he won one competition, the stallion would be his. Osman Ferid was confident; he knew he could shoot, ride and fight better than most of his friends.

As the sun rose over the hills, the Shapli aoul woke to a hub of bustle and expectation to host guests from far and wide on this prestigious day in their calendar. Dignitaries, comrades-in-arms, tribal heads, relatives and friends arrived on horseback, in carriages or on foot, delighted to meet friends as they gathered around the stadium-like green shaded by huge walnut and oak trees.

Women, magnificent in their costumes and bejewelled headgear, took their places to the left of the green; young girls sparkled, giggling with anticipation while their married sisters sat sedately surrounded by their children forming a delightful rainbow of colour and grace. Chiefs, noblemen and warriors rode into the aoul on fine stallions. They looked tall and handsome in their chain-mail, steel helmets and soft red leather boots; precious swords and kinjals hung from their belts, a bow and arrow sheath slung over their shoulders. They walked to the right of the green, leaving the centre to the Shapli family, princes, elders, and visiting imams. Behind every prince was an aide-de-camp bearing the banner of the family insignia. It was a scene from ancient times, of knights-in-armour surrounded by beautiful ladies.

Silence fell as Chief Hasan rose to welcome the guests and congratulate the young boys who would soon to be accepted as warriors in their tribes. The imam prayed for the Sultan and Caliph of All Islam and the protection of their honoured warriors. Chief Hasan stood at the head of a line of Adyghe and Abhaz chieftains. The cadets, more than a hundred in all, lined up in troop formation ready to step forward as their names were called.

"Shapli Bereketuko Osman Ferid."

Osman Ferid marched to the centre of the green. He knelt to receive the blessing of the imam then walked towards his father. Chief Hasan bowed his head and handed him a silver kinjal and sword, safe talisman, the treasured trophies of his acceptance as a warrior.

Bowing in front of each chieftain he returned to his place, his heart beating so fast he thought it might burst. He saw his mother, Kudenet, sitting with Ismail on her knee. She smiled, brushing away tears of pride as she watched her eldest son, the first member of her family to be presented.

Following the ceremony, a member of the Khadzhi-Berzek family rose; he spoke of the ancient Adyghe nation and its heritage. Since antiquity, they had fought for the freedom of their lands. Ubykhs were known for their military organisation and discipline, qualities rarely found amongst wild Caucasian mountaineers. He spoke of the responsibility young warriors carried in the struggle for independence from the infidels. In unison, the young warriors swore an oath of allegiance to their tribe.

The young men rushed off to prepare for the sports display

and competitions, while guests mingled on the green talking to friends and relatives, cheering the winners, and sympathising with the losers in good spirit. Osman Ferid, much to his parent's delight, carried off four first prizes.

Feasting and dancing were heralded with fire torches and music. Trays were laden with succulent roast lamb, chicken red with pimento, eggs, pilaf, bowls of yogurt and honey, goats' cheese, millet cakes and puddings, cakes of millet, dried fruit and nuts, almonds, raisins and spices. Samovars of tea and flasks of shuat and fruit juices were placed on low tables. Etiquette demanded all beverages be drunk three times. Girls with silver and beaded plaited hair and warm, shy smiles served the guests with charm and grace. Religious chants and songs of past glories were sung while epic poems of battles were recited by strolling troubadours to the accompaniment of duduks, thin reed pipes, the tar or the pandour, a three stringed kind of cittern.

The highlight of all Caucasian gatherings is the traditional Circassian dances performed by young men and girls in national costumes. These exquisite ballet movements, danced on their toes, express the wealth and diversity of the traditions and conflict in their lives. The dancers performed the gavotte, galliard fling with vigour and rhythm. At times enacting the melodious, smooth movements of peace-loving villagers, the sensual passion of lovers or the ferocious leaps and sword fights of feuding mountain-warriors, all the dancers performed with superb grace and delicate movements.

The music, played with a *sc'epsine*, (a violin-like instrument) *psine*, *bjamiy*, and *sontrip* that led with an insistent beat loud and wild or soft and melancholy set the rhythm for the intricate, fiercely energetic jumps, sword and war dances or the slow and sensual movements of a courtship.

Festivities continued until the sun began to set at dusk. Chief Hasan and his family bade farewell to their guests, congratulating each of the young warriors. As the last wagon disappeared,

Osman Ferid led his magnificent stallion to the stables. He stroked the horse's long black nose, pressing his face on his silky neck and whispered in his ear,

"What a wonderful day we had; the beginning of a new life together, -let it be long and great - a man's life – let's ride with the wind together."

Young men of Circassia, rush forth to the battle

For brave youths always love war,

If ye fall, ye become martyrs, and if ye survive, ye have half that glory!

—19th century Circassian war song

Osman Ferid's childhood faded with the setting sun. He was thirteen. He was a boy warrior.

CHAPTER 4

Freedom Fighter

Make bare the sword, oh people!
Come to our help:
Bid goodbye to sleep and quiet;
I call you in the name of God.
　　　　　—Imam Shamil's battle hymn

Bravery in battle and vengeance for honour and country was the code of conduct for Circassians as it had been in the days of Homer's Greece. In *The Travels in Circassia* Captain E. Spencer wrote,

"A Circassian cavalryman has no equal in the world. His sight gives an expression of great ferocity. When one sees that warrior mounted on his fiery steed, armed and equipped for battle, brandishing his sabre in the air, bending, turning and stopping at full gallop with unequalled agility and grace of action, one realises every idea of Homer's Hector."

Chief Hasan promoted Janbolat to cavalry commander with Osman Ferid a cavalry-soldier in his company. Osman Ferid was thrilled; he moved into the soldier's quarters then rushed to the stables in search of Janbolat where his long-time friend and mentor was tending to the injured leg of a horse with firm but gentle hands.

"Janbolat, Janbolat, I am so happy. I prayed to Thae I would be recruited into your company. Now we can fight together, side-by side."

Janbolat rose, stroked the horse and signalled Osman Ferid to follow him to his quarters.

Janbolat's room was large and bare except for a long, rough table, a few chairs and a narrow cot in the corner; it was dark with narrow-slit windows, two lamps hung from the ceiling above. The walls were covered with gun-racks and swords, the floor with boxes of ammunition. Janbolat sat down. The table was covered with tools, rags, brushes, tins of oil and jars of waxes, pistols and ammunition parts; he took a rag in his hand and began polishing the silver handle of a kinjal. Osman Ferid sat down puzzled by Janbolat's indifferent attitude. He had not looked at him or even congratulated him. Without raising his eyes, Janbolat spoke in a low but kind voice,

"Osman Ferid, I am honoured your father chose to place you under my command. I have looked after you since you were a child. You did me proud on your presentation day. I know you will be a brave and worthy warrior. But you must realize our relationship has changed; it is not the same as it was when you were a child. Now I am your commander. You are a cavalryman in my unit. You will be treated the same as all cavalrymen under my charge. I make no exception because you are the son of Chief Hasan. At daybreak tomorrow, we leave camp and ride hard; we may meet the enemy and have to fight. Your duty is to obey my commands without question. This is not a game: we fight for our lives and the safety of the aoul. I depend on your obedience and discipline as a warrior; you can depend on my command."

Janbolat rose, stretched out his hand and looked the young cavalry-man in the eye.

"Welcome to my company."

Osman Ferid jumped up taking Janbolat's hand.

"Thank you," he said.

"Forgive me for being so impulsive. It won't happen again; I promise. I would not want to be treated differently. You can depend on my obedience and loyalty, sir."

He turned and walked briskly towards his quarters.

Sleep was impossible. Osman Ferid tossed and turned in his cot, upset and embarrassed by his childish outburst. He had not acted like a warrior. He should have shown more respect, understood the change in their relationship. He would always love Janbolat and he knew Janbolat loved him, but it would never be the same. He prayed to Thae for strength in the future to control his emotions whatever the circumstances.

At sunrise, while the aoul slept, Janbolat and his men set off silently, riding out of the forest into the open valley then upwards along the precariously narrow ridges towards the mountains. They rode throughout the day, camping at dusk under towering pines, wrapped smugly in their bourkas from the cold.

The following day, they happened on a supply group of Russian soldiers carrying medical supplies and clothing to a nearby Russian fortress. Osman Ferid was ordered to the rear-guard on scout duty during the skirmish. So much for fatherly protection, he thought, obeying orders at the double. The attack was sharp and swift; a dozen men, with slight wounds, escorted the prisoners and their booty to camp while the rest of the cavalry moved forward.

A few days later, while on patrol, Osman Ferid stumbled upon an Abzah scout hiding behind thick bushes. Abzahs belonged to a large Circassian tribe called Adyghe, neighbours of the Ubykhs. The scout had fallen asleep from exhaustion having ridden throughout the night to warn his chief that a Chernomorsky Cossack unit was advancing in the direction of their aoul from the north.

They rode back to camp where Janbolat questioned him about the Cossacks, the aoul, the strength of their weapon and the surrounding terrain. The scout was fed, given a fresh horse and then urged to ride hard to warn the headman of the impending invasion, evacuate the aoul of villagers and prepare every available piece of armoury and ammunition. They would follow as soon as possible.

Janbolat was in the habit of drawing a plan for every raid on the ground with a stick before the attack. His motive was to protect the safety of his men as far as possible, for while a guerrilla ambush might be the same, the terrain and circumstances required different methods to charge. He would draw one move for one group, another for the second group. The skirmish consisted of attack, withdrawal, counter-attack, and withdrawal until the invaders ran amok like clucking hens and a final attack of devastation on all sides could be made. The force was divided into vanguard, rearguard, then into three parts. They rode in files of two and raided, if possible, at night just before dawn. This was basic mountain guerrilla warfare strategy, the dread of the Russian army because it was difficult to address.

Janbolat's Ubykh cavalry of 120 men set out for the Abzah village along the narrow, rocky path cut out of the mountainside, making their way towards the flat lands.

Cossacks were the original Tartar hordes of Genghis Khan who had swept fear and destruction through Asia and medieval Europe; they roamed the Asiatic steppes from the Carpathians to China and from Taiga to the Pamirs. The history of these nomads date back thousands of years. When they were not pillaging they tended their cattle and horses.

Even though there were eleven Russian and Ukrainian Cossack hosts (tribes), the Cossacks lacked a sense of unity. They developed no racial, cultural, linguistic or religious ties. Their lives were spent fighting, host against host, until the Russians realised it took a Tartar to defeat a Tartar. For centuries, Cossack warriors had served the Tsars as a fierce mercenary force, keepers of Russian borders. To further their own political end, Tsars, as well as Ottoman sultans, incited Cossacks against one another, while the Cossacks, loyal to none, profited from any hostility.

In *The Horsemen of the Steppes* Albert Seaton recalls observations of Doctor Wagner and Leo Tolstoy during their travels in the Caucasus. In 1843, the government in St Petersburg ordered an official Cossack escort to accompany Doctor Wagner on his journey overland along the Kuban on his way to Persia. The doctor noted in his diary that Cossack horsemen of the Black Sea were by themselves unable to counter the Circassian raids. The doctor was amazed at the respect, even fear, with which Don Cossacks regarded Circassian horsemen. The Don Cossacks found lances to be useless. In 1853 lances were removed from the Black Sea Don Cossack hosts as being 'of no use' against the hill men in hand-to-hand combat with swordsmen, particularly since the enemy riders were more agile and swifter than the Don Cossacks.

In the event of an attack, the Don Cossacks told him, they intended to flee, cutting the traces of the carriage horses after first mounting the doctor on one of them. Doctor Wagner noted that the Cossacks would have fought to the death had they been with their Russian lancer squadrons, but for this type of warfare, when in small groups faced by a Circassian enemy bolder than themselves, they were of doubtful value. The doctor saw the Cossacks as generally full of cunning and dissimulation, remarkable among a people so uncultivated. They had a great propensity for theft, being in truth without gratitude or generosity and being a people of degraded character and "...yet, concluded Wagner, "all Cossacks contributed much to the Russian army mobility, resourcefulness and elasticity, those qualities that were lacking in the ponderous Great Russian."

In 1851, Leo Tolstoy served for a short time in the Caucasus as an officer in the Russian army. His observations and descriptions of the Grebensk Cossacks were exact and colourful:

"The Grebensk Cossacks were closer to the mountaineer enemy than to the Russian soldier billeted in their villages, for among the men it was the height of style to dress like a Circassian and their Russian speech was interlaced with foreign words. The Cossack copied the Caucasian for the Caucasian practised lounging, indifference and nonchalance and gave himself dignified and imperious airs; and among these impressive Caucasian gentlemen, the Circassian was the lord of all."

A sentry met them as Janbolat's cavalry approached the outskirts of the aoul. Women and young girls with bags and sacks tied on their backs clutched the hands of their children as they guided the sick and old into groups to move through the forest to their hideout. Each aoul or fortified settlement had a shelter to which to escape in times of danger. Depending on the local terrain, these shelters might be a cave in the mountain or a cottage or mud hut deep within the wild, tangled greenery of the forest. The path leading to the opening was hidden by thorny hedges or thick bracken. Villagers planted specific trees and shrubs with markings to guide them. Larger tribes built camps similar to their aouls with thatched roofed buildings of mud and wattle, fully equipped with bedding, food, dried meats, flour, maize, water-wells and buried deep underground, guns, ammunition and swords. They could survive in relative comfort for months if necessary, until a return to the aoul was safe. Six warriors, three in the front line, three at the rear escorted and remained with the refugees during their stay.

Janbolat explained his plan to the Abzah chief and his men. The chief, aware of the exploits and successes of Chief Hasan's warriors against the Russians, gave a sigh of relief as the cavalry rode into the aoul to their rescue.

"My Thamata," said Janbolat addressing the chief formally, "the Chernomorsky Cossacks are fierce and brutal. I don't know their numbers or strength but I know their weaknesses. Our strategy depends on your cooperation; half of your force will hide in the cottages, the others will spread around the square and at the entrance to the aoul. We will hide in the nearby woods. When the Cossacks find a poorly defended aoul, their tactic is to terrorize the people by charging full force through the aoul to gather on the green in the centre. That is when we make our move. We will attack and gallop off while your men attack from the cottages and square, thus giving us time to relocate for a counterraid."

Hours passed before a scout reported the sound of horses' hooves advancing from the northern hills. Janbolat guessed there were approximately 300 Cossacks. Osman Ferid felt his throat go dry; his heart thumped as he watched the Cossack cavalry gallop through the valley over the flat pastures to the entrance of the village. He had heard of their brutality, how they raped women and children, burned villages and spent nights in drunken orgies. Suddenly the silence was broken by frightening animal-like screams. Smoke from muskets filled the air; bullets whistled as Cossacks, shooting at the Abzahs guarding the entrance, scoured the land as they swooped down towards the centre of the village. At that precise moment, Janbolat whirled his sabre above his head to charge. Swords outstretched, the Ubykhs galloped out of the wood at tremendous speed. The Cossacks, taken by surprise, stood their ground against the ferocious slashing thrusts of the Circassian cavalry as the assailing force rode through the aoul. The deadly attack was swift before Janbolat and his men disappeared into the bush. The Abzah warriors hiding in the houses fell upon the Cossacks in hand-to-hand battle giving Janbolat and his men time to lead a second attack.

Osman Ferid fought off one assailant after another with a sabre stroke or a deadly kinjal thrust as the wild horde fought back. At that moment, Osman Ferid saw four Cossacks bearing down on Janbolat from the rear. He spun his horse galloping towards them to break the charge, slashing his sword to the right, to the left; one rider fell; another was struck badly in the arm. Seeing a Cossack advancing with his sword outstretched, Osman Ferid dropped over the side of the belly of the horse to spring up with the agility of a tiger in time to thrust his kinjal into the Cossack's chest just as Janbolat turned and shot the last attacker. It was over in a second.

When a skirmish seems too intense, Cossacks flee, galloping off leaving the wounded to be captured with their dead. They screamed a loud retreat as they disappeared into the forest under a rain of bullets. An eerie silence fell over the aoul; the air was thick with the smell of gunpowder, walls potted with bullet holes. The few casualties received immediate attention while the battle weary men leaned on their muskets or sat on wooden steps or the ground, tired but grateful to have survived the Cossack onslaught. A scout left for the mountain camp with the good news. Osman Ferid, wet with sweat, propped his rife against the wall and crouched behind a building. His hands covered his face; his stomach churned as he relived that gallop towards those four Cossacks. Madness, he thought, I could have been killed. He felt a hand on his shoulder.

"It's all right; it's all right Osman Ferid."

It was Janbolat.

"We all felt the same on our first raid. Fear drives us to perform feats of bravery we never thought possible. You saved my life; thank you I am grateful. Your father will be proud of you when he hears his son fought like a Shapli chieftain warrior against the Chernomovsky Cossacks."

Osman Ferid wiped the tears from his eyes in embarrassment.

"Drink this hot soup; there is a cot inside; rest now for we leave at sunrise."

Janbolat gave him a small smile, a half salute then walked away.

Osman Ferid went into the cottage and sat on the bed; the soup warmed his belly. Folding his hat into a pillow, he lay under his bourka. He might have fought like a warrior but he felt afraid and insecure. He was still a child, a child-soldier in the harsh Caucasus Mountains. Staunch in battle, boys grew to men only to be consumed by war.

Osman Ferid awoke with a thumping headache, village noises sounding outside. Uybyk and Abzah warriors lounged around the green exchanging vivid accounts of the attack. A few young women had already returned from the hide-out, delighted at the victory. They rushed to and fro setting up tables, carrying trays of food to the centre of the courtyard for a feast of thanks. When Osman Ferid appeared, the men welcomed him with a grin and heavy congratulatory pat on the back. He felt bashful, still suffering from the sickening pain in his twisted gut. He looked at the prisoners sprawled on the ground, tied hand and foot with ropes to one another near the entrance of the aoul.

Wretched and pitiable, they bore little resemblance to those cruel, ferocious fighters of yesterday. They would be sold to the Turks, used as labourers or exchanged for Caucasian prisoners. After the meal, the company prepared to leave. The Abzah chief rose thanked the warriors, embraced Janbolat then beckoned to Osman Ferid.

"This is a gift for your father."

A groom leading a magnificent young white stallion handed the reins to Osman Ferid.

"Tell him his son carries his name with honour and was one of the brave warriors who fought to save my people. I shall come to visit him, until then, Thae be with you."

Mounting their horses, amid cheers and gunshots, Janbolat and his men galloped out of the aoul.

Decades of continual conflict in the North-Caucasus war had afforded little success or containment for the invading Russian Army or the defending Caucasian forces. The fluctuation of power and influence and a series of interrelated issues necessitated a change in the political stance forcing the government in

St Petersburg and the ruling tribes in the Caucasus to address new objectives in its strategy. But the fundamental reason lay in the fact that the conflict had become unsustainable for both sides: the war had gone on too long. The outcome of the Crimean War had hammered the final nail into the Circassian coffin.

Many historians argue that the Crimean War could have been averted. It had not been deliberately sought by any of the participants. Peace could have been preserved had Russia's aggressive policies to reassert her declining influence in Turkey been contained by the concert of Europe, which had, unfortunately at that time, ceased to function.

The British Foreign Minister, Palmerston, spoke with good sense of Turkey:

"No empire is likely to fall to pieces if left to itself and if no kind neighbours forcibly tear it to pieces."

Since Tsar Nicholas I's initial irritation with "that mountain terrorist, Shamil," Russia's military strategy of "Hacking" had changed the terrain of the war-zone and its policy of bribing defectors with large sums of money and promises of sanctuary against Shamil's revenge had achieved far-reaching results.

Following his death in 1855, the emperor was succeeded by his thirty seven year old son, Alexander II. On his death bed, Nicholas I whispered into his son's ear.

"I am handing you command of a country in a poor state."

Very different in character from his autocratic father, the new Tsar had, in his youth, been influenced by his aunt, the Grand Duchess Elena Pavlovna, an enlightened, worldly lady. Tsar Alexander was a benevolent ruler who supported the liberal ideas of his contemporaries and understood the urgency for change and reform if Russia was to retain her position as a world power.

Determined to modernise the country, the Tsar lost no time in initiating his reform programme with what he considered the most pressing problems of the land. The first was the abolishment of the institution of serfdom. In a famous speech to the nobility of Moscow, he said, "Better that the reform should come from above, than wait until serfdom is abolished from below."

The second objective was to end the war in the Caucasus. This task was handed to his trusted, childhood friend, Prince Aleksander Ivanovich Bariatinskii, a controversial colourful aristocrat and brilliant general. He was appointed Viceroy and Commander-in-Chief to the Caucasus. This saw the beginning of an aggressive military attack with a force amounting to three armies against Shamil and his Murid mountaineers in Chechnya and Daghestan.

On the Circassian front, decades of fighting had taken its toll on the war-weary mountain people. Although Shamil continued to win inspiring victories, they were outweighed by the greater loss of lives and suffering. Various phases, crucial incidents and climaxes over the years had influenced events and the lives of people. The devastation of aouls and families and the physical and mental exhaustion of the unending war had torn their country apart, exhausted their physical strength, and weighed heavily in their hearts. Although news of a victory could stir their spirits and invigorate their souls, the mountaineers were troubled by one thought: life could only get worse.

Shamil's desperation was expressed in an appeal to Sultan Abdülmecid in 1853.

"Gracious and Great Caliph, we, your subjects, having for a long time fought the enemies of our faith, have lost our strength. Furthermore, we, your subjects, have been (continuously) hardpressed year after year (to such an extent that) now we have no force to furnish against our enemies. We are deprived of (all) means and are now in a disastrous position."

Ottoman travellers, be they devout imams or Turks who came for trade or commerce constantly heard, "We have known the Russians only with arms in their hands; that nation has always shown the greatest desire to take possession of our territory. Our valour assisted by the power of the sultan has fortunately opposed their designs."

But the assistance was never enough, despite the fact that European weapons superior to Russian flint locks were being smuggled through by Turkish and British gun-runners.

In a letter addressed to Queen Victoria, Shamil wrote,

"For years, Oh Honoured Queen, we have been at war against Russia, our invaders. Every year we must defend ourselves against the invader's fresh armies which pour into our valleys. Our resistance is stubborn; altogether we are obliged, in winter, to send our wives and children far away, to seek safety in the forests, where they have nothing, no food, no refuge against the severe cold. Yet we are resigned. It is Allah's will... We beseech you, we urge you Oh Queen, to bring us aid."

Shamil sincerely believed help would come from England, but his letters remained unanswered. Many Caucasian tribes, tired of the iron grip of Shamil's naibs, their cruel authority and austere life-style, succumbed to the lesser of the two evils under Russian protection. Without doubt, Shamil, great leader and warrior, hero for more than 25 years, was revered by all Caucasians but time was against him. He had aged; the country and its people were exhausted, while expectations for freedom or independence from the Russian yoke remained as distant as ever.

Moshe Gammer, in his book *Muslim Resistance to the Tsar* writes: "Shamil was a born leader, commander, diplomat and politician. He repeatedly out-manoeuvred the Russians in battles, intrigues and negotiations. The greatest gift a leader may possess is the ability to appoint the right person to each position. Shamil's ability to do so was far from negligible, though his ability to keep such persons in key positions lagged quite markedly behind."

After fierce fighting in June, 1859, Vedeno, Shamil's seraglio and last stronghold fortress fell into Russian hands. In July, the fortress of Tchokh surrendered, with many naibs deserting to the Russian side. Shamil's miraculous escape from the hell of Vedeno drove him to prepare a last stand at Mount Gunip with his remaining handful of faithful Muridis.

Shamil, with stoic fatalism, accepted that his destiny was to die fighting with his Muridis. His battles had been fought in mountains and on plains far from his aoul and family. But at Mount Gunib, perched on the top of the mountain, he was surrounded by his extended family, women and children of his followers and retinue. His son, Ghazi Mohammed, was given the agonizing task of informing his father that Prince Bariatinsky's third and final ultimatum was unconditional surrender or the bombardment and death of every woman and child living in the aoul. Imam Shamil surrendered on August 24, 1859, to save the lives of his family. J. F. Baddeley wrote, "Shamil had failed because it was no longer possible for him to succeed."

News of Shamil's surrender shocked the mountaineers throughout Circassia. An emergency meeting of princes, chiefs, Vorks and noble Thamatas was called at the Shapli aoul. They galloped into the centre green lit with flaming torches, sober and tense, exchanging greetings in low voices as they made their way into the inner circle. Osman Ferid sat behind his father watching as the assembly gathered. Warriors on horseback guarded the entrance. The eldest Shapsugh leader rose to address the meeting.

"Brothers, it saddens me to announce that Imam Shamil was forced to surrender to Prince Bariatinski. He was persuaded to do so by his son, Ghazi Mohammed, in order to save the lives of the women and children in his household and those of the 400 warriors who remained with him at Vedeno. He had no choice but to surrender with the dignity of a great leader.

"Naib Mohammed Emin has deserted to the Russians. It was

a mistake on our part not to inform the Imam of the naib's mis-rule. It might have changed the course of events. Daghestan has surrendered; the Chechens and Adyghe of Kabarda are defeat-ed and the Karatchai have been subdued. Here on the Black Sea coast, we are alone in our fight. Most of the land southeast of the Kuban River is occupied by Russians. Should we fight, we will face the full might of the Russian army and navy. I urge you to join me and my tribe in our last stand —in the name of Imam Shamil, our leader. It is our duty to carry on the fight until the very end. Thae, God be with you."

The assembly remained still, heads bowed; only the rustle of wind in the trees made a sound.

"We'll fight, won't we, father? We won't give in; I'll fight by your side," ignoring ceremonial correctness, Osman Ferid rushed to his father's side to whisper.

Looking at his young son, Hasan remembered how he had been fired with feelings of national pride at his age. Now weary and disillusioned, unsure of the future, all he wanted was for this mayhem to end; he wanted peace for the Caucasus, his tribe and family, peace which even the great leader, Shamil had been unable to achieve. What hope is left for my people, he thought as he lowered his head in prayer.

Chief Hasan rose to address the assembly with military stiff-ness and a cold, impassive face:

"We have in the past won many victories against the Russians; today we are called upon to make the most important decision in our lives as Circassian warriors, whether to fight for freedom or surrender. I say we fight as our forefathers did before us; I say we must unite with every tribe on the Black Sea coast to avenge the injustices suffered by Imam Shamil and our country. Let us resist with all our might. I say, as a Circassian chief, we have no choice but to defend our people and country to the end. God, Thae be with you."

Chief Hasan's speech was met with empty cheers by some, silence by others. They agreed to meet at a later date, departing with a poor show of false hopes and bravado as they rode into the night.

Greater adversity was to come. The seriousness of their plight became more apparent as the Black Sea Caucasians faced the full might of the Russian army, an army determined to use its military and naval strength to crush the remaining resistance in the Caucasus once and for all. Two hundred thousand Russian soldiers and Cossacks were sent to the Caucasus to fight the poorly equipped, wretchedly outnumbered, defenders.

On August 20, 1860, a Russian infantry regiment with a Cossack cavalry unit attacked the Shapli aoul. Women, children and the elderly fled to the hideout in the hills behind the next valley out of reach of artillery attacks. Warriors resisted the bombardment and gunfire, charging and recharging from all quarters. Deadly and fast as they were, the warriors made little impression against the precision and artillery strength of the enemy. On the second evening of the siege, Chief Hasan called Osman Ferid, whose unit was employed in guarding strategic secret pathways to the aoul. These paths, wide enough for a horse carriage, were lifelines into the forests and mountains in times of siege, camouflages for surprise attacks and paths for neighbouring tribes with extra light artillery and ammunition to join the fight.

His father was deep in discussion with four of his comrades and Mahmut, a Turkish friend and merchant from Istanbul who was about to leave for Istanbul. When they saw Osman Ferid, they moved away. His father nodded to him to sit.

"Son, it seems this siege will last for four or five days. Although our defence is strong, we are outnumbered and the Russians have powerful weapons. Word has arrived that a large Adyghe reinforcement is on its way to join us. I am confident we can defend our position until they arrive; even so, I have decided to move the women–folk to the mountain camp. Janbolat and his unit will accompany the move and remain with them until I send word. You leave tonight. May Almighty Thae protect you and our people".

His father rose; Osman Ferid jumped up. Chief Hasan embraced and kissed him, then nodding his head, he smiled a sad smile before turning sharply to walk towards his men. Osman Ferid was about to speak when Mustafa, his father's commander-in-chief, stepped in front of him, shook his head, lifting his finger to his lips. He put his arm around Osman Ferid leading him to the door.

"This is no time for words, Son, your father and chief has ordered you on a mission; your duty is to obey."

He gave Osman Ferid a gentle push and closed the door.

Janbolat was waiting behind the mosque.

"The supply carts have left; we leave at nightfall. Ready your horse."

Obediently Osman Ferid walked to the stable to prepare his horse and baggage, but his brain screamed to rebel, rebel against his father, against the war, rebel against the Russians and the injustices carried out against their world. Soldiers were not allowed the luxury of emotions they were expected to obey orders. Why? screamed his head, why? Why couldn't he stay and fight with his father?

By the time he arrived at the hide-out, preparations completed, everyone was busy checking and rechecking their belongings, lifting children on to saddles and helping the elderly onto carts. Osman Ferid saw his mother holding the reins of her horse in one hand and Ismail in the other, counting heads as the refugees passed in front of her. She put Mehmet and Ahmet into Zissi's care, climbed on her horse, lifting Ismail onto the saddle. Kudenet led her horse to the front of the convoy, nodding to Osman Ferid as she passed. If warriors are denied emotions, so are their womenfolk, he thought looking at his mother's blank, white face. They could hear the reports of cannons and rifle blasts down the valley and smell the burnt gun powder in the air as they moved stealthily through the thick, dark, forest upwards towards the snow line of the high mountains.

Shadows in the night, they moved slowly and silently without a stop until the following evening when they reached the top of the first hill on high ground. Janbolat called for a rest. He and Osman Ferid rode over the crest of the granite crags to the precipice where, far below, the Shapli aoul was just visible. Janbolat focused the binoculars then, with a strangled cry, handed them to Osman Ferid. Instead of the green Circassian national flag, the twin-headed eagle of the House of the Romanov flew above the aoul. The village had fallen. They had narrowly escaped with their lives. There had obviously been no reinforcement; otherwise the aoul would not have been taken so quickly. His father had lied to him; he and his men would have fought to the end rather than surrender.

"You are chief now," Janbolat said in a low voice.

Osman Ferid lowered the binoculars, trying to control his breathing. He felt his gut twist and thought he would vomit. Mounting his horse,

"Say nothing. We move at once; the Russians must be aware of our escape. If we can make it to the camp, they won't bother to climb that high. Say nothing until we reach camp."

Janbolat and Osman Ferid avoided eye contact; there was no time to waste, no time to mourn. Fate had changed their relationship once more. Osman Ferid was chief, Janbolat, his commander. They needed at least a day and a half to climb the treacherous, at times, crumbling, narrow ridges, chasms and river rapids before reaching camp and safety. Not returning his mother's searching looks Osman Ferid urged them to move faster and faster. On the evening of the third day the exhausted refugees reached their old camp. It was not a welcoming sight. It looked desolate and abandoned after such a painful journey.

Two days later, a young boy, led two badly wounded warriors into camp; miraculously they had escaped the burning aoul. In a choking whisper, he related the final moments of carnage and death.

Osman Ferid went in search of his mother. She was sweeping the floor of an empty cottage having removed the beds, chairs and tables outside. Kudenet straightened up and set the broom aside when she heard Osman Ferid's voice.

She took his hand, "I know, son."

She kissed him on both cheeks holding him tight.

"I knew the day you refused to look at me on the first hill. Your father could never look at me when he had bad news to tell."

She stroked her son's face as grief poured out of her body, her eyes glistening with the tears she refused to shed.

"There is much to do; the children and I will look after the camp. You are chief now Osman Ferid. May God, Thae, help you make the right decisions for your family and tribe".

Janbolat presented Osman Ferid with the Shapli seal and banner with a short, sad speech; those present offered muted congratulations and blessings. He was seventeen and was chief of the Ubykh Shaplı tribe scattered in aouls around the Black Sea. The villagers in the camp expected his guidance and protection in this remote spot, high in the formidable mountains soon to be wreathed in the black clouds and mists of winter. Osman Ferid thanked them briefly. The imam prayed for Chief Hasan and the warriors who had so bravely given their lives to save them. The ceremony was short, funereal, their circumstances too painful to permit mourning.

It was a large refugee camp, spreading over terraced platforms of rock, sloping forests and to the south, land which could be tilled for planting. Work began in earnest. Cottages were repaired, a common area cleared for meetings, prayers, lessons and a playground for children. Winter crops were planted, barns repaired for storing food and ammunition, and four broken watch-towers reinforced for guards-watch day and night. Men, women and children worked side by side preparing the camp for winter and against attack, which was most unlikely. Mountaineers galloped in and out with news from other camps of skirmishes and raids along the Black Sea.

One morning Osman Ferid received an invitation to join the Circassian forces gathering under the flag of the Free Princes.

Torn between wanting to accept the invitation and his concern for the camp, Osman Ferid went to consult his mother. Kudenet had prepared a fine breakfast for the family, after which she sent the children outside so that she could speak privately to her eldest son. He told her his dilemma, his deep desire to join the Circassian forces but his fear at leaving the camp with few guards, even though Russians soldiers rarely climbed so high into the mountains. They preferred to fight in the safety of the valleys below.

Since she had arrived, Kudenet had taken charge of the daily running of the camp. Working from sunrise to sunset, she never spoke about her husband or the tragedy of the Shapli aoul. She was concerned and kind to the children but she no longer laughed. The children longed for the sound of her lusty, infectious laughter when her thick, black hair spilled over her face. When she suddenly galloped off into the mountains for hours, they knew that she was overcome by sorrow and despair and needed to be alone. Osman Ferid had given her the stallion presented to him by his father. It was a magnificent horse, fast and sure footed; his mother was a superb rider, but even so, Osman Ferid, worried for her safety when he saw her gallop out of camp. Still he feared to reproach her.

Closing the cottage door, Kudenet sat facing her son:

"Osman Ferid, I respect your position as chief of the tribe and head of the family, but first I wish to speak to you as your mother. I intend to send the children to Istanbul. I have discussed it with our dear, trusted friend, Mahmut Bey. Your father realised the fight for our country was over when Imam Shamil surrendered to the Russians. It was then he began to consider a move to Istanbul. You know it has always been my desire to live there, in that beautiful, peaceful city, where we could be safe and happy. Your father wrote to Imam Shamil and was about to discuss it with Mahmut Bey. Our plan was to send the children, including you, Osman Ferid; then, when arrangements for the tribe and aoul had been completed, we were to join you."

Kudenet paused, silent tears ran down her bloodless cheeks. She looked out of the window watching the children at play.

"Then the Russians attacked the Shapli aoul. It is too late for me, but not too late for the younger children. Do your duty, Osman Ferid. I will care for the aoul, have no fear, but your brothers and sister go to Istanbul."

She turned, looking defiantly at her son, daring him to object. For the first time in his life, his mother had spoken to him as a man sharing her deep love for his father, her secret desire and thoughts with him. He looked lovingly at her,

"Nan, dearest Nan, of course the children will go to Istanbul if that is your wish. In respect to my father's memory, I will join the Circassian Princes but I swear, on Thae, on my return, we shall both go to Istanbul."

Kudenet ran into his arms, crying, hugging and kissing him like a child. To share her plans and know that her son supported her was an unbelievable relief.

"Your father and I were soul mates; we had one heart. I knew I would never see him again when we left the Shapli aoul. You remind me so much of him. I hope you find a love like ours; God bless you and thank you my dearest son."

The Abdzakhz, Shapsughs and the Ubykhs entered into an alliance to form a national government, a Meclis in Sochi.

Osman Ferid, his brother Ahmet, Janbolat and the warriors galloped off to the headquarters of the Ubykh Chief, Hadj Berzek. The large aoul was an assemblage of princes, chiefs, Thamatas warriors from different tribes and regions in North –Caucasus, the last of the Kabardan chiefs, Bshaduk chiefs, from the Kuban River, proud Shapsughs, even a Bey from the Karatchais and a Chechen chieftain.

The imam began proceedings by offering condolences and prayers for Chief Hasan and welcoming his son, Osman Ferid. His father had served with Hadj Berzek during the time of the

Congress of United Princes and Chiefs in Circassia. During the debate everyone had the opportunity to voice their opinions; this was followed by a heated discussion that continued until sunset. Finally it was decided to send two representatives abroad. Berzek would seek an audience with the Ottoman Sultan, while Pshi Kosanekou Ismail would lead a delegation to England to meet with Queen Victoria's ministers to explain the urgency of their plight and request aid and political intervention.

Osman Ferid and Ahmet shared living quarters and duties in the mountain stronghold. Although very different in character, they became very close, which would have been impossible at the aoul. Ahmet was cheerful and outgoing. He loved to hunt, hang out with the officers, play jokes and enjoy himself. Ahmet, like his brother, was not fond of study, but he was exceptionally talented with his hands and would spend hours dismantling or repairing guns, filling gun powder into bullet capsules, or restoring the handle of a sword with the finest silver filigree. Osman Ferid was quieter, far more introspective. He tolerated the antics and rough play of the warriors with humour but never participated himself.

One of their duties was to assist a Turkish merchant, Hüseyin Memişoğlu, who supplied ammunition and taught Turkish and English to commanders so they might read the manuals and correspondence that came with the equipment imported from Turkey and the west. The Daghestanis, Chechen, and Circassians were of different ethnic groups. In addition to speaking their own languages, the Shapsugh, Ubykhs, and Abzahs all spoke at least one other language as well.

Much to Ahmet's surprise his brother insisted they attend the Turkish classes regularly. Osman Ferid decided to cultivate his friendship with Hüseyin, spending more and more with him. Hüseyin was delighted when he offered to help him and eventually they become close friends. As a token of this friendship Osman Ferid presented him with a silver inlaid kinjal when Hüseyin married a Circassian bride.

One evening, a messenger arrived from camp. Eager for news, the brothers greeted him warmly, but realized from the young man's face that the news was not good. Their mother, Kudenet, had died.

They saddled their horses and set off at once, leaving Janbolat to take over their duties and explain their absence. They covered the rocky mountainous distance in record time without stopping for food or rest.

The villagers had gathered outside Kudenet's cottage for prayers; litanies were sung in her honour. Zissi and Ismail, red-eyed and tearful, embraced their brothers. Funeral arrangements had been postponed until their arrival. It was a sombre, quiet ceremony without the rites and glory awarded to the wife of a chieftain at a Circassian burial. Friends spoke of her unstinting sense of duty and hard work and how she had transformed the camp into a warm, welcoming aoul. She found a home, food and work for anyone who happened to find their way there. Zissi told them how she worked from sunrise to nightfall, eating little but full of nervous, burning energy.

"She prayed for your safe return, but she missed father so much, every evening, no matter how cold or how exhausted she was, she would wrap up in a shawl, walk up to the edge of the highest ridge and sit staring down into the valleys."

"Why should she be homesick? She saw the same mountains from the fort as she did from her village- and that's all these savages want."

(From *A Hero of Our Time* by Mikhail Lermontov.)

"Mahmut Bey has taken Mehmet to Istanbul and arranged for him to enter the Military Cadet School. She told us time and time again when you returned we would all go to Istanbul. That hope kept her alive. She began coughing a few weeks ago, then caught a slight fever but still refused to rest. One morning, I went into her room. She was too weak to get out of bed. She told me she felt tired and wanted to rest; she kept repeating how she missed father and that we were not to worry. She made me promise to look after Ismail, send a messenger to you, and when you had fulfilled your promise to her, all would be well."

Zissi fell into Osman Ferid's arms shaking, tears pouring down her young, pale face. All through the night, he cradled her in his arms, while Ismail and Ahmet sat in silence.

Osman Ferid, Zissi, Ahmet and Ismail stood side by side as they buried their mother. Songs of her beauty, strength and love echoed through the valleys as messengers carried the sad news of her death. It was a clear day; the snow glistened; rays of sunshine escaped through the cold blue shadows that lay over the mists hiding the peaks of the mountains, wild, isolated and utterly unspoiled, the leaves of an old gnarled tree rustled in the wind. It was a dramatic and magical burial ground, a worthy resting place for beautiful Kudenet.

Osman knelt besides the fresh grave.

"Rest in peace dearest Nan I promise I will keep my word and take our family to Istanbul, I promise."

Kudenet was thirty-five years old.

CHAPTER 5

Last Battle and Exodus

In the spring of 1863, Hüseyin Memişoğlu called on Osman Ferid. He seemed deeply concerned by the worsening situation in the country:

"It is too threatening and dangerous for us to stay here. I see no future, my dear friend, I have decided to leave as soon as possible and would be obliged if you took over my remaining duties."

This was the moment that Osman Ferid had been waiting for. He told his friend of his plan to send Zissi and Ismael to Istanbul to join Mehmet. He asked Hüseyin if they could accompany them on the journey. At first Hüseyin seemed doubtful; the Black Sea crossing was dangerous with Russian navy patrols frequently intercepting boats from the Caucasus. Two children would be a serious responsibility. Osman Ferid showed him the letter Mehmet had written praising the royal protection offered to Circassians by order of the sultan. Mehmet, a second-year cadet, was making splendid progress. Osman Ferid had added that his Circassian wife would be warmly received by the Circassian society if she were to escort the children of Chief Hasan of the Ubykhs to Istanbul. After some hesitation, Hüseyin agreed to chaperon them on the journey. Janbolat was sent to prepare the children for their departure with instructions to give them the family valuables and accompany them to the boat into Hüseyin Memişoğlu's charge.

Osman Ferid and Ahmet soldiered on in Hadj Berzek's army for another year. One day the Russian general Evdokimov invaded the Berzek headquarters with such a mighty force—columns of rifle battalions, a brigade of Cossack foot and mounted soldiers—that they had no choice but to retreat into the mountains.

The Adyghe Circassian tribes in the north, the Kuban, Bhjaduk, Abzah, Makkosh and Kymirguay tribes capitulated under the fire of the Russian generals. Thousands of refugees, their pitiful belongings, horses, cattle, herds of sheep and goats crossed from the occupied territories into the last unconquered land near the Black Sea. It was in this free zone that the last fighting force, the Shapsugh, Ubykhs and southern Abzahs, gathered.

Osman Ferid, now a commander in the Light Cavalry guard regiment, was assigned to protect refugees crossing into the free territories. One day on patrol, they came across a group of refugees—women and children from the Kuban—being attacked by a group of Cossacks moving south. The unit galloped towards the convoy desperately trying to ward off the charging Cossacks. The cavalry charged from both sides, positioning themselves between the refugees and the Cossacks, forcing the invaders uphill away from the convoy. Osman Ferid led the attack until a Cossack's sword pierced the top of his thigh. He was about to fall off his horse when he felt his orderly's support and, to his relief, saw the back of the Cossacks as they galloped off, shrieking and shooting.

Osman Ferid's wound was deep and slow to heal. Unable to join his regiment, and much to Ahmet's surprise, he spent his time writing to his brothers and reading Turkish military catalogues and books on Istanbul.

Shamil's capture had allowed the migration and settlements of Cossacks and Russian peasants into the fertile lands of the Caucasus. Crushing the resistance of the remaining insurgents was simply a question of time. By 1860, the conquest of the Caucasus was near completion except for a few tribal warriors who refused to capitulate. In 1862, Tsar Alexander II visited Ekaterindar where he received a delegation of Circassian leaders and chieftains. The Tsar offered land on the northern side of the Kuban on condition they withdrew from their mountain aouls and settled in villages in the lowlands under Russian sovereignty. Two Abadekh tribes accepted the proposal. Ubykhs Shapsughs and Abdzahkhs, insulted by the Tsar's arrogance, defiantly refused.

Enraged by their continued opposition, the Tsar ordered an immediate mass migration from the Caucasus to regions far afield in the empire or deportation to Turkey.

Prince Gagarin, Governor–General of Kutaisi, described the situation among the Circassians at the time:

"I must give our enemies their due. The Circassians have not lost either their heads or their hearts. On the contrary they have decided to fight for their independence but with an energetic appeal to foreign powers."

On May 9, 1864, a congress of 'elected elders' held in the Sochi valley, outside the village of Achipso decided unanimously to make a last stand against the advancing Russian army. Everyone volunteered— men, women and children.

Women prepared the gunpowder, children carried provisions, men dug ditches and built barricades; the elderly sat cleaning, oiling and loading muskets, rifles and pistols and sharpening lances. Achipso lay near a creek overlooking the Hodz valley of the Kuban. It was a peaceful pastoral valley, its green meadows enhanced by the crystal, clear water of a winding river flowing through its thick undergrowth. One day a messenger from the north galloped into the aoul with news of a full-force Russian advancement.

General N. Dubrovin, official historian of the Tsarist Government, described the Ubykhs' military organisation at that timed:

"Before undertaking an expedition... Ubykhs would choose a leader. He could only be a man noted for his bravery. During the expedition the leader could rely on the complete obedience of his party. The leader acted on his initiative. An uninhabited pass usually served as an assembly point for the party. Only weak, old men and small children did not take part in the expedition. Everyone undertook to provide the necessary clothes and food.

"When a force of from eight hundred to three thousand had assembled, the leader went to the assembly point to inspect the clothes and provisions of those present. After inspection the force was split up into a vanguard and a rearguard. Men from the same village were formed into units of ten to a hundred men. Each unit had its commander who gave orders, led his men and in important cases, reported to the leader to obtain instructions and to confer.

"The Ubykhs marched in two files. They raided only at night, before dawn. Before a raid, the leader divided his force into three parts, the first two, consisting of the most able for the attack and the third consisting of the old and young, cooks, tree fellers, formed the reserve."

The Imperial Army marched from the north of the Hodz Valley, the double-headed eagle of the Romanov banners bearing regimental colours fluttered in the wind. There were infantry battalions, a lancer cavalry of Hussars from the Tsar's regiment, Grebensky, Chernomorsky and Kuban Cossacks and in the rear, the artillery, twenty thousand troops in all. Before sunset the Russians took up positions north of the valley.

Facing this mighty force were four thousand stout-hearted determined freedom fighters, the remnants of the Circassian army. A regiment of horse cavalry escorted princes and tribesmen, magnificently dressed in chain mail or flowing white Tcherkesskas, who rode ahead of the cavalry also in chain mail, steel helmets and carrying lances and heavy swords. These were followed by foot soldiers with long-barrelled muskets, pistols and a kinjals.

Janbolat held the National Standard – Sandjak-i-Sherif– bearing three crossed arrows with twelve stars on a green background high above the other coat-of-arms banners. Ahmet held the Shapli banner on his lance.

Nikolai Ivanovich Evdokimov, General Count Evdokimov, commander of the Russian Army, a veteran of many battles in the Caucasus, was cunning and courageous, well experienced in mountain warfare.

He respected his opponents' fighting skills, admiring their stand for independence but, as he looked across the valley at this martial scene of medieval knights in shining armour glittering in the morning sun, he was saddened by the futility and unnecessary bloodshed these warriors would suffer in this desperate last stand. Evdokimov ordered an emissary to ride across the valley with a white flag on the slim hope that the Circassians would accept negotiation and an honourable surrender. It was, as he expected, refused.

Hell broke loose at the theatre of war in Hodz Valley. Cannons blasted through the valley as the Russian offensive began its deadly siege. Flashing sabres, wild roars of battle cries, a hail of bullets from Circassian musketeers positioned behind rocks and bushes filled the air as Grebensky and Kuban Cossacks and Circassian cavalry galloped across the southern slopes to collide in a bloody struggle.

At first the sheer fanatical force of the Circassians, their mobility, courage and superb marksmanship held their aggressors at bay, but without the raison d'etre of guerrilla warfare, they were overwhelmed by the sheer number and power of their besiegers and forced to give way. Surrounded by a tight ring of Russian forces, with most of the warriors killed, the Ubykhs were forced to capitulate. General Evdokymov sent word to his commander, Field-Marshall, Prince Bariantinsky that the last stand of the Circassian resistance was over after 150 years of guerrilla warfare.

On March 6, 1864, the armistice negotiations between Ubykhs and General Heiman, according to the orders of Tsar Alexander II, stated:

"Those who wish to go to Turkey should assemble in encampments on the sea coast at the mouth of the rivers Shakhe Varane and Sochi where Turkish ships may come. Those who wish to join us should begin at once to move to the Kuban where land will be allotted to them."

Past the bitter glare and smoke of torched villages, some thirty thousand Ubykhs made their way to the Black Sea coast to begin the precarious sea voyage to Turkey. The families that remained were removed to the Kuban and later resettled in the Kostroma province. On May 21, 1864, the Tsar's Governor-General in the Caucasus, the Grand Duke Michael reported to St Petersburg that "the Caucasian war has come to an end."

Ahmet's cavalry had been about to charge when he saw Janbolat's horse galloping past towards the oncoming Cossack warriors with Janbolat hunched across the saddle.

He whipped his horse into a gallop to follow, shooting wildly at the oncoming enemy to ward them off. Janbolat rode a magnificent stallion that galloped like the wind through the raging battlefield towards the hills beyond. Ahmet circled the fighting zone, racing into the woods, desperate to reach the narrow fork in the path on the lower hill in time to grab the reins of the frightened animal. The horse responded and stopped.

Ahmet lifted Janbolat gently from the saddle and set him on the ground, cradling his head in his arms, his jacket was wet with blood; his face grey.

"Janbolat, Janbolat it's me Ahmet," Ahmet whispered in his ear.

"Ahmet is that you?" Janbolat answered faintly, opening his eyes.

"I prayed to the good Thae to die fighting in these mountains and He has answered my prayers.

"Ahmet, find Osman Ferid. Tell him it is time for him to honour the promise he made to your mother. Leave for Istanbul; carry your heritage with pride. Tell the world about the last stand our brave people fought to save Circassia. Thae be with you."

Janbolat's hand fell limp and Ahmet closed his eyes. Janbolat's face wore a peaceful, serene expression rarely seen in his lifetime. Ahmet removed his kinjal and sword, then buried him in the woods.

Gathering the reins of Janbolat's horse, he waited for nightfall before making his way back to camp. When he arrived, he found Osman Ferid searching for him among the wounded. His elder brother gave a sigh of relief when he saw Ahmet and greeted him heartily until he saw Janbolat's horse.

Osman Ferid put his arms around his brother and in silence they mourned the death of their beloved Janbolat.

Numbed into painful silence, the two brothers, overwhelmed and unnerved by the sudden turn of events, prepared to leave for Istanbul. They rode to a harbour on the Circassian coast, their belongings in packs slung over the back of Janbolat's horse. For two weeks they stayed in the house of a relative until they found a berth on a Turkish schooner. On the last evening their cousin, Fazil, prepared a farewell feast. He had been to Istanbul many times and was full of sensible advice, handing them letters of introduction to friends. As he said goodbye, he pressed a leather pouch of gold coins into

Osman Ferid's hand, in remembrance of their dear mother, he insisted. In turn the brothers presented him with their three magnificent stallions.

As they sailed out of the harbour on the overcrowded schooner, Osman Ferid and Ahmet stood on deck watching the jungle-thick forests and snowy ranges of the frosty Caucasus mountainous chain. The sky was a deep gentian blue, the snow dazzlingly white. As the mountains receded the peaks shone golden until on the horizon, the farthest crests and thin streaks of cloud took on a rich amber tint. A luminous, transparent haze spread over the lowlands softening their features. They stood on deck, unaware of the biting cold until the landscape disappeared into a grey, shadowy outline in the sky.

Osman Ferid grasped the rails trying to overcome the physical and mental agony and wretchedness he felt. He knew he would never return to the Caucasus, the mountains and home of his childhood where so many of his loved ones were buried. That night as he crouched on the deck, he wrote on a small piece of paper,

"Erkek insan kendi göz yaşlarını kimseye göstermez (a real man never shows his tears to anyone).

Carefully he folded the paper and put it in his pocket. (Osman Ferid carried that small, creased piece of paper with him for the rest of his life; after his death, his son Şamil found it in the worn, leather pouch that never left his father's side.)

He touched shoulders with Ahmet, young, tired and despondent,

"I don't know what the future holds for us in Istanbul, Ahmet, but I promise you, I will do eveything in my power to fulfill Nan's dream so that our family lives in safety and peace."

When the sun is overturned
When the stars fall away
When the mountains are moved
Then a soul will know what it has prepared.

The Circassian exodus was horrendous, the tragedy of a people uprooted, displaced.. Villages were wrecked, burned, homes destroyed, families separated; farmers burnt crops, killed cattle and herds. Proud warriors shot their horses rather than sell them. Before they embarked on the waiting ships, their precious belongings stuffed into carpet bags, they fired three times into the air, a salute to their beloved mountains and chanted a curse against the infidel.

"Oh sacred Oshamaphe (Circassian name for Mount Elbrus, the highest peak of the Caucasus mountain chain) with your far reaching summits decorated in eternal snow and ice, you are now the sacred home of our fallen brothers whose spirits will forever grieve the loss of our nation. Oh sacred mountain, the mists that fall on the valleys are mists that carry the souls of our fallen heroes. Your thunder and lightening once echoed with our honour and glory, now it carries our cries of anguish and defeat; the rains pour our tears on the forests valleys and plains. Curse the enemy, Oh Oshamaph, curse the invaders of our magnificent mountains."

I sketch
A sound of the violin;
There is a tree that grows
In a deep mountain gorge,
A green tree on which
A bird sits, and
This tiny bird composes
A beautiful melody about
A tiny bird who does not
Want to leave
Its native tree,
Whose song sounds
In the mountain gorge
Like the voice of the violin.

Nalbiy Kuek (Adig poet) translated by Ana Shiloff

PART TWO
TURKEY (1864-1878)

A real man never shows
his tears to anyone.
                    –Osman Ferid Pasha

CHAPTER 6

In the Service of the Sultan (1864-1878)

The refugee boat was silent, dry-eyed, overcrowded and uncomfortable. Its voyage weighed heavily in the hearts of its passengers. Their baggage carried the apathy and wretchedness of the past, rather than any optimism or cheer for the future. Even the prospect of a family reunion could not lighten the brothers' deep despair. They spent the voyage on deck, wrapped in their bourkas, crouched in a corner protected from the wind, until early in the morning they saw, in the distance, the magnificent skyline of mosques and minarets: Istanbul. Osman Ferid wondered how his mother would have felt standing on the deck of the boat as it ploughed its way towards the city of her dreams. Would she have felt joy, expectation and relief or would she have been dry-eyed and silent?

Edmondo de Amicis, a late nineteenth century Italian traveller, wrote,

"The best way to see the glories of the city was to approach by sea. To the right, Galata, her foreground a forest of masts and flags: above Galata, Pera, the imposing shapes of her European palaces outlined against the sky: in front, the bridge, connecting the two banks, across which flow continually two opposing, many-hued, streams of life; to the left, Stambul, scattered over her seven hills each crowned with a gigantic mosque with its leaden dome and gilded pinnacle.

"The sky throws everything into marvellous relief while the water, of a sapphire blue and dotted over with little purple buoys, reflects the minarets in long trembling lines of white."

This romantic image of the city was deceptive. Istanbul was run-down and neglected.

Osman Ferid and Ahmet searched for Mehmet among the noisy, excited crowd swarming the dockside, desperately seeking relatives and friends among those disembarking.

"Look, there he is with Ismail amongst a group of cadets near the entrance," Ahmet pointed, shouting and waving both arms.

Grabbing their luggage, they scrambled down the gangway, elbowing their way through the motley throng. The four brothers jumped on each other, wrapping their arms around one another in poignant embrace, shaking hands, before they laughingly embraced again and again, overjoyed at being reunited. Mehmet looked handsome in his military uniform. He was a senior cadet with one more year before graduation. Ismail had grown tall; he blushed and was shy but soon his freckled face broke into a huge grin. Mehmet ushered them into a waiting carriage, asking after friends in the Caucasus. Were there any from the Shapli tribe on board?

Too excited to take in their surroundings, they talked and joked as they drove through the streets firing questions at each other until the carriage stopped in front of a small house in the district of Fatih. Zissi had been sitting in front of the window for hours; when she saw the carriage draw up, she ran into the street, threw her arms around Osman Ferid and, burying her head in his chest, sobbed and murmured how much she had missed him.

Zissi and Ismail lived with an old Caucassian couple, Ömer Bey and Zübeyde Hanım, who had kindly taken them under their wing while Mehmet boarded at the military school barracks. At weekends he would arrive armed with presents, warm blankets, fruit, halvah and sweets; in the evenings he and Zissi visited friends or attended social gatherings of the Caucasian community.

Zissi had inherited her mother's fine features, porcelain white skin framed in a shock of dark hair. She was polite and popular, and much sought after by Caucasian ladies with marriageable sons, but she firmly resisted any romantic advances.

"I am waiting for my family to come to Istanbul," was her reply.

She had prepared a Caucasian feast of sweetmeats, lamb, rice, chicken with walnuts and beans, filling their glasses with sweet tea until they begged her to stop.

They talked until the early hours of morning, each with a story to tell: happy, sad or traumatic. It was an exhilaratingly emotional evening and the young people were intoxicated with happiness at being together in this foreign land. They had kept their promise to their mother and were together in Istanbul, having survived the horrors of war and the loss of their parents and beloved country.

When the young Shapli family gathered around the table next morning, Osman Ferid stepped comfortably into the role as head of the family. The first task, he said, was to find a house as they could not impose on Ömer Bey's kindness much longer.

Zissi surprised her brother when she handed him their mother's jewel box and bag of gold still wrapped in cloth. She explained how they had survived without spending the inheritance. Mehmet helped with a small monthly allowance while she earned their keep caring for the dear Circassian couple who treated her as a daughter. She also made a little extra pin-money baking Caucasian sweets that a friend sold in her shop in the bazaar. Zissi was an excellent cook and rightly proud of her little enterprise. Every morning she took Ismail to school, delivered her daily quota of sweets, shopped with friends, and then collected Ismail from school in time to prepare the evening meal.

Mehmet told them of the large contingent of soldiers from the Caucasus recruited into the Ottoman military services and how the Circassian community assisted new arrivals finding homes, employment and schools for children.

In the afternoon the brothers set off to explore the city. They walked through crowded, crooked streets lined with wooden houses from Beyazit to Hagia Sophia, along the Divanyolu, through the noisy spice and flower bazaar to the harbour at the entrance of the Golden Horn. The bridge connecting the Golden Horn was one of the busiest spots in the city.

De Amicis described the scene on the bridge:

"Standing there, you can see all Istanbul pass by in the course of an hour. The crowd surges by in great waves of colour, each group of people representing a different nationality. Try to imagine the most extravagant contrasts of costume, every variety and type of social class, and your wildest dreams will fall short of the reality; in the course of ten minutes, and in the space of a few feet, you will have seen a mixture of race and dress you had never conceived of before."

He summed it up:

"It is an ever changing mosaic, a kaleidoscopic view of race, costume and religion, which forms and dissolves with a rapidity the eye and brain can with difficulty follow.

"Except for the commercial centre, where people of different religions and groups worked side-by-side, neighbourhoods were ethnically organised. Muslims, the largest group, lived in the central part of the peninsula; Armenians, Greeks and Jews concentrated along the Marmara shore and the Golden Horn was crowded with Greek and Jewish settlements."

In 1826 the Rev. R. Walsh wrote in his narrative of a journey from Istanbul to England:

"The Turks call the different people who reside under them by names indicative of the estimation in which they hold them. The Greeks, *Esir* or slaves, as they were considered to have forfeited their life at the taking of Istanbul and hold it ever since on sufferance; the Armenians, *reyas* or subjects, as they were never a conquered people, but merged insensibly into the population of the empire. But the Jews they call *mousaphir* or visitors, because they sought an asylum among them. They treat them, therefore, as visitors with kindness and hospitality."

Caucasians were given similar treatment to that of the Jews.

Most of the Circassian immigrants gathered in communities around the Fatih-Beyazit district; some had moved on to Central Anatolia, Izmir and Adapazar, while the more adventurous had travelled further afield to Syria, Jordon and Iraq.

In the evening, tired but exhilarated by the hub of the great city, the Shapli family gathered around the table to enjoy Zissi's delicious suppers, everyone prattling away at the same time. At first the brothers were overwhelmed by the sheer noise of the crowds and constant trading in a city of grand palaces, mosques, konaks, bazaars and dirty crumbling wooden houses in the back streets resided in by a variety of races, Muslims, Christians, Greeks, Jews and Armenians, all dressed in different costumes. Since his arrival, Ahmet lived in a fever of excitement; every day was an adventure, exploring new places, making new friends. Osman Ferid's reaction was more restrained; he began to feel apprehensive and troubled as he realised the huge challenge that faced the family in this cosmopolitan Ottoman capital.

In *The Last of the Dragomans* diplomat Andrew Ryan wrote,

"Nature and art alike contributed to the charm of Istanbul. I came to love it in all its moods, even the angriest, when thunderstorms swept the surrounding hills. In the city there was much squalor, but even the meanest buildings and some of the larger incongruities merged somehow in a beauty of ensemble. The mystery of Istanbul was, one might say, symbolised by the latticed screens, called in Turkish 'kafes' or cages which protected the outer windows of the women's quarters of all Muslim houses."

These wooden houses, especially in the old city caused constant fear of fire. The dreaded sound of the fire-brigade's bell ringing warnings never stopped as they raced through the city.

"The English writer, Edward Lear wrote to his sister,

"You will have heard of the frequent fires, and their extent... you will not be surprised to hear since I came there have been eight dreadful burnings - the least of which 60, the largest 5,000 houses - and reduced hundreds and hundreds to wretchedness."

He goes on to describe the Pera fire in 1848,

"As it was only 300 houses were burnt! No lives lost—they very seldom are!-all the property is carried through the suburbs to the cemeteries etc - and there the poor people live till another wooden suburb arises in less than a year's time. Such is life in Istanbul."

To escape the fear of fires, wealthy families moved into stone houses in fashionable neighbourhoods around the foreign embassies of Galata and Pera, renting their large wooden *konaks* to three or four families of limited means. Ömer Bey suggested they share a konak with two Circassian families, but Osman Ferid politely refused. He had seen the devastation fires caused in the mountains and besides he did not want to share a house; he wanted the privacy of their own home. Every day he set out to look for an affordable, *kârgir* building of stone and brick to rent.

Edmondo de Amicis described the helpless agony of residents in Istanbul in the face of fire disasters.

"The word fire means for the inhabitants of Istanbul 'every misfortune' and the cry *Yangın Var* is charged with a dread meaning, terrible, fateful, carrying with it dismay - a cry at which the entire city is moved to its very depths, and pours forth as at the announcement of a scourge from God."

Osman Ferid spent days walking the streets of the old city until he happened upon a house he liked; it was in Beyazit, a large two-storey with a brick exterior, surrounded by a walled garden. The next day they moved.

Isolated communities attach great importance to the tradition, customs and rituals of their tribes on notable occasions. Memorial ceremonies for dead warriors were strictly observed in the Caucasus. Their coat-of-arms and weapons were treated as sacred belongings and displayed on the walls of their houses as a tribute to bravery.

When Osman Ferid discovered Zissi had brought his father's weapons, he suggested they arrange a wall display in their new home. The brothers set to work preparing a tribute to their father, Shapli Bereketuko Hasan. Ahmet designed a large Shapli coat-of-arms in rich mahogany to hang against a green felt background. Osman Ferid and Mehmet arranged the shield, gunpowder-flask, silver embossed kinjal, a set of pistols and medals engraved with precious stones around the insignia, then added Janbolat's kinjal, sword and the Circassian flag that had flown on his banner in that last battle.

Osman Ferid said,

"This coat-of-arms is a testimony of the bravery and loyalty of the Shapli family in the Caucasus. Let it be a testimony to our new life in the Ottoman Empire; together we will be brave and loyal against all odds."

They cheered, raising their glasses of tea as a toast. For the first time since he had left the Caucasus, Osman Ferid felt at home.

Months passed. The Shapli family settled comfortably into life in the busy, noisy city. Zissi went about her chores humming happily, delighted to mother her brothers. The money she earned from sweet making was spent on extra luxuries for the house; her latest purchase had been wooden benches with a table so that on warm summer evenings they could dine in the garden, watching the stars as they had in their mountain aoul.

Mehmet's influence acquired a place for his younger brothers at the military schools; Ismail gained entry to the cadet academy and Ahmet was accepted into the Cavalry Corps.

Good fortune smiled on the Shapli family at last, except for Osman Ferid, who found himself in a singularly frustrating predicament. From childhood he had been trained as a warrior; he had no other talent. Too old to apply to the military academy, the only option open to him was to recruit as a regular soldier in the Ottoman Army but with his three younger brothers about to graduate as officers, it would cause an embarrassing and awkward situation within the family.

After weeks of indecision, he decided he had no choice but to learn a trade. Thousands of Circassians had become prosperous and well-integrated tradesmen and members of the Turkish society. He would seek help from the Circassian community.

Osman Ferid's Daghestani friends were famed as artisans and craftsmen for their exquisite, fine work in metals, iron, silver and gold, set with precious and semi-precious stones. They owned jewellery and silver shops in the Grand Bazaar, forged beautifully embellished blades and handles for kinjals, swords and weaponry. Blacksmiths worked within the Royal compound, while peasants made their way to farms on the outskirts of the city seeking work as horse trainers and farm-hands.

Osman Ferid was chief of the Ubykh tribe, a warrior who had fought in the last battle. To this day, Caucasians remain loyal to descendants of the ruling class. Princes, chieftains and noblemen are entitled to the respect and honour they commanded in the past. The Circassian community was well aware of Osman Ferid's predicament, but it would have been improper to suggest a menial post to a chieftain and Osman Ferid was too proud to ask.

He became more and more disillusioned. For the first time in his life he felt inadequate and unsure of himself; these were deeply disturbing emotions for a responsible young man in a strange city. In the evenings, not wanting to burden the family with his problem, he invented amusing stories of places and people he met during the day. But alone in his room, he tossed and turned, waking up in a sweat; he longed for the open spaces, mountain air and the physical activity of a ride or hunt. He longed for the countryside. He felt imprisoned in this noisy metropolis which offered little hope of a decent living.

Mehmet was a pillar of support, rushing home for brief visits during the week and spending the weekends with his elder brother. Ahmet had joined a Circassian dance group and rushed off to the community centre in the afternoons.

"Why don't you come; you will meet pretty girls," he winked as he waved goodbye.

One Saturday morning, Mehmet suggested they visit an officer friend in charge of preparations for a royal hunt party at the Sultan's lodge at Therapia on the hills overlooking the Bosphorus.

Boarding a ferry boat at Karaköy, they sat on deck looking at the white palaces, shining domed mosques, wooden yalıs and clusters of houses by the waterside. The boat lurched against the landing stage to let crowds off and on, before it lurched to a start. Osman Ferid enjoyed the boat ride along the Bosphorus.

"Mehmet, if I can't live in the mountains, I want to live near the sea or the desert. I need space. I feel claustrophobic in this city."

He laughed ironically shaking his head,

"What am I going to do?"

They disembarked at Therapia to find Ghazi, a handsome Caucasian officer, waiting with a horse-driven carriage cab. They drove past wooded hills of pine and cypress trees to the Sultan's lodge. An army of soldiers were hard at work painting and repairing, while gardeners watered greenery, planted flowers and cut unsightly foliage. The young men passed through the elegant rooms and immaculate tiered lawns towards the stables.

"The Sultan has a string of magnificent horses and stallions. I am in charge of exercising them until the hunt, would you care to ride with me?"

Osman Ferid stroked the black, silk-like coat of a horse.

"It would be a pleasure; I miss the smell of stables," he joked as he took the reins of a fine thoroughbred.

They spent the afternoon riding through the woods, past fig gardens, Judas trees and the high walls of private villas. Riding through this glorious countryside, Osman Ferid forgot his troubles as the horse responded to his touch. Ghazi was delighted when Osman Ferid performed a few equestrian disciplines, whose origins were used in military practices, before galloping off like the wind, leaving them far behind. They found him in the stables, flushed and smiling, rubbing down the horse.

Osman Ferid grinned, "I apologise for galloping off like that, but I miss a good gallop in the country on such a fine horse."

"Thank you," responded Ghazi.

"You are a pleasure to watch.. Mehmet said you were one of the finest horsemen in the Caucasus, now I believe him." It seemed other officers on duty had watched him ride, for they congratulated him on his horsemanship and invited him to join them for dinner. Talk circled around life in the army. Osman Ferid felt at ease in the convivial atmosphere of the barracks with their loud, high-spirited camaraderie; he prayed the evening would never end.

A few days later, Ghazi made a surprise visit to the Shapli home. Looking smug and pleased, he handed Osman Ferid a large envelope stamped with the royal seal. It was an official invitation to take part in the *Djighitovka*, an equestrian tournament performed by royal command once a year. Ghazi explained how the invitation had come about.

"The reason Mehmet had arranged the visit to the Sultan's lodge on Saturday was to introduce you to my brother officers at the academy. He was determined to present you as a candidate for the *Djighitovka* tournament. There are certain qualifications required to enter; the candidate has to be a recent immigrant, unmarried and nominated as a worthy contestant by twelve officers serving in the Sultan's royal forces. My fellow officers and I have unanimously agreed to invite you to represent the Military Academy as our nominee this year.

"Long before you came to Istanbul, Mehmet kept telling us about your exploits as a soldier and horseman. He gave me no peace until I helped him arrange that day at Therapia. We are all impressed and think you stand an excellent chance to win. The first ten competitors win a place in the Sultan's Guard Regiment, the Circassian Musketeer Guards."

Ghazi shook Osman Ferid's hand as he stood there speechless, quite overcome. I must be dreaming, he thought.

Mehmet called Zissi, Ahmet and Ismail to share the good news; they squealed with delight dancing around their brother but Ghazi lifted his hand to silence them.

"This tournament is highly competitive and the competition will be even keener this year due to the large influx of immigrants. I have seen the list. Many are from well-known warrior families. You will have to work hard to win. My father has a stud farm at Yeşilkoy outside the city. It is the perfect place to train; he always needs an extra hand, but I warn you, he is a hard task master."

Ghazi's father, Hamit Bey, was from Abkazia and had met Chief Hasan and his tribe at Sochi. In 1859, after losing an arm fighting in Cape Pitsunda, he migrated to Turkey to set up a stud farm. A man of few words, he was large and autocratic, embittered by his physical handicap; he made it clear from the start that he preferred the company of horses to men.

After they rode around the farm, which spread over the downs along the coast of Yeşilkoy, he showed Osman Ferid his living quarters, a small, bare room near the stables, gave him his duties for the coming week and rode off.

The next morning at sunrise Osman Ferid rose with the farmhands, fed the animals, cleaned the stables, felled trees in the woods, repaired paddocks and outbuildings and finally, just before sunset, set off to exercise the horses over the sand dunes and through the woodlands. He looked forward to those long solitary trail rides every evening, taking time to brush down the horse with loving care, thoroughly enjoying his arduous labour.

Two weeks later, Osman Ferid was told to meet Hamit Bey in the lower fields.

He was stroking a magnificent white Arab stallion.

"This is the horse you will ride in the tournament. He is a favourite of mine, fast, intelligent but temperamental. You must win his respect to get the best out of him. From now on you are relieved of all duties."

Hamit Bey handed him the reins.

"Good luck," he said as he rode off.

"Thank you sir, thank you," Osman Ferid shouted to the disappearing figure.

Weeks passed. Osman Ferid spent every waking moment with the horse, grooming, riding, feeding and whispering Circassian orders in his ear until a trust grew on both sides. He taught the horse to stay at the sound of a rifle or gunfire, to stand beside him when he dismounted, and to move through sharp turns to full gallop.

Their relationship had a magical quality. Osman Ferid felt he was back in the mountains preparing for his presentation. He felt strong, bursting with energy and vitality, confident that he had the endurance and stamina to win the competition.

One warm, September evening, Hamit Bey sent word that they were to leave for Istanbul the following day. The tournament was to be held within a week. Osman Ferid felt well prepared, physically and mentally confident, motivated not by burning ambition or vanity, but by a strong sense of duty. He had been taught since childhood that his duty was to protect the tribe and family. Circumstances might have changed, but his duty remained the same, to provide and protect his family: winning the tournament would open doors to the military career he had prayed for and, at the same time, would guarantee prosperity for his family. He would win.

He looked dashingly handsome, tall and slim in his impeccable white Tcherkesska with his father's kinjal and Janbolat's sword attached to his belt.

The tournament was held outside the walls of Yıldız Palace. It was the sporting event of the year, attended by a large crowd from Istanbul and Anatolia, wealthy Ottomans and Christians from far and wide. Many came, not only to enjoy a day of superb equestrian sport, but in the hope of hiring guards or personnel from this elite group of competitors. Excitement heightened as the royal guards rode into the arena to a fanfare of trumpets and drums announcing the arrival of Sultan Abdülaziz and his entourage.

During the time he was heir apparent, Sultan Abdülaziz had spent his life as a country squire on the hills of Therapia, far removed from the intrigues and power of the Palace and Porte, until in 1861, at the age of thirty-one, he succeeded his half-brother, Abdülmecid, to the throne. He was a large, outdoor man, weighing over 225 pounds, loud-spoken, of intemperate habits, who delighted in wrestling, cock fighting, hunting, fishing and shooting; he was known and feared for his explosive temper. He looked magnificent in the imperial uniform, seated on a white stallion with a gold saddle, escorted by Circassian Royal Guards, and followed by the grand vizier, ministers of the Porte, ambassadors, diplomats and foreign guests. Osman Ferid thought the sultan looked, as he was often described, a "handsome giant with a full face and large staring eyes and a beard streaked with grey even when young, the finest of his race for 400 years, looking every inch a sultan."

As he rode towards the royal enclosure the crowd parted cheering in unison, "Padişahım Çok Yaşa - Long live our Sultan" three times.

The sultan's mother, Pertevale Sultan, a Circassian, was a powerful, strong-willed woman who played an influential role over her son's affairs. Not only did she handpick the Circassian beauties in his large harem, it was rumoured that it was her influence and crafty politics that had persuaded Sultan Abdülaziz to offer sanctuary to the hundreds of thousands of Muslim Circassians expelled from Russia.

Silence fell as the sultan's chief of staff rose to address the crowd. He welcomed the new arrivals in the name of the sultan, expressing the importance and significance of the event for the competitors and the Ottoman Armed Forces. The Sheikh- ul - Islam read the prayer, blessing the Sultan and Caliph of Islam, the contestants and spectators. All eyes turned to the sultan in anticipation as he bowed his head, the sign to begin the tournament. A dazzling spectacle of two hundred riders circled the arena dressed in a myriad of colourful costumes seated on supremely agile horses, "the fittest of all for a king in the day of triumph" with ceremonial bridles and manes.

The first event in the horse trials was a show of equestrian arts. The contestants were divided into groups of twenty, from which two would qualify for the next round. Deafening applause and name calling accompanied the riders as they went through their paces.

It was a lively circus-like contest involving challenges for horse and rider. Proud in their tribal costumes, the contestants strove to outwit their opponents with speed and precision as they rivalled for a place in the second round.

Wild mountaineers dressed in black fur stood on the stirrups of their horses as they galloped around the arena, swinging their sabres in the air and attracting the greatest excitement and roars.

There were three Kabardan warriors in shining chain mail, two fierce-looking Shapsugh chiefs, a number of Abdzakhs, a member from the Berzak family and twenty Ubykh, some of whom Osman Ferid had known in Circassia. The first round ended with loud cheers and fanfares as the winners rode in front of the royal box to salute the sultan before retiring for the second half.

Ahmet, Mehmet and Ismail ran to congratulate their brother.

"Be mindful of the Kabardans and the Shapsugh chief," Ahmet advised.

"They are aggressive."

"I think Bhaduk Djighit is your strongest adversary. Does he remind you of anyone?" asked Mehmet.

"Yes, Janbolat," answered Osman Ferid.

"He has that same panther-like agility and self-assurance."

The bugle and drum-roll sounded the start of the second and final contest. The crowds rushed to their places; sellers gathering their wares, scurried to the edge of the arena.

The second half was a gruelling event that demanded the ultimate in fitness, stamina, agility and obedience. The speed and endurance part was designed to test the horse's fitness and training. At a gallop, contenders jumped ditches and fences and fired at moving targets until the final free-for-all battle, gathering flags tied to poles. One-by-one, contenders were sent off the field, penalized for faults at obstacles, falling, foul play, lack of control or failing to hit the target, until only ten remained to race for the flags. The contest was played out with the fury and energy of gladiators, all intent on winning the prize that would change their lives. The air was filled with noisy expectation as the last ten—now assured of their place in the Circassian Musketeer Guards—prepared for the final test.

The final challenge was to load a pistol while circling the field at full gallop, shooting at the target at the far end of the field three times. This demanded physical and mental coordination and steady nerves. Seven were instantly disqualified, leaving three to contend for first place: Bhjaduk, the Kabardan warrior, and Osman Ferid. The three nodded with sporting spirit as they took their places.

The crowd chanted,

"Bhjaduk, Bhjaduk, Bhjaduk," as he galloped into the field shouting warlike cries, firing into the air and raising dust into swirling clouds.

He galloped as he loaded and reloaded his pistol from the charges in his pockets with huge, dramatic gestures. He had one hit and two misses, but the crowd cheered him with roars of delight.

Osman Ferid was next. He cantered onto the field, sitting straight and tall in the saddle. He bowed low in front of the sultan and his guests before urging his horse into a gallop circling the field. With perfect precision he fired, loaded and reloaded three times: two hits, one miss. The crowd went wild with excitement, shouting his name

"Osman Ferid, Osman Ferid."

The last contestant was the trim Kabardan, arrogant in his fine, chain mail costume. Ignoring the royal spectators, he galloped towards the target shooting, reloading, shooting three times and scoring three hits. The crowd let out a tremendous roar, cheering, clapping, and chanting his name. He accepted this adulation with an elegant bow, firing into the air as he galloped around the field.

The sultan nodded with pleasure as the winners rode past for the presentation ceremony. The director of the Military Academy, a Caucasian pasha, presented the medal of accomplishment with the invitation to enrol into the Royal Guard regiment.

Amidst a fanfare of trumpets, drums and shouts of 'Padişah, çok yaşa' the royal party departed. It was then the festivities and celebrations began in earnest. Osman Ferid was smothered with hugs and kisses from family and friends; every passing spectator shook his hand or gave him a congratulatory slap on the back. The military band played; minstrels wandered around improvising poems and songs in their honour; gypsies threaded through the crowd offering to read palms or poke wretched bears with sharp sticks to dance for a few kuruş.

Sellers shouted their wares as they walked carrying large trays of rice, sweets and baklava strapped around their necks, followed by water sellers with pitchers of cool water or sweet lemonade. Colourful baskets of fresh flowers filled the air with perfume; stalls were laden with mouth-watering home-made breads, biscuits and cakes. Osman Ferid went to the stables where he knew he would find Hamit Bey.

"Hamit Bey," Osman Ferid shook his hand,

"Thank you for permitting me to ride such a fine horse; he did us both proud. I owe my success to him."

Hamit Bey smiled,

"I enjoyed the competition. It was one of the most exciting I have seen for a long while. This year the competitors were an exceptional group. I knew you would ride him well and appreciate his temperament and sensibilities. Congratulations on your commission. You will make a fine officer. Come visit me sometime."

Osman Ferid was pleased to receive the invitation.

"It will be an honour sir; I am grateful and deeply indebted to you and Ghazi. Thank you."

Hamit Bey nodded and led his horse away.

Osman Ferid felt elated but emotionally drained. As he walked back to join his family, he thought how much he missed not having his father or Janbolat at his side. He looked up to the sky, his eyes glittering like the stars above,

"Thank you Thae, thank you. Rest in peace, Nan, your dream has come true."

Early next morning he reported to the Guard Headquarters at Taşkışla. New recruits were met by a Circassian officer who gave a short initiation speech. They swore loyalty to the His Imperial Highness and Caliph, Sultan Abdülaziz, the Ottoman Empire and the Ottoman Military Forces, with a special prayer of thanks for the sultan, who had so generously bestowed upon them the honour and opportunity to serve in his regiment.

At the age of twenty Shapli Osman Ferid was commissioned as Master Sergeant in the Circassian Musketeers. He was tall, 6 ft 4, and handsome with a mop of brown hair, pale complexion and serious but expressive eyes. After nine months of strenuous military training, he was promoted to lieutenant by royal decree on April 16, 1866.

He moved into the officers' mess where his pleasing, well-mannered attitude, hard work and quiet efficiency were soon noted by his senior officers

But Osman Ferid was not one of the boys like Mehmet and Ahmet. Dependable, good-humoured and friendly though he was, he remained apart, at times even aloof. Even though he did not join in their lively pranks and high-spirited adventures, secret parties in the mess-room or rare midnight escapades into the city, it was to him they turned when a problem arose or to seek advice. He became known as a man who spoke little but listened well and could be relied upon for a frank and impartial opinion.

Within a short time, he had won the respect and trust of the company. They teased him about his natural reserve and need for privacy but admired his strong sense of identity and his genuine concern for the well-being of the group. He was keen to learn about the new military technology and equipment introduced into the Ottoman Army. His spare time was spent at the sultan's stables, grooming and exercising the royal horses. On weekend leave, armed with presents, he rushed home. It was here with Zizzi, Ismail, Ahmet and Mehmet in the privacy and warmth of his own house that Osman Ferid dropped his inner defensives and enjoyed the intimacy and love of his family. He played games with his brothers, oiled and polished rifles and the family swords for hours; he enjoyed teasing Zissi about her lack of admirers and playfully scolded Ismail and Ahmet. Much to the family's dismay he insisted they speak Turkish. When he made mistakes, which was quite often, he was held to shame.

He and Mehmet, a lieutenant, were inseparable. They spent every spare moment together. Mehmet introduced him to prominent Circassian families, many with beautiful daughters who served coffee with shy, lowered but flirtatious eyes. Many young men yearned after Zissi but, awed by her brothers and her cool attitude, few had the courage to ask her hand in marriage. Zissi remained happily indifferent, quite content preparing for the family gatherings at the weekends; she, like her mother, wanted to keep the family together as long as possible.

In April, 1867, Sultan Abdülaziz hosted a boar-hunting party for members of his court and foreign guests at the Royal Köşk (lodge) in the wooded hills above the Bosphorus. These invitations were highly prized, for it offered not only a day of superb hunting in extravagant luxurious surroundings but a rare opportunity to catch the ear and eye of the sultan or his grand vizier. Fine drapes, silk and velvet embroidered cushions of every hue were strewn on silk carpets and on the lawn, while sumptuous feasts prepared in the royal kitchens were served on huge silver trays heavy with succulent meats with vegetables and herbs fresh from the royal gardens and delicious warm breads from the royal bakery. The meal was followed with tray upon tray of honeyed sweets, baklava and fruits. An army of servants and courtiers attended to the guests.

The Guard Regiment accompanied Sultan Abdülaziz, astride his magnificent white stallion, along the shore road of the Bosphorus, past wooden konaks standing high in large gardens, sleepy villages and forests to the entrance of the köşk. Cheering crowds gathered to greet the illustrious sultan as he rode past. Osman Ferid had been assigned to accompany dignitaries from the French Embassy. A bugle sounded the start of the hunt as they followed a drove of servants banging tin boxes to entice boars out of their lairs. They had been hunting for several hours without any sign of an animal when suddenly, from behind a large rock, a wounded boar pounded out towards one of the hunters. Osman Ferid pushed the guest to the ground, sprung forward, leaped over him, and shot the boar head on.

The boar slumped to the ground; Osman Ferid turned to find the gentleman still on the ground.

"I am sorry, sir," he muttered in confusion helping him to his feet and brushing away leaves and dirt from his suit.

"Non, non, young man."

The Frenchman was shaken, but smiled when he saw the dead boar.

"I am all right. What is your name, please?" he asked as they made their way back to the köşk, followed by servants carrying the large boar in hammock-fashion tied to sticks.

A month later, Osman Ferid was summoned to Dolmabahçe Palace for an audience with the sultan. Osman Ferid sat stiff and straight on a plush velvet chair in the corner of the ornate Mabeyn-i Hümayün, the Selamlik or waiting chamber, for what seemed hours, until a court chamberlain beckoned to follow him up the wide red-carpeted stairs along a corridor with heavy brocaded windows and gilded mirrors overlooking the Bosphorus.

"Wait here," he was told.

Behind the door he could hear voices.

"Keep close to me. Do not speak," whispered the chamberlain as they entered the Kabul Odasi, a vast, rococo, throne room.

Sultan Abdülaziz sat on the throne surrounded by officials, while silent servants offered sherbets and sweets on silver trays. The chamberlain walked towards the sultan bowing low,

"Your Majesty, Lieutenant Shapli Osman Ferid of the Circassian Musketeers'

Abdülaziz looked at the young man standing in front of him. He remembered his fine performance at the *Djighitovka* tournament. He admired Caucasians for their excellent horsemanship and loyalty to the House of Osman.

"Your act of courage at the hunting party at Therapia has been brought to my attention in a letter from the French Ambassador. He wishes to express his gratitude and reward you for saving the life of one of their most distinguished guests. As your Sovereign, it befalls upon me to reward you. I promote you to the rank of captain. You will join my personal guard regiment as aide-de-camp. Go with God."

"Reward this officer with a hundred pieces of gold," he ordered the chamberlain.

The sultan nodded, and then turned to his guests. Before he could murmur his thanks, Osman Ferid was ushered out of the room.

"Don't worry; there is no need to thank His Majesty," said the chamberlain.

"He never forgets a face or a good deed."

Osman Ferid rushed home to share his good fortune with the family. He described his audience with the sultan, the splendour of the courtiers and the palace where he would soon resume his duty.

The Circassian Muskeeteers was made up of North Caucasians from Daghestan, Chechnya and Circassia assimilated into a Caucasian Guards Brigade. This brigade was frequently dispatched to remote areas of the Ottoman Empire to stamp out uprisings.

By royal edict, in May, 1867 Lieutenant Shapli Osman Ferid was promoted Captain of the Guards and aide-de-camp to Sultan Abdülaziz.

CHAPTER 7

Visit to Europe

Throughout its history, reform within the Ottoman Empire inevitably caused some form of controversy, opposed by radical, conservative mullahs, hailed by the enlightened few. In 1839, Sultan Abdülmecid had proclaimed a constitutional document, the Hatti-Sherif of Gülhane in the Gülhane Edict, known as Tanzimat (reforms). This charter gave political, legal and social rights to all Ottoman subjects, Muslim and non-Muslim.

The charter, although modelled on the western system of government, kept strictly within the framework of the Islamic law by reconfirming the supreme power of the sultan and his government. The aim of the charter was two-fold: first to address the declining state of the Empire by instating reforms for modernization according to European standards and secondly to appease growing concerns of foreign powers for the protection of non-Muslim, Christian and Jewish subjects who resided within the Ottoman Empire. These reforms were welcomed by the European community. While keeping a careful eye on their progress, Lord Palmerston, British foreign secretary, hailed it as a grand stroke of policy.

The reforms ensured that Muslims and non-Muslims alike were entitled to equal rights in matters of law, property and taxation, education at civil and military schools and the right of

118

enrolment in the armed forces or civil service. While this law addressed the concern voiced by foreign powers about Christian Ottoman subjects, the sultan's grand vizier, Ali Pasha, expressed his concern for the plight of the Muslims. He wrote:

"The (unequal) privileges enjoyed by different communities arise from inequalities in their obligations. The Muslims are absorbed almost entirely in the service of the government. Other people devote themselves to professions that bring wealth. In this way, the latter establish an effective and fatal superiority over Your Majesty's Muslim subjects. Muslims must also devote themselves to commerce, agriculture, trade, industry and crafts. Labour is the only durable capital. Let us put ourselves to work, Sire, that is the only way to safety for us."

This included the hundred of thousands of immigrants who had poured into the Ottoman Empire from the Caucasus. It meant they were entitled to the same legal rights (with the exception of those in the harem, who remained the sultan's prerogative). This influx was to cause serious social and political upheaval as well as stretch the resources of the Porte.

Since 1839, European powers had been pressing the Porte for sustained continuance in its reform programme.

By 1860, the social and political unrest that was sweeping through Europe had begun to gather momentum on the streets of Istanbul. Crowds of frustrated, disgruntled subjects attended meetings at public squares throughout the city. The government was in a dilemma; the liberal-minded vizier and his ministers were torn between external pressure from France, Britain and Austria demanding enforcement of the reforms and growing internal pressure from a small, but influential radical group, known as 'Young Ottomans' (Yeni Osmanlılar), who campaigned vigorously against the reforms.

Articles written by the Young Ottomans appeared in newspapers and journals opposing the Tanzimat reforms as too Western in ideology. Their goal was to promote the controversial and sensitive issue of constitutional and social reform. They wanted reform within the system rather than a revolution; their call was for constitutional monarchy with a sultan who would understand and respect the new intelligentsia. The group founded a secret society in France inspired by the writings of Namik Kemal, political journalist and essayist, Ibrahim Şinasi and Ziya Paşa, brother of the Khedive of Egypt, Mustafa Fazil Pasha and other enlightened men. Their ultimate objective was to limit the autocratic powers of the sultan and introduce social reforms according to Islamic traditions. It was the first call for Ottoman patriotism - their slogan was *Hürriyet* – Liberty - while the slogan of the Tanzimat reforms had been *Adalet* - Justice.

An American missionary, van Lennep, wrote in his diary in 1864,

"There is a party chiefly composed of men educated in Europe who may be denominated 'Young Turkey,' whose object is to introduce a general and radical reform into all branches of the administration."

Lord Kinross in the *The Ottoman Centuries*, wrote,

"Namik Kemal drew on the liberal, parliamentary constitution of England with its indomitable power of public opinion against authority; he saw it as the 'model of the world' in political principles."

The grand vizier, well aware that any whisper of resistance to his absolute rule and sovereignty aroused Abdülaziz's explosive temper, attempted on every possible occasion to broach the subject of the Young Ottoman Movement to the sultan but always in vain.

Early in his reign, Sultan Abdülaziz had shown an interest in the reforms, especially in the introduction of new technology and costly projects for the military forces. He encouraged plans to link the Ottoman capital to central Europe by a network of railways. The Imperial Ottoman Bank was established in 1863.

But this interest soon waned when the sultan was informed of a lack of financial resources at the Porte – the state was near bankruptcy. He was simply unable to curb his personal extravagances and expenditure even when told of defaults in interest payments on the huge loans from European banks.

The newly crowned Emperor of France, Charles Louis Napoleon III, was young, ambitious, and misled by a love for glory. Determined to establish himself as a leader on the world stage, he hoped to settle affairs in Europe and find a solution to the "Eastern Question" in favour of France. In 1867, in an effort to symbolize the glory and grandeur of the Second Empire, the emperor decreed that he and his beautiful wife, Empress Eugenie, would host a state visit on the occasion of the opening of the Great Universal Exhibition of Paris. Invitations were sent to members the Royal Houses of Europe and Heads of State, including the Sultan of the Ottoman Empire.

The grand vizier, Mehmet Emin Ali Pasha, shared power at the Porte with Fuad Pasha, the foreign minister. A most able statesman, Ali Pasha was the first Ottoman spokesman to sit among the victorious peacemakers at the Peace Congress in 1856, following the war against Russia. He had been well received and his speech warmly applauded. The Congress reaffirmed the principles of Gülhane, asserting equality for Muslims and Non-Muslims within the Ottoman Empire, direct collection of taxes, and the writing of official decrees in simpler Ottoman Turkish. Foreign powers had no right to interfere in relations between the sultan and his subjects, nor in the internal administration of the empire.

The relationship between the grand vizier and foreign minister was one of concord and mutual support. They were convinced that the future of the empire lay in education and commerce, with strong social, political and cultural ties with the west. Dedicated to reform, and sympathetic to the cause and liberal views of the "Young Ottomans," they believed honest governing could solve many political problems. They envisioned their roles in government as mediators between the state, the western powers and the Young Ottomans. Both strongly opposed the conservative views of the mullahs. Ali Pasha welcomed the invitation from the Emperor of France as a step towards closer relationship with Europe.

The advent of electricity and the telegraph in 1855 greatly affected the speed of the decision-making process of the Porte; dispatches to embassies in London and Paris were received within hours. After months of delicate, secret negotiations with European heads of state and ambassadors, the British Ambassador, Lord Derby, along with the German and Austrian Ambassadors, approached the Porte to suggest the visit be extended to include other European countries. The day arrived when Ali Pasha was prepared to present the invitation to Abdülaziz.

Ali Pasha had on a previous occasion written to the Sultan:

"We have to establish stronger relations with Europe. It is essential to identify Europe's material interests with our own. Only then can the integrity of the Empire become a reality rather than a diplomatic fiction.

"In making the European states interested directly and materially in the conservation and defence of the country, we entered into many partnerships necessary for the regeneration of the Empire and the development of its riches."

Fuad Pasha accompanied Ali Pasha to Dolmabahçe Palace. As they waited in the selamlik, the grand reception room with its magnificent crystal chandelier, a gift from the Austrian Emperor, they watched the caiques skim silently across blue waters of the Bosphorus.

A royal chamberlain showed them into the throne room where the sultan greeted his grand vizier. Bowing low, Ali Pasha presented the royal invitations for a state visit from the Emperor of France, Queen Victoria and the German Kaiser. Ali Pasha, who prided himself on his fluency and good judgment, presented the proposal for the visit, emphasising its importance as the first visit by a reigning Sultan and Caliph of the Ottoman

Empire to Europe. He exercised subtle praise and flattery, elevating the sultan's self-absorption and vanity. He stressed the prestige and honour a visit by His Imperial Highness would have upon the wealthy, powerful heads of states in Europe, noting it would encourage foreign trade, new investments, and opportunities to negotiate for the extension of interest payments and provide a common ground for further larger loans. His royal visit would be 'a blaze of glory' throughout Europe.

Leaning towards the sultan, the grand vizier also made much of the adverse and harmful effect such a visit would have on the Young Ottomans, who would see the Caliph of the Ottoman Empire rub shoulders with leaders of liberal, western countries; this would proclaim the sultan's desire to become a modern ruler to all his subjects. The journey was to last 47 days. The sultan and his party would sail from Istanbul to Toulon and then travel by rail to Paris, before crossing the English Channel to England. The return journey would be overland by train with visits to Prussia and Austria before sailing from Varna to Istanbul on the last leg of the journey. Manufactured in 1866, the imperial train coach was elegant and comfortable. It had been presented to the sultan by the Midland Railway Carriage and Wagon Co, Birmingham who were building the Izmir Kasaba Railway.

The next day Ali Pasha received an acknowledgement from the palace. Abdülaziz had accepted the invitation.

News of the proposed visit spread like wildfire through the city, arousing controversial reactions from the sultan's subjects. It gained whole-hearted support from the foreign communities and from moderate Muslims and liberal- minded intellectuals who welcomed the visit as a positive step towards improved relations and understanding between Istanbul and Europe.

Conservative, religious mullahs and their followers were outraged that the Caliph, Supreme Head of all Islam, should have agreed to visit the "Countries of Infidels." It was the subject of discussion in elegant villas on the Bosphorus, crowded, wooden houses in the poorer quarters, on the streets, in cafes and bazaars, on boats, and in schools, the madrasahs and mosques. Bureaucrats argued. Imams raged from the mimbar (pulpit). Ladies smiled as they strolled along the Pera, anticipating the latest Paris and London fashions in their favourite shops on the sultan's return. Politicians and ministers spoke in whispers; walls had ears and the situation remained delicate and uncertain.

The Royal Guards, aware of the sultan's dislike for pomp and formality, were surprised at his acceptance, but any diversion from the strict daily routine was welcomed. The immediate question uppermost in the minds of the officers was who would be chosen to accompany him on the journey. At night in the barracks names of likely officers were shouted at random, bets made, arguments quelled. Names changed every evening. Osman Ferid's name came up a few times; he was popular and had impressed his brother officers and superiors, besides the sultan favoured big men like himself.

Osman Ferid shrugged off the rumours with a smile. He had been in the regiment less than a month and lacked the qualities of officers from the military academy who were fluent in French or English.

When he went home at weekends he was bombarded with questions about the goings on at the palace; there was little to tell. Life behind the high walls was secret, respectful and isolated. Zissi and Ismail heard much more in the streets; there were huge orders from the Porte for silks, brocades and jewellery. Caucasian goldsmiths worked day and night to meet demands for medals inlaid with precious stones, the finest silverware, presentation arms and a hundred more valuable gifts commissioned by the Porte. Osman Ferid grinned as Zissi remarked,

"I am sure you will be chosen; who better to serve the sultan than my handsome brother?"

Mehmet had been on guard duty at the Porte.

"So many carriages passed through the gate that it was difficult to control. I saw Müzürüs Pasha, ambassador to Britain, Cemil Pasha and the ambassador to France, who were received immediately while other diplomats and bureaucrats waited for hours."

A few days later, Osman Ferid was about to leave the palace for duty at Therapia, when orders arrived for all military personnel to return to Taşkışla barracks and report for inspection in full military uniform the following morning.

The Royal Household Regiment parade rode along Dolmabahçe Road passing Camlı Köşk from where, it was whispered down the line, the sultan and his ministers watched. A few days later the names of those to accompany the sultan on the royal tour were posted on the bulletin board. Much to his surprise, Osman Ferid had been selected.

Orders to remain in barracks until departure date meant Osman Ferid was unable to say good-bye to Zissi, but his brothers were able to visit him at barracks. As departure date drew near, the solemn formality of the palace disrupted into a hive of activity, with visits from worried-looking ministers, frowning, arrogant ambassadors, bureaucrats carrying mountains of paperwork and dossiers, and fussy tailors waddling along the corridors, followed by assistants struggling under bales of silks, velvets and brocades of every shade.

Besides their daily duties at the palace, the chosen few were measured for parade uniforms, attended classes on the logistics and details of the programme, the general culture of the countries to be visited and were instructed on their duties during the visit. Every possible precaution for the comfort and safety of the sultan and his party was checked and rechecked; nothing was overlooked, no detail too trivial. Ali Pasha was determined the royal visit would be a success.

At night, the officers fell into their bunks too exhausted to talk about the pending tour. Osman Ferid lay on his bunk revising the programme in his head; the thought of visiting Britain filled him with anticipation. He had asked Mehmet for a list of the names of the Englishmen who had supported the Caucasian cause in the hope he might have an opportunity to meet someone who knew them.

The day before departure, his brothers came to say good-bye.

"Take care of yourselves and Zissi. Tell her I miss her."

They embraced, and with a smart mocking salute bade a proud farewell.

Friday, June 21, 1867 was declared a public holiday. Sultan Abdülaziz' historical departure became an opportunity to display the power, wealth and grandeur of the Ottoman Empire to its subjects. The departure procession was accorded strict protocol; the court, ambassadors, guests and ministers took their positions on the waterfront of Dolmabahçe Palace. The Ottoman navy anchored at Beşiktaş joined the fanfare as cannons were fired from the Maiden's Tower, informing the city of the departure of Sultan Abdülaziz and his retinue.

The *Bostancıs* in charge of the rudders of the Imperial caiques standing in formation at Maiden's Tower bowed low in respect. Firework displays from the Asian and European shores of the Bosphorus lit up the sky as drums rolled and siren-whistles blew as the sultan's subjects gathered along the banks of the shore, shouting and waving 'Padişahım, çok yaşa - long live our Padishah' three times or more.

To humour his Royal Highness, whose dislike for sea voyages was well known, the royal yacht, the *Sultaniye*, had been completely overhauled and luxuriously refurbished according to his specifications. Hasan Bey, the most experienced seaman in the empire, captained the yacht. He had been relieved to learn the voyage was to take place before the September winds blew gales in the Marmara Sea.

Regally attired in ceremonial uniform, Sultan Abdülaziz boarded the yacht with three imperial princes, his son, Prince Yusuf Izzetin Efendi aged 12, and two of the sons of his late brother, Abdülmecid Efendi: Prince Murad Efendi, the Crown Prince who was 27, and his younger brother Prince

Abdülhamid Efendi, aged 25. He was attended by Grand Vizier Ali Pasha, Minister of Foreign Affairs Fuad Pasha, Grand Master of Ceremonies Kamil Bey, Cemil Bey and Hafız Mehmet Bey, Imam Hasan Nani Efendi, Halil Pasha, Diplomat Nazırı Keçeci, Ömer Faiz Efendi, First Chamberlain Cemil Bey, Second Chamberlain Kalid Bey, the principal physician to His Majesty, Marco Pasha, the principal interpreter to the Divan, Arifi Bey, several secretaries, chamberlains, aide-de-camps and a number of officers, military and civil, in the personal service of the Sultan. The *Sultaniye* was escorted by the *Pertevniyal* yacht, two warships, the *Aziziye* and *Orhaniye*, and the *Forben*, which carried the French Ambassador, Count Beureau, and the first secretary of the British Embassy.

As the yachts sailed into the calm, turquoise Marmara Sea, hundreds of His Majesty's subjects escorted the navel convoys in caiques, ferries, tugboats, takas and rowing boats as far as the Princes' islands, waving enthusiastic farewells.

Edmondo de Amicis describes a similar scene,

"The waterway resembles an unending port with a fleet of Ottoman merchant ships coming from all four corners of the globe with their shining armour, multi-coloured sails and strange prows. In front of the onlookers lined up along the shore, we see excursion caiques, darting like arrows, vying to pass each other. Crowded caiques of all shapes and colours come and go between the numerous piers on both sides of the continents and sandals glide between the columns of huge cargo-laden mavnas. Flagged sloops, fishermen's sandals and gilded Pasha's caiques zigzag among Istanbul's steamboats, full of turbans, fezzes and veils, to stop at all the piers."

The days passed calmly; the sultan and his party remained in their quarters. Osman Ferid idled the hours away checking the names his brother had given him and reading the information booklet about the countries to be visited, especially Britain.

Whenever he practised a few phrases aloud in French or English, his fellow officers overhearing would tease him.

"Don't worry, Osman Ferid," they laughed, "all you have to do is speak with your eyes. The lovely Parisian ladies will surely fall in love with your handsome, Caucasian looks."

Leaning on the rail of the deck one evening watching the fading light shimmering on the sea, he remembered that nightmare journey with Mehmet: two desperate émigrés from Circassia crossing the Black Sea. How traumatic it had been; it seemed a lifetime away, but it had been only three years. They had left their country in chaos and ruin. The aftermath of war is long and bitter. He had left the Caucasus for the sake of his brothers and sister and to keep his promise to his mother. Had he been alone, he would have remained in the mountains he loved so dearly.

Osman Ferid had a clear, self-disciplined mind when it came to making decisions, refusing to give in to adversity. Like his father, he believed his energy and belief came from Thae, god of the mountains, the reason perhaps for his sometimes childlike faith and beliefs. He was exiled physically rather than mentally; a part of him remained in the Caucasus. That image of being with that and those he loved—of not being disconnected—was the most powerful driving force within him. It was his inner strength. He was deeply grateful for the sanctuary and opportunities the sultan and Ottoman Empire had given his family and the thousands of Circassian immigrants. He would serve the Ottoman Army as a loyal officer – but would remain at heart a guest - someone who came in from the cold. Osman Ferid grimaced. He rarely reflected on the past for it brought back too many painful memories and inner anxieties.

On the fifth day, the royal yacht sailed through the blue Mediterranean Sea to its first port of call, Naples.

That Italy was torn by civil war did not hamper King Emmanuel II from honouring his illustrious guests with a royal welcome. A group of representatives of the monarch, including members of the royal family, the prime minister, and members of the cabinet, along with leading dignitaries from the Vatican, stood at the harbour during a presentation of arms by the Italian Royal Guards. These sights plus the lively tunes of the military band entertained crowds of Italians who lined the harbour waving Italian and Turkish flags and shouting "Viva Turchia." Their hosts boarded the *Sultaniye* to pay their respects to the Ottoman sultan and his entourage. Each guest was given an Ottoman decoration; the prime minister was presented with an exquisite jewelled Order of the Ottoman Empire, a gift to the absent but honourable king. As the royal yacht sailed towards the French coast the sultan and his entourage were pleased by the warm reception they had received from a Christian country.

Little could spoil the pleasure of the voyage until one morning the weather changed; low ominous clouds darkened the sky as though a storm was about to brew. Sultan Abdülaziz ordered the yacht to return to the nearest Italian port, but Captain Hasan rolled the ship with the waves until the sea calmed and they were able to continue on course, to anchor at Toulon harbour. There, on behalf of Emperor Napoleon, Abdülaziz and his suite were welcomed with an impressive naval reception by the Duc de Tarante, the Marquis de Coeau and General Bevillemet. The masts of the French fleet were hung with Turkish and French flags and the harbour crowded with welcoming French people waving flags and cheering the procession as it boarded the royal train for Paris.

The *Illustrated London News* reported:

"The scene at the Paris terminus of the Lyons and Mediterranean Railway on 1st July, the day of the Sultan's arrival, when the Emperor Napoleon went there to meet him and conduct him to the palace of the Tuilleries, was a moment in history. Many thousands of people assembled in the streets near the Place de la Bastille to see their Imperial Majesties pass, and the houses were decorated with flags. They cheered, waved flags, shouting "Viva Turkey, Viva France, Viva Sultan, Viva Napoleon."

"The interior of the railway station was adorned with a long streamer and banners attached to a row of tall flag staffs richly gilded; the waiting room was splendidly fitted out, and seats were ranged for the accommodation of privileged spectators. The special train bringing the sultan from Toulon arrived at a quarter past four. The Emperor Napoleon met him and shook hands with him on the platform. The two sovereigns immediately entered a court carriage and proceeded by a detachment of lancers, drove off to the Tuilleries. The Emperor Napoleon was dressed in a military uniform; the Sultan also wore a military uniform, richly embroidered and crossed by the ribbon of the Legion of Honour; on his head was a fez.

"He attempted very eagerly to enter into conversation with the Emperor but it is said he cannot speak French with enough ease or fluency so as to make himself understood. The carriage in which they took their seats was followed by nine other imperial vehicles, containing the suite of the sultan and the Turkish ambassador at Paris. As on previous occasions when these visits take place, the sultan was conducted by the Emperor to the Tuilleries where he was introduced to the empress and the officers appointed to attend his Majesty during his sojourn in the French capital. The sultan then took his departure for the Elysee where he has been lodged."

Paris was more splendid than ever, enjoying the halcyon days of the Second Empire as Napoleon III and his beautiful wife, Empress Eugenie, hosted the rulers of Europe, royalty and heads of state at the first Paris Exhibition in the Champs de Mars. It was a manifestation of France's power and grandeur; the ambitious Emperor had orchestrated brilliant gala performances, receptions, balls, concerts, a *son et lumiere* spectacular, and other functions with ostentatious exaggeration, which Parisians, flanking the tree-lined boulevards, watched with wonder and pride.

On July 1, Emre Aracı wrote in the introduction to his album *London to Istanbul,* "Napoleon greeted his royal guests with a patriotic French Hymn dedicated to himself and "his valiant people," composed by Rossini and played by the military band at the Palais de L'Industrie."

The sultan of the Ottoman Empire and his suite remained the centre of attraction throughout the visit. Abdülaziz was an imposing figure in his bejewelled uniform and red fez, accompanied by tall, handsome aides-de-camp, immaculate and sober in their gilded uniforms. Their hostess, beautiful, elegant Empress Eugenie, expressed delight at the retiring disposition of her Oriental guests. Sultan Abdülaziz received, besides others, the King of Saxony and Marshal Conrobent, the Queen of Prussia, the King of Wustemberg and the ambassadors of the pope.

At first the splendour and brilliance of the receptions, honours and fanfaronade of the exhibition pleased the sultan, but he soon began to tire. His natural distaste for pomp and pageantry aroused flashes of disapproval and anger at the familiarity and intimacy of the French court. Added to this was the irritating presence of the French speaking Khedive Ismail of Egypt, who had studied in Paris in his youth, and the interest showered upon his young nephew. Prince Murad was handsome, cultivated and socially inclined. The prince's mother, Şevkefza Sultan, was known for her intelligence; she had encouraged her son to learn French fluently, play the piano and appreciate the arts. He delighted in dancing and had developed a taste for champagne, much to Abdülaziz's disapproval. Murad's brother, Abdülhamid, remained a quiet, unassuming figure in the background while Prince Murad made such a pleasing impression on the empress that she expressed a desire to meet him. The sultan's displeasure was further aroused when he learned that Mustafa Fazil, a wealthy Egyptian prince who had held ministerial posts in Istanbul before his forced exile, lived in Paris. He had written a letter to Sultan Abdülaziz implying the problem of the empire lay in its outmoded political system and that its remedy lay in the end of absolutism with the adoption of a written constitution with freely elected assemblies of delegates from each province. These minor irritations exploded into a violent temper when Abdülaziz learned that the results of discussions between ministers for more substantial loans had not been as generous as expected, while Ismail, Khedive of Egypt had been promised larger loans.

Osman Ferid was overwhelmed by the fine buildings, broad avenues and wide arrow-straight boulevards, the spruce green spaces, beautiful parks and gardens, where boules were played, the elegant ladies who strolled arm-in-arm with well-dressed men or rode in horse-drawn carriages, people chatting at colourful side-walk cafes, and charming small antique shops with magical lights. Despite this, he also found Paris to be a city full of extremes and Parisians overpowering. Accustomed to the order of precedence, rigidly observed at the Ottoman court and army, he was bemused by the Parisians' savoir-faire attitude.

One evening he visited the palace stables to inspect the emperor's horses only to find a groom lying asleep on the straw with an empty bottle of wine by his side. The groom opened one eye, looked at Osman Ferid and murmured, 'Vive la Turk,' before falling into a drunken stupor.

Although officially on duty, officers attending the sumptuous evening receptions were plied with glasses of champagne; some stealthily accepted, while others, like Osman Ferid, politely declined. Beautiful ladies at court amused themselves, giggling and smiling flirtatiously at the handsome, Ottoman aides-de-camps standing at attention in the background; these women seemed particularly drawn to the shy, retiring Osman Ferid, much to the amusement of his fellow officers who teased him mercilessly. Even his superior officers noticed and commented on his success with the young ladies at court. He was extremely embarrassed and awkward, not knowing whether or not to respond to their friendly advances. With the exception of his mother and sister, he had always felt uncomfortable in the presence of women. A French officer kindly took him to Bon Marche, the first recently opened fashionable department store in Paris, where Osman Ferid bought Zissi a pair of white silk gloves and ribbons for her hair.

Abdülaziz showered the emperor and empress with exquisite gifts and a gracious invitation to visit Istanbul as he and his party bade farewell before boarding the *Reine Hortense*, Napoleon III's Imperial yacht at Boulogne to cross the English Channel. Unfortunately the yacht had great difficulty approaching the Dover harbour due to stormy weather.

The *Illustrated London News* covered the visit of Sultan Abdülaziz in detail. It wrote rather pointedly after the Sultan's visit to Paris:

"The national hospitality of England, whether deservedly or undeservedly we shall not stay to discuss, is not in the highest repute, although it is assigned a much lower place we suspect, by her own sensitiveness than by any seriously expressed opinion of her foreign neighbours. If she is not quite *au fait* at receiving and entertaining royal personages and is somewhat lacking in the imagination and the taste indispensable to state pageantry of the highest order, her insular position will perhaps be accepted as accounting for her deficiency in part at least. Possibly she cherishes affectionate loyalty to her own Sovereign more sedulously than she does an indiscriminate and semi-superstitions veneration of crowned heads in general. Perhaps also she attaches less importance to barbaric splendour as a means whereby she may testify sincere respect, than she does to simpler but more expressive ways of showing her heartiness. One thing is certain, whomsoever she delights to honour she never fails before he quits her shores, to make fully cognizant of the fact by spontaneous demonstrations of popular goodwill, which tell more effectively upon her guests than the roaring of cannon, the display of bunting, the magnificence of processions or the festivities of court... Within the last few days this country has had ample opportunity of proving its hospitality. The Sultan, the Viceroy of Egypt and the Belgian volunteers have been our guests. The visit of the Sultan takes precedence not merely on account of his rank or of the vast extent of his territorial and spiritual dominion but because it is an event which has no historical precedent. It is the first time that the supreme head of the followers of Mohammed, the autocratic ruler of the Turkish Empire, has left the seat of his sovereignty on a peaceful visit."

In their profile of Sultan Abdülaziz the *London Illustrated News* wrote:

"His Imperial Majesty Abdülaziz Khan, Commander of the Faithful and Sultan of the Ottoman Turks, is the thirty-second Sovereign of the line of Othman, chief of the Oguzian Tartars and founder of the Turkish Empire; and he is the twenty-sixth since Mahomet II took Istanbul and made it the capital of his dominions. He is the second son of Sultan Mahmoud and brother of the last sultan Abdülmecid. He was born in February 1830 the 1245th year of the Hegira and ascended the throne in June 1861. The beginning of his reign was marked by some valuable administrative and financial reforms. He maintained in their functions all the ministers of the late sultan except one whom he dismissed and ordered to be arrested on a charge of embezzlement; reduced his civic list to one fifth of what it was in his brother's time; confirmed the Hatti-scherif of Gülhane which is regarded as, in some sort, the charter of the Ottoman Empire; promised equality to all his subjects, non-Mussulmen as well as true believers; re-commanded order and economy, of which he set the example; abolished the worthless *caimes* or depreciated paper money, and replaced them by a metallic currency. He visited in person the public establishments and mastered the details connected with them; reformed the administration of justice, broke up the seraglio, and kept in the palace only the sultanas – the mother of the Princes. He placed his nephews in the military service and created the eldest a Pasha instead of following the unnatural usage of the Turkish court, which dooms all the presumptive heirs of royalty to the closest seclusion, lest they should anticipate the legal succession. His own son, then four years old, had been brought up in secret, though with the consent of Abdülmecid, as a Prince. The present Sultan, amongst other acts of his reign, has decreed the sale of the vakoofs, or estates in mortmain belonging to religious corporations which had long been unproductive and ruinous. He has granted a certain degree of independence to the tributary Princes of his empire - the ruler of the Danubian province, Wallachia and Molovia, now united bearing the name of Roumania; the Viceroy of Egypt, the Bey of Tunis, the Prince of Montenegro, and the Prince of Servia. The treatment of foreign Christians residing in Turkey has been greatly improved. They are now permitted to acquire land in all parts of the empire with the single exception of Hedjaz on the same conditions as Turks. Christians, who become possessors of land under the new laws, are to be subject to all the burdens imposed by the Turkish code on landed proprietors."

Edward, Prince of Wales, with his entourage, met the sultan and his suite at Dover with a salute from the British Navy before escorting his guests aboard the royal train to London. At Charing Cross the official welcome was attended by the Lord Chamberlain, Lord Steward, eighty- five members of parliament, members of the House of Lords, their wives and ladies of the court after which the royal procession escorted by the Royal Horse Guards drove through the cheering crowds waving British and Turkish flags on the streets of London, down the Mall to Buckingham Palace. On July 13, the sultan was invited to meet Queen Victoria at a luncheon given in his honour at Windsor Castle. Crown Prince Murad Efendi, Prince Yusuf Izzettin, Prince Abdülhamid and the Khedive of Egypt, with his brother Mustafa Fazil Pasha, were present.

Queen Victoria was forty eight years old. A mother of eight children, she had been devoted to her husband, Prince Albert. After his death she retired from public life to the solitude of her beloved home, Balmoral Castle in Scotland, from where she conducted state affairs with great tenacity. She was deeply loved, even revered, by her subjects, always dressed in black and, although she appeared stern and autocratic, was known to possess a sharp wit and keen sense of humour on occasions. Abdülaziz won Queen Victoria's approval as he took her arm and escorted her into lunch. She wrote to her daughter, Crown Princess of Prussia.

"I like the true splendour of soft brown oriental eyes; he never touched wine."

On July 15, the sultan's party, accompanied by the Prince of Wales and the Duke of Cambridge, attended a gala performance of *Masaniello* by Auber at the Royal Opera House. The following day, in the company of the Prince of Wales and the commander-in-chief of the army, the sultan visited the Arsenal, a munitions factory at Woolwich, and watched with pleasure an impressive manoeuvre display. That evening the Prince of Wales hosted a magnificent Royal Command performance on behalf of Queen Victoria at the Crystal Palace in honour of the sultan. The previous year a fire had seriously damaged the Palace; Abdülaziz had donated one thousand pounds towards the restorations to the building.

At an official display of fireworks, the sultan noticed a few red fez hats in the crowd. Enquiring who they were, his foreign minister replied, "They are your Majesty's opposition." Namik Kemal and his group, having been politely asked to leave Paris during the Royal visit, had come to London.

In *Istanbul to London*, the text that accompanied his CD, Dr Emre Aracı descibes the music played that evening: "The piece was called a *Turkish Ode* which included a cantata composed and conducted by Luigi Arditi and sung in Ottoman Turkish by a British chorus of 1,600 voices. Arditi had directed the Naum

Theatre in Istanbul for six months for a season in 1856-57. He had been received at court and had given a violin recital at Dolmabahçe Palace before Sultan Abdülmecid for which he received the Ottoman Order of the Medjidie, fourth class."

The Musical Times, August 1867, wrote:

"Whether the words which reached the sultan's ears sounded to him a bit like Turkish we have no means of ascertaining but as music is a universal language, we have little doubt that the notes at least found their way to his heart, and must have convinced him that his welcome to this country was not a mere matter of conventional form."

The sultan and his suite visited Woolwich Shipping Yard and a cotton mill in Manchester which imported Turkish and Egyptian cotton; later they took a trip along the River Thames, visited the Tower of London, the Armoury and the City of London. On Wednesday, July 17, the royal party travelled by road to Spithead near Portsmouth to attend a naval review by the Royal Navy; this was the climax of the visit and was held in the presence of Queen Victoria.

Sultan Abdülaziz, Edward, Prince of Wales, Lord Derby and the First Lord of the Admiralty boarded the *Osborne*, Queen Victoria's yacht. Sadly, the weather worsened as a strong wind gathered and the sea became choppy and rough. Queen Victoria, realising the sultan's discomfort, suggested they view the review from the steady and solid bridge of the battleship, *Victoria and Albert*.

The *Illustrated London News* reported:

"Taking part were wooden ships headed by Victoria with 102 guns, the iron- clads, the turret-ships and the twin-screw ships and the *Waterwatch*, a vessel on the hydraulic principle. There was an excellent opportunity for comparing the aspect of the wooden ships with that of the iron-clads. It was generally remarked that while the former presented the most magnificent appearance, the invulnerability and irresistible armament of the latter appealed most strongly to the imagination. The firing of the broadside and great guns was tremendous; it was heard, some say, at Malvern and Monmouth, a distance of more than a hundred miles. The fire was kept up on both sides with great spirits, presenting a most animated sight. The illumination of the fleet after dark in the evening was less successful as the weather prevented the spectators on land from seeing much of the lights shown by the fleet at Spithead."

At the reception that followed Queen Victoria decorated Sultan Abdülaziz with the "Order of the Garter." It was a historic moment in the history of Britain, the first time for a non-Christian to be so highly awarded. There was a burst of applause from those present. Emre Aracı wrote,

"The Queen in her letter to her daughter said, 'It was an act of great devouement (devotion) to my Oriental brother; the whole ship was swarming with Turks! I fastened the garter round him myself - and he smiled and laughed and coloured and was very much pleased.' Queen Victoria noted in her diary. 'It must have been a curious sight, the sultan and I sitting outside the deck saloon, the others beyond. The sultan feels very uncomfortable at sea. He was constantly retiring below and can have seen very little, which was a pity, as it was a very fine sight'."

At the Guildhall, members of the royal family, including the prime minister, Disraeli, members of the House of Lords including Lord Derby and Lord Romilly, members of the House of Commons and a body of foreign ambassadors—in all more than 3,000 people—attended the sumptuous banquet in a huge marquee. The British excel at royal pageantry. They displayed the pomp and glory of its past as 150 members of the council with gartered legs and powdered wigs moved in a stately manner down the aisle to the amusement of the Turks. A magnificent official naval departure from Dover brought an end to the successful meeting of two of the greatest royal houses in Europe. Crowds lined the street waving flags and cheering a warm farewell. A gun salute boomed as the Royal Navy escorted the *Sültaniye* and her sister yachts out of the harbour. The sultan

expressed his admiration and esteem for the reserved but powerful dignity of the queen while Queen Victoria felt empathy for
the larger-than-life Ottoman Sultan with soft brown eyes.

Whereas Paris had overwhelmed him, Osman Ferid felt at ease
in London. He might lack the capacity to learn languages, but he
understood enough English to carry on a simple conversation,
which gave him a degree of confidence when he visited the
Royal Guard officers at Hyde Park, Chelsea and the Wellington
barracks near Buckingham Palace.

He befriended Hikmet Efendi, a Caucasian first secretary to
the Turkish Ambassador who had lived in London for many
years. Osman Ferid showed him the list of names of those who
had assisted the Caucasian cause, David Urquhart, James Bell, J.
A. Longworth and Captain E Spencer. These names had gained
the attention of the queen who sent an emissary to the
Caucasus. Osman Ferid was delighted when Hikmet Efendi
told him he had met David Urquhart.

"He stayed as a guest with one of my father's cavalry com-
manders, Janbolat, at his aoul when he travelled in the
Caucasus," said Osman Ferid as Hikmet Efendi related David
Urquhart's story.

Urquhart came from an aristocratic Scottish family and
served as an eminent diplomat under Lord Ponsonby, British
Ambassador in Istanbul. Strongly anti-Russian, he was chief
British propagandist against the Russian Empire; this stance
appealed to the subjects of the empire although he actually had
little sympathy either for the Ottomans or their civilization.
Lord Ponsonby, known to be sympathetic to the Circassian
movement for Independence, encouraged young Urquhart to
travel on a mission to the Circassia with Captain Lyons in
August, 1834. This journey changed Urquhart's life.
Enamoured by the majestic beauty of the mountains and
courage of the brave mountaineers, on his return he gathered a

group of like-minded men, who carried their Russophobia to such extremes that they refused to recognize any Ottoman or Circassian fault. He influenced the ambassador, Sir Henry A. Layard, published articles, wrote books, and lectured in Istanbul and in London. In 1861, Urquhart financed a mission by selling the family silver (said to be 32,000 thousand English pounds) to promote an insurrection in the Caucasus against the Russians and financed Caucasian envoys to travel to London to appeal for funds to buy arms and ammunition from the government and influential friends. He achieved a certain success, raising awareness of the plight of the Caucasians. Although they received substantial funds, the needs of the mountaineers were much greater than he or his organization could ever achieve. During the first tragic immigration of thousands of Caucasions to Ottoman territories, David Urquhart set up a relief committee for refugees in Istanbul. He was often guest of honour at the Ottoman Ambassador's dinners.

Osman Ferid admired the discipline and spirit of the British officers he met. They were pleased to accommodate a guest officer, especially when he expressed admiration for the power and discipline of the British military. They were taken on a tour of the barracks, the mess-room and living quarters, parade grounds, and early one morning Osman Ferid was invited to join a mounted cavalry on a practice ride at Hyde Park. The horses were healthy and the stables immaculately clean.

He was impressed by the Houses of Parliament standing tall and imposing on the bank of the river Thames; its architecture seemed to endorse law and order. The Naval Review was unforgettable. Although no sea-lover, he saw the huge advantage a modern powerful navy held in warfare.

Abdülaziz presented Queen Victoria with a superbly jewelled brooch and members of the royal household with other exquisite pieces. In return, the Ottoman guests received trophies according to rank and position. Each aide-de-camp was given a fob watch.

At one of the last receptions, Osman Ferid asked to speak to Hikmet Efendi in private.

"I wish to ask a favour, sir." He mumbled, "As a Caucasian, I am grateful for the support Britain, the Queen, gave to my forefathers and people during their fight for freedom from Russia. I saw a photograph of Queen Victoria at a store and bought it. Do you think her Majesty would sign it? I would treasure it all my life."

Hikmet Efendi was amazed and not a little amused by this shy, young man's request as he continued to express his admiration for the queen and for the warm welcome the sultan and his retinue had received during their visit.

Hikmet Efendi nodded, smiling.

"Wait here," he said as he went off. Osman Ferid bit his lip. He had doubted the wisdom of asking Hikmet Efendi, now he felt foolish. An officer signalled that the royal party were preparing to leave when Hikmet Efendi reappeared, accompanied by a tall, imposing gentleman in a frock suit, one of the queen's chamberlains, an old friend.

'This is Lord Garfield, a dear friend. Please tell him what you told me."

Osman Ferid was horrified; this was quite unexpected. Taking a deep breath, and without looking at the two men, he repeated his request in painfully slow English. When he had finished, he glanced at the gentlemen standing in front of him.

"Well, that was quite a speech, young man." Lord Garfield smiled, "I followed the war in the Caucasus very closely. I admire Imam Shamil and his brave highlanders, a great tragedy. I am a friend of the Urquhart family and sent a donation for one of his shipments of firearms. I will see what can be done."

They shook hands.

"Thank you," Osman Ferid replied.

Lord Garfield grinned.

"I respect your request, Sir, and your nerve, but you really must improve your English."

"Well done," said a quiet voice behind them.

They turned to see Prince Abdülhamid standing close by.

"I hope you grant this young officer his request, Sir, the effort is worth the prize, don't you think?"

They laughed, nodded to Osman Ferid, and walked off together. Even the prince found me amusing and they hadn't even taken the photograph, thought Osman Ferid ruefully as he rushed to join the other officers. Still, he was pleased to have made the acquaintance of Lord Garfield.

On the last day, before leaving for the official royal departure at Dover, the sultan and his suite attended a luncheon party hosted by the Ottoman Bank. Osman Ferid saw Hikmet Efendi deep in conversation with the Turkish Ambassador and ministers from the Porte. After a while he approached Osman Ferid and handed him a slim package.

"Here you are, my son, an autographed photograph of Queen Victoria. She expressed her pleasure at your loyal sentiments and wishes you God speed."

"Thank you; thank you very much, Sir," said the delighted Osman Ferid.

The royal party journeyed by train to Belgium to be greeted by King Leopold II at a grand military ceremony in the sultan's honour, then on to Prussia where King Wilhelm I hosted a state reception at Koblenz Castle. The splendid buildings and monuments in Vienna were dressed in Turkish and Austrian flags.

Emperor Franz Joseph, Sultan Abdülaziz, and the princes attended a command performance in their honour at the Vienna Opera House, a magnificent ornate building. The royal train passed through Hungary to the banks of the Danube where the royal guests boarded the *Zeshenyi* to sail to Rumania, a vassal principality of the Ottoman Empire.

On Wednesday, August 7, 1867, the royal yacht *Sultaniye*, accompanied by warships and a splendid naval escort, sailed into Istanbul to the greetings, cheers and jubilation of thousands of subjects lining the shore waving and shouting "Padişahım çok yaşa." The Maiden's Tower fired cannons informing the city of Sultan Abdülaziz's arrival. The Bosphorus teemed with caiques of all shapes and colours; private and fisherman sandals darted between crowded steamboats, while gilded Pasha Caiques zigzagged between ships with multicoloured sails and strange prows, blowing their horns and waving flags of welcome.

The journey was over, the first and last royal visit of an Ottoman Sultan to Europe. The following day Mehmet came to meet Osman Ferid at the palace. After a little friendly back-slapping and jokes with friends, they left for home. The door flew open. Zissi, Ahmet and Ismail jumped on Osman Ferid, pulling him inside.

"We want to hear all about your trip."

"Just a minute," he laughed as he gave them their elegantly wrapped gifts.

Zissi kissed Osman Ferid's cheek and unwrapped her presents, a pair of silk white gloves and ribbons from Paris, and a length of pure English cloth for a gown. Hikmet Efendi had taken him to a well-known store specialising in English cloth.

Osman Ferid showed them picture books of Paris, London and Vienna.

Zissi had prepared Osman Ferid's favourite food, Circassian chicken with beans, rice, yogurt and salad. They sat around the table listening to his adventures.

He told them of the pomp and glory of Paris, the flirtatious court ladies, and described in detail the magnificence and huge halls of the Paris Exhibition. He spoke warmly of the visit to England, the imperial, but kindly, Queen Victoria. Proudly he showed them the inscribed framed photograph of the queen, telling them how embarrassed he had been.

"Tell us in English," they joked. Osman Ferid kept the photograph of Queen Victoria by his bedside until he died. It was said on one occasion when asked who the lady was, he replied, "the Virgin Mary."

He spoke of the power of the British navy with its modern warfare and the ironclad ships, the comfortable, clean but practical barracks for soldiers and officers, the spacious stables, and the fine horses he had ridden. He took them stage by stage on the journey through the capitals of Europe.

"But it's good to be home."

Osman Ferid smiled as he rumpled Ismail's hair. They plied him with questions. Zissi wanted to know about the fashionable ladies in Paris and London. Ahmet, fascinated with new technology, was delighted with the manuals on arms and weapons. They talked until the early hours of the next morning; exhausted but happy, they retired.

The next morning Mehmet and Osman Ferid strolled down the narrow streets to the Golden Horn, stopping at a coffeeshop on the pier to watch the heavy water traffic between Sirkeci and Eminönü.

Osman Ferid confided in his brother.

"The journey was beyond my wildest dreams. Sultan Abdülaziz received the highest honours of any foreign head of state. The cities were magnificent; the French capital seems to dictate the art, culture, science and romance in Europe, but I preferred Britian. Europeans are more modern, sophisticated and less traditional, but still friendly and hospitable. The sultan and his retinue were pleased with the gracious receptions they received from the Christian countries throughout the visit."

He laughed.

"My most difficult moment was when a lady addressed me at one of the evening receptions. I didn't know whether to respond or not. I have no court or social manners. Mehmet, you have to help me; you know how to charm the ladies."

It was Mehmet's turn to laugh.

"I would be delighted, but I doubt you will be a good student."

They left the coffeeshop to return home.

"The same vibrant movement for change is happening

Major Osman Ferid, Captain of the Guards at the time of his trip to Europe as aide-de-camp to Sultan Abdülaziz. (May 1867)

Shapli Bereketzade Ismail.

Shapli Bereketzade Mehmet Pasha.

Kazım Bey, Osman Ferid's son from his first wife. İstinye, (1905).

Shapli Bereketzade Ahmet Pasha (1897).

DAVID GAZALA   BAGDAD

Dağestanlı Mehmet Fazıl Pasha.

Beşiktaş Konak at Serencebey Yokuşu.

Cherkess Hasan.

Osman Ferid Pasha.

Taşkışla Barracks.

Dağestanlı Mehmet Fazıl Pasha, 1916.

throughout Europe, as it is in Istanbul. Technology, social services, and education are all far superior there than in the Ottoman Empire. Even so people demand more.

"If the Ottoman Empire hopes to maintain its position as a world power, it will have to speed up its programme of reforms in the state, the government and the military forces. Otherwise, I fear, the situation doesn't look too bright for this country."

Osman Ferid looked at his brother, as if he had an afterthought, and added,

"We must not forget we are guests in this country, Mehmet. We emigrated from the Caucasus to live in peace as Caucasians in the service of Ottoman Empire, loyal to the sultan. Thae willing, we shall work hard and carry on with our lives. The politics of this country are not our concern."

CHAPTER 8

Drawing Lots

The success of the sultan's European tour filled his subjects with hope and expectation for a more prosperous future. The city was jubilant and rich and poor alike were optimistic, proud the Sultan and Caliph had received such acclaim in the foreign press. They were confident that the long awaited reforms within the government and political system would receive his blessings. Reform, new laws and modern technology were the talk of the day in the konaks and yalı of the wealthy, in the coffeehouses and on the streets; the Ottomans looked forward towards a more liberal system of government led by an enlightened sultan who had seen the benefits of modernity in western countries. Trunks laden with goods were carried through the long corridors of Dolmabahçe Palace to the royal harem and palaces of the Imperial princes.

Foreign and Turkish ladies flocked to the smart shops in the Rue de Pera to admire the colourful window displays of fine silks and satins from Paris, linen and wools from England, lace and embroideries from Brussels and Vienna, or to browse over rows of delightful bottles of expensive colognes, perfumes, elegant gloves and stylish hats.

But behind the heavy doors of the Porte's ministerial offices, the atmosphere was far from jubilant. The grand vizier and ministers were faced with overwhelming political and financial problems. The tour might have been a personal success for the Ottoman sultan and his court, but the talks between ministers for further loans and extensions on the interest payments of previous loans had not been as forthcoming as expected; in fact, Napoleon III had pledged more to the Khedive of Egypt than he had to the Ottoman sultan. The death of Fuad Pasha in Nice a few weeks earlier at the age of 54 had caused more concern and apprehension in the foreign office. Abdülaziz flew into a violent, black rage when he was told of the lack of generosity of the European governments. In a mood of sheer defiance, against the advice of his ministers, the sultan demanded the modernization of the military services, the purchase of ironclad ships from England and the revised plans for the railway line to link Istanbul to Europe be continued—expensive projects for a country on the brink of bankruptcy.

On their return from the royal tour, aide-de-camps and officers found themselves in great demand at tea parties and evening soirées hosted by royal princesses and pasha wives with marriageable daughters, for whom they hoped to find a suitable husband with good prospects. Osman Ferid was twenty three. Zissi made a point of inviting her dearest girlfriends to tea when Osman Ferid was at home. Although polite and friendly, he refused to consider any serious relationship. He preferred the company of his fellow officers in the mess-room or a gallop over the hills on one of the sultan's magnificent stallions to the thought of a staid, married life.

His friends, Hasan and Mahmud, decided to marry into the royal family and teased Osman Ferid.

"Come on Osman Ferid, you are a Royal Guard officer of distinction, have all the qualities needed of a royal damat (son–in–law) family background, good-looks; you could have your choice from the beautiful princesses we meet."

One day Osman Ferid received an invitation from his commanding officer, Murat Pasha, to attend a reception at his home. Taking Zissi on his arm, they set off by boat for Yenikoy. It was a warm, pleasant day. Officers and friends from the Taşkışla barracks mingled with the royal society in the garden of the konak overlooking the Bosphorus waterway.

Zissi ran off to find her friends, leaving Osman Ferid watching the boats and caiques skimming past. Suddenly an elaborately decorated caique pulled up at the quay and a slim girl, her veil flying in the wind, jumped out. Raising her gown above her ankles, she ran up the hill towards the konak to join a group of young men and women. It was Ayshe Shamma, one of the richest and most sought after young ladies in society.

As Osman Ferid went in search of Zissi to take their leave, Hasan, a fellow officer, drew him aside, whispering in his ear.

"Ayshe wants to meet you."

Ayshe approached them as they walked through the garden into the salon.

"Hello, Osman Ferid, I am Ayshe Shamma."

She smiled at him, beckoning him to take a seat. Ayshe was charming; she laughed and talked with surprising ease. When she asked about Paris, he told her how awkward he had felt at the receptions and social gatherings. She smiled. Touching his arm, she assured him he had no reason to be shy with her.

Ayshe was the daughter of the famous Circassian Shamma family who had fought in the war against the Russians. Her father, a wealthy merchant, had traded between Turkey, Eastern Europe and the Caucasus, supplying the guerrilla fighters with arms and ammunition at great personal risk until the last stand. Ayshe, whose mother had died at childbirth, had been raised by a series of foreign nannies. She spoke French fluently, was beautiful, confident and sophisticated, without any of the inhibitions or shyness of her Caucasian sisters. She reminded Osman Ferid of the lovely ladies in Paris.

A week later, Osman Ferid was summoned to the Shamma konak. Ayshe's father received him in the selamlik. They talked about the Caucasus, mutual friends, family and his future. He left the konak engaged to Ayshe Shamma. He was over-

148

whelmed with happiness. She was different, and excited him as no other girl ever had. He rushed home to share the good news to his family. Zissi had expected it; hugs and kisses hid her doubts and fears for Osman Ferid's future happiness. Ayshe was rich and spoilt and would demand much from her young husband.

Ayshe and Osman Ferid married on December 15, 1867. They made a handsome couple. Ayshe looked exquisite in a long white robe and veil as she stood smiling radiantly next to her husband, immaculate in his military uniform. The reception was held in the spacious hall at the Shamma residence, with members of the Ottoman household, foreign guests and Caucasians mingling with prominent figures in society and the military forces. The festivities carried on until late in the evening with Circassian songs and dancers leaping and flying through the air, swinging and clashing swords. Ahmet and Zissi joined in a folklore dance.

The happy couple settled into a comfortable house at Tophane, a wedding gift from Ayshe's father. Every evening Osman Ferid rushed home from the palace eager to spend the evening with his wife. Ayshe was enchanting, full of surprises. She played the piano, prepared delicious suppers and delighted in introducing her handsome husband to her large circle of friends. On September, 1868, to their joy Ayshe gave birth to a son, Kazım.

The following year Osman Ferid was promoted to First Captain of the Guards in the Royal Household Regiment. He believed sweeping changes should be made within the armed forces and that military technology and education were the keys to building and maintaining a powerful modern army. He introduced new regulations. Osman Ferid was obsessively neat and punctual and expected the same behaviour from others. Some evenings he worked so late he slept at the serasker dairesi (security station). His experience as a mountain warrior had taught him to reduce a problem to its bare essentials and then tackle it.

A stickler for detail, he worked indefatigably. He looked forward to the Djighitovka tournament every year, working to improve conditions on the field for competitor and horse. In a short speech to the competitors, he spoke of his personal experience, reminding the winners of their duty and loyalty to the sultan and the Ottoman Army.

After his capitulation, Imam Shamil spent ten years in comfortable confinement at Soukhotine House on Ranievsky Street in Kaluga, Russia, where he was treated with respect and honoured by the Tsar. A small mosque was built in the garden and his library brought from Daghestan. Shamil had always felt a deep bond of respect towards Britain for the part she had played in the Crimean war; he sent a portrait photograph of himself and his son Ghazi Mohammed taken by the famous Russian photographer, Andrei Denier in Moscow to Queen Victoria with an inscription on the mount in Arabic and French, *'Hommage du plus profond respect a Sa Majeste, La Reine Victoria'*.

In 1870, Tsar Alexander consented to the imam's request to make a pilgrimage to Mecca. When Sultan Abdülaziz learned of the imam's journey to Saudi Arabia, he invited him to Istanbul as his guest. The streets were lined with cheering crowds. Ottomans, Muslims, and Christians joined the Caucasian community who travelled from far and wide throughout the Empire to catch a glimpse of their hero, Shah Shamil, Imam of Daghestan, Lion of the Mountains—a legend in his lifetime.

The imam was given a state welcome with a 21 gun salute as he rode in the Imperial carriage to Dolmabahçe Palace. Shamil, elderly and in ill-health, still retained the dignity and presence of a world leader, demanding respect, even fear, as he walked into the palace attired in the simple white robe of an imam, his stern, autocratic face, piercing eyes and thick white beard silencing the crowd. Standing on guard at the entrance of the palace, Osman Ferid froze as Shamil passed, for here was the hero who had inspired his grandfather, father, Janbolat and all the brave warriors who had fought and died in his name.

A week later, he was ordered to deliver a gift from Sultan Abdülaziz to Shamil at the Koska Konak in Aksaray, a fifty-room mansion with a private mosque on its grounds. He was shown into the selamlik where the imam sat with his son, Ghazi Mohammed, and friends from the Caucasian community. Osman Ferid knelt to kiss his hand. He was invited to join them for tea.

As the imam's granddaughter, the beautiful Sofiate, served tea and Caucasian sweets, Osman Ferid felt the imam's eyes on him.

"I appreciated the loyalty and bravery of the Shapli family in our fight for independence. I met your grandfather and your father when he was very young, perhaps your age. Now you are chief of that noble family. Only Allah can tell what the future holds my son. Whatever your fate maybe, carry your heritage with pride."

The head of the community presented the imam with a detailed report concerning the funding and education of Caucasian children arriving from the Caucasus. As Osman Ferid took his leave, Shamil inquired about his life and family in Istanbul and wished him well.

"Do not regret leaving the Caucasus. Carry the mountains in your heart and Allah will protect you."

On February 4, 1871, Shamil the Avar, Imam of Daghestan, died in Medina.

Osman Ferid was promoted to Major on August 27, 1874. His army career was deeply satisfying. His earnestness and regard for the men and officers in his unit were appreciated. He looked forward to the day's challenge; usually the first to arrive in the morning he was the last to leave at night. But there was another reason for spending long hours at the barracks; all was not well at home.

The pressure of work was an excuse to avoid his wife's continual complaints when he was at home. Ayshe was finding that her husband's idea of a happy marriage was very different from her romantic thoughts. She had expected Osman Ferid to join in her social whirl, to attend receptions on the arm of her handsome husband and have him at her side when entertaining at home, but Osman Ferid was proving to be a dull major. Ayshe was not interested in his military career. She found the Shapli family gatherings boring, while Osman Ferid's sole interests lay in his military career, his family and the sultan's string of thoroughbreds.

His wife had lived a comfortable, pampered life as the only child of a doting father. Now living on the meagre salary of a major was proving tiresome and frustrating. As time passed, the difference in their interests seemed to divide them increasingly. She did not understand why her father could not help them financially. One evening, angered by her husband's passivity, she suggested they speak to her father. Osman Ferid was furious and deeply offended. He bluntly refused to discuss the matter. That night he sat up until the early hours of the morning brooding over their relationship; he loved Ayshe and his son Kazım, but he realized he could never be the person she desired. He lacked the qualities to satisfy her needs, socially and financially. He had tried to be a loving, dutiful husband, accompanying her on visits to friends, but after a while, restless and out of place in the opulent, crowded, smoky salons and lacking in polite small talk, he usually found a quiet corner and waited until his wife was ready to leave. Osman Ferid knew his wife loved him and he sympathized with her frustration and increasing sense of loneliness. She was young and beautiful, had been the centre of attention of a large group of friends with a bevy of servants at her command. She had not imagined marriage on a limited income in a smaller house with an absent husband. As weeks passed, their relationship resorted to cool politeness; the excitement and intimacy of their first love was lost.

When Osman Ferid was assigned to divisional field duty a

year later, both gave a secret sigh of relief; a period of separation might ease the strain on their marriage.

Osman Ferid left for camp with the field forces. After the sedate pace at the palace, the training was gruelling, but he soon regained his old fitness and physical strength, enjoying the athletic out-door existence that reminded him of happier days in the Caucasus. Every day he rode out of camp to the hills beyond, stopping at a village to talk to the locals. When Mehmet and Ahmet came to visit, they cantered out of camp and then whipped their horses into a wild gallop over the hills, racing like children through the village, much to the sleepy villagers' surprise. Six months later Osman Ferid was recalled to barracks.

As the euphoria of the European tour died, the public had become increasingly disillusioned, angered at the sultan's indifference to the reforms. Discontent, intrigue, political instability and financial crisis permeated the very atmosphere of the city, but seemed to make no impression on the sultan's personal extravagances. Beylerbey Palace, on the Asian shore, was completed at great expense in 1865. An Imperial Mosque was commissioned in the name of his mother Pertevniyal in Aksaray in 1871. The modernization of the armed forces continued with an expensive order for ironclad warships from England. The first stretch of the Istanbul-Paris rail line from Istanbul to Sofia was opened in 1873 and plans to continue the line were underway. In spite of loud opposition from ministers against these huge investments, the sultan's demands and extravagances continued unabated. The Ottoman debt, within twenty years, had risen to two hundred million pounds.

The Porte was finally forced to declare a moratorium. People took to the streets. The powerful conservative Ulema blamed the Tanzimat reforms and foreign policy for the financial crises and unrest within the country. News of floods, drought and famine and the pitiful plight of the Anatolians reached the capital. The Young Ottomans were joined by religious students in their thousands, angered by the Porte's submissive response to

Russia, Austria and Hungary concerning increased taxation in Bosnia and Bulgaria. The revolt in Bulgaria had been severely stamped out by the Ottomans and many Muslims, as well as Christians, had been killed. Mass meetings were held in the main squares, criticising the government, demanding the dismissal of the pro-Russian grand vizier, Mahmut Nedim Pasha, and the empire's leading Islamic official, the Sheikulislam Hasan Fehmi Efendi. By the end of the month the city was on the verge of civil war. In the spring of 1876, the British ambassador, Sir Henry Elliot wrote,

"From the pashas down to the porters in the streets and the boatmen on the Bosphorus no one thinks any longer of concealing his opinions. The word "constitution" is in every mouth and, should the sultan refuse to grant one, an attempt to depose him appears almost inevitable."

Osman Ferid returned to duty at Dolmabahçe Palace. Life behind the high walls of the palace continued in its seemingly peaceful fashion. The sultan had completely withdrawn from court life, never leaving the palace except for Friday prayers. He lacked self-restraint, flying into black rages when approached by ministers concerned with the alarming state of affairs. He retired into the harem, sending messages by eunuchs to chamberlains and ministers. Aide-de-camps and officers were ordered to keep a low profile and under no circumstances to incite the anger of the sultan. Duties completed, they would gather in the mess-room to discuss the general concern at the growing crisis on the streets and more importantly, for them, how it might affect the army. Some even talked of a constitutional government, the need for radical change and of an impending coup.

Usually these meetings led to heated arguments. Many agreed with the Young Ottomans and the demonstrators on the streets; others sided with the government and sultan, but all were unanimous in their concern for unity within the ranks of the army. Osman Ferid was deeply distressed by news that the

"Bulgarian Atrocities," as they were called, had been blamed upon the Circassian forces in that area.

"We are officers in the Ottoman Army, answerable only to our superiors. Our duty is to obey without question, so let's not argue amongst ourselves but wait for orders."

Mustafa, a close friend, rejoined.

"Osman Ferid, we cannot remain observers or be dogmatic at such a time; the scale of the political unrest in a country can lead to civil war and we should be prepared"

Osman Ferid saluted him.

"I believe the military forces to be above politics, as officers our duty is to carry out orders and remain silent. I advise you to do the same."

In the evenings, Osman Ferid ferried to his father-in-law's konak where Ayshe and Kazim had stayed during his absence. They had settled into a respectful, cordial relationship. Ayshe was a dutiful wife and Osman Ferid an often absent, husband.

On Tuesday, 30th May, 1876, Sultan Abdülaziz was deposed in favour of his nephew, Prince Murat.

It was a bloodless coup d'etat, brilliantly orchestrated by the Minister of War, Commander General of the Ottoman Army, Hüseyin Avni Pasha. It was the first time in the history of the House of Osman that a sultan had been deposed by a coup d'e-tat. Hüseyin Avni Pasha was an ambitious man driven by personal motivation. As the situation worsened and tension and violence grew on the streets, he used his formidable power of persuasion first to influence and convince the grand vizier, Mehmet Rüştü Pasha, and the director of the Military Academy, Süleyman Hüsnü Pasha, that the only way to quell the riots was by deposing the present sultan in favour of his nephew Murat. Armed with their support, the minister of war approached the president of the Military Council, the Şeyhülislam, Hayrullah Efendi, and other key figures in the army and navy.

Hüseyin Avni Pasha's influence spread throughout the bureaucracy, even to the private chamberlains at the palace. He knew by name every officer serving in the Royal Guard elite corp. With foresight and great cunning, a forty hour leave of absence was issued to those he thought might be troublesome, a small group of Caucasian officers that included Caucasian Hasan and Osman Ferid.

Timing was of the utmost importance. Two operations were carried out simultaneously with military precision. Under the cover of darkness, Prince Murat, legal heir to the Ottoman throne, was escorted first by caique and then carriage from his palace to the War Ministry at Beyazit. At the same time, two battleships edged silently in front of Dolmabahçe Palace; heavy weapons were rolled above the hills. The perpetrators of the coup d'etat swore an oath of allegiance, proclaiming Murat Khan V, Sultan of the Ottoman Empire, while cannons fired from the battleships woke the sleeping sultan in the harem who was hastily informed that he had been deposed.

Abdülaziz and his family were huddled into a caique and ferried across the Bosphorus to Topkapı Palace in time for Sultan Murat Khan V to be proclaimed sultan from the minarets of every mosque in the city.

The following day, Abdülaziz and his family were moved to more appropriate quarters at Çirağan Palace. His favourite wife, the beautiful Caucasian, Nesherek Nesrin, was heavily pregnant and died of pneumonia a week later. She had been roughly treated by a soldier who accused her of smuggling jewellery under her cloak; desperate and fearful, she had dropped the cloak as she boarded the caique.

On June 4, 1876, the Porte issued an official declaration signed by foreign and Turkish doctors which stated Abdülaziz had committed suicide by slashing his wrists. Many believed he had been murdered.

In the stillness of the morning the sunrise spread its golden glow over the hills and dark waters of the Bosphorus. Osman Ferid's carriage drew up outside the gates of the palace. He had heard the cannons and assumed the shadowy outline of the two battleships were preparing for exercises; he wondered why the night guards were not in their usual posts, drinking tea and smoking outside the palace gate. As he entered he was told to hand over his weapons and to join the officers of the royal guards at the assembly room for roll-call. They stood at attention as Raşid Pasha, Colonel of the Guard Council, entered to address them.

"An important announcement will be made shortly. Please remain seated until I return."

He left the room, bolting the heavy door behind him. After a while, the muffled sound of the muezzin could be heard through the heavily drapes and closed shutters. At that moment, the door flung open and armed troops followed by Raşid Pasha surrounded the room. His piercing eyes searched the faces in the assembly hall; then, in a slow commanding voice he announced the deposition of Abdülaziz for the succession of Murat V.

He ordered each officer to take an oath of allegiance to the new Ottoman Sultan and Caliph, Murat Khan V. To refuse was treason, punishable by death. Not a sound, not a move was made except for the loud ticking of a clock. As the minutes ticked by, silence blanketed the room. Osman Ferid felt nauseous; hostility filled the room to breaking point. His mind screamed to rebel against such an ultimatum but he just stood motionless looking in disbelief at the trigger happy soldiers pointed their weapons at their comrades in arms. He remembered the law of the mountains.

Expressionless, benumb and stiff, he stepped forward. Two armed guards sprang to his side, rifles cocked. Raşid Pasha brushed them aside, looking directly into his eyes. Osman Ferid stood at attention to pledge oath to the new Ottoman Sultan and

Caliph, Murat Khan V. The clock ticked louder in the silence. At first one, then another officer followed until the unit stepped forward to pledge oath to the new sultan. It was over; the coup d'etat had succeeded. They were confined to barracks unarmed until the following Friday, when they would accompany Sultan Murat Khan V to Friday prayers at Yıldız Mosque.

Cramp twisted his gut; this was the same physical pain he had suffered when forced to obey his father the last time he saw him alive. While his whole being screamed to rebel, it was over-ruled by a desperate need to protect the safety of unarmed offi-cers surrounded by troops ready to shoot; they would surely have been gunned down.

With the crowd appeased, the streets and squares emptied; theological students returned to the madrasahs while the Young Ottomans and their supporters looked forward to a new era of change and progress. Everyone had been impressed by the sophisticated manners of the young prince during the royal tour. He had charmed the Parisians with his command of French and his joie de vivre as he enjoyed champagne and danced the night away. These were qualities, thought Osman Ferid, that Ayshe admired, but as he accompanied the sultan on his first official public outing to Yıldız Mosque for the Friday prayers, the sultan looked pale and ill at ease. Rumour had it that events had triggered a serious mental instability brought on by alcoholism.

Ayshe and Kasım returned to their home at Tophane. Late one afternoon on June 15, a servant announced a visitor. It was Circassian Hasan, agitated and overwrought. He had been told of a decree, signed by Hüseyin Avni Pasha, ordering his imme-diate posting to Baghdad. Ayshe retired to her room while Osman Ferid attempted to calm his friend.

Hasan, born in 1850, was the son of Zish-Brakee Ghazi Ismail Bey, a close friend of Osman Ferid's father. Their fathers had fought together. Hasan and Osman Ferid had been playmates, competing in friendly competition. Hasan had immigrated to

Turkey with his sister during the 1864 exodus. After attending military school, he began his military career as a lieutenant.

Hasan was tall, dark and handsome, charming and courageous. His beautiful sister, Neşerek Nesrin, fourth wife to Abdülaziz, had introduced him to the pleasures and exclusivity of palace life. He was promoted captain and assigned first aide-de-camp to Prince Izzettin Efendi, eldest son of Abdülaziz. Since the coup d'etat he had been confined to barracks without weapons, where he was closely watched by Hüseyin Avni Pasha's spies. Hasan had become increasingly moody and aggressive, barking orders and handing out severe discipline for minor offences. Many officers, apprehensive and stressed themselves, complained that his disruptive behaviour was undermining the morale of the soldiers. The decree came as no surprise.

Hasan ranted and raved incoherently, making little sense. He grabbed Osman Ferid by the arm shaking him.

"I will have no peace until I revenge the death of my sister and the sultan. Do you understand Osman Ferid? The rumours I hear are too painful. I am confused and cannot sleep. Those horrific deeds, the deaths, rumours and now this. Hüseyin Avni, the perpetrator of all this evil has the audacity to exile me as though I am a traitor.

"This would not have happened in the Caucases. There revenge is just and swift. I will avenge the death of my beloved sister and Abdülaziz. They shall see blood flow; they shall pay with their lives for carrying out such treacherous acts."

Hasan fell into a chair, burying his face in his hands, sobbing with anguish. Osman Ferid looked at him with pity.

They were so different. Hasan was passionate, volatile, lion-hearted and fearless. He did not consider the consequences of his actions or words. Since the coup, Osman Ferid had relived those moments a thousand times; he believed he had acted in good faith. His duty as major was to protect his men, to keep a sense of normality in an abnormal situation. Had they rebelled they would have been shot as traitors; even so, time and time again he was riddled with doubt that he had acted too hastily. The situation in the country had not improved; the government was still in a state of crisis and the sultan, too unwell to attend public functions, spent his days in the harem.

Looking at Hasan, dishevelled, hunched in the chair, he wondered whether there were other officers who doubted his actions. No one spoke of that day, as though they feared to voice the incident aloud. It had been a custom to gather in the officer's mess to relax after a tiring day, now everyone was eager to leave the palace as soon as possible. The mess was deserted, quiet and tidy, without the noise and horseplay of young guards off duty.

Osman Ferid sat next to his friend.

"Hasan, listen to me, and listen carefully. We all share your grief. We know how devoted you were to your sister. If there is a question of honour, as your senior ranking officer, the honour of the guards is my duty, not yours. Vengeance was the creed of our forefathers in the Caucasus. I thought it would not happen here, but perhaps I am wrong. If revenge is to be taken, it is I who will bear the consequences."

Hasan was taken aback by Osman Ferid's response. Objecting loudly, he reminded him of his responsibilities to his wife and son, but Osman Ferid stood firm. Hasan looked at his friend. He admired his physical confidence, military superiority and concern for the men in his unit, but he knew how stubborn and unbending he could be. Hasan rose and walked to the table.

"Let's draw lots. The one who pulls the longest straw will murder Hüseyin Avni and so avenge the death of my sister and the sultan."

Hasan paused, looked intensely at his friend, then shaking his head, he laughed aloud.

"My friend you can be as stubborn as an old goat. But first, share a bottle of wine with me. I know, I know you don't drink, but who knows what the night might bring; make this an exception for me. Let us toast our past."

5

He gave a bitter laugh.

"We might not have a future."

Osman Ferid nodded. "Well, just one glass." He would have agreed to anything to humour and calm his volatile friend.

Osman Ferid offered the first draw to Hasan, who drew the short straw. Hasan threw the straw to the floor in disgust. Shouting and cursing, he circled the room again and again.

"No, no, this is not a game. It is I who will avenge my sister's death, not you."

They argued until the early hours of the morning. Hasan kept shouting, crying, and forcing his friend to drink, until Osman Ferid simply could not stand any longer. His head ached. He felt sick as he tried to calm his friend, fearing the noise would wake Ayshe and Kazım.

"Hasan, for Allah's sake that's enough. It's done. It was a fair choice. I will prepare a plan and then call you. Now please go home. Try to rest. We are both exhausted." Hasan leaned heavily on Osman Ferid.

"Promise me one thing: This will be our secret, a secret we take to our grave."

Hasan filled his friend's glass with the remaining dregs.

"A last toast to you, Osman Ferid, to the Caucusus where revenge is sweet and swift. You are my beloved brother. Whatever happens, remember I love and respect you and hold you to your promise.'

They embraced. Hasan saluted his friend with a tender smile, holding Osman Ferid who slipped into a chair overcome with emotion and alcohol. Hasan disappeared down the street.

Cherkess Hasan rushed to the home of his brother-in-law, Ateş Mehmet Pasha, on the pretence of bidding him farewell before leaving for Baghdad. He knew the pasha kept his weapons in the library. He took a Derringer pistol and kinjal dagger from their cases and then made haste to Hüseyin Avni Pasha's konak at Paşalimanı, where he was told the pasha was attending a cabinet meeting at Midhat Pasha's konak.

The members of the new government were assembled on the upper floor of the konak. Those present were Mütercim Rüştü Pasha, the prime minister, Hüseyin Avni Pasha, the foreign minister, Raşid Pasha, the minister of education, Cevdet Pasha, Ahmet Pasha, the commander of the admiralty, Yusuf Pasha, the royal accountant, Halet Pasha, the secretary of the grand assembly, Midhat Pasha and three secretaries. The agenda included the uprisings in Montenegro and Crete.

The sentries at the gate saluted Hasan as he made his way to the second floor where the guards on duty asked his business.

"I am leaving for Baghdad early in the morning. I have come to pay my respects to my Commander-in-Chief. I shall wait."

He paced up and down the corridor until the guards returned to their room, then ran up the stairs to the third floor where the meeting was being held. Hasan nodded to the guard outside the cabinet room as he sat on a chair near the door to wait for Hüseyin Avni Pasha. After a few minutes, he ordered the guard to fetch him a glass of water while he stood guard. As the soldier disappeared down the stairs, Hasan rushed into the chamber, locking the door behind him before the ministers realised what had happened. 'What is the meaning of this?' shouted a minister as Hasan pointed the gun at Hüseyin Avni Pasha.

"Revenge for the death of my sister and Sultan Abdülaziz," was his reply as he fired two shots straight at Hüseyin Avni's heart.

The pasha died instantly. Hell broke loose in the room as the ministers shouted for the guards to open the door. Admiral Ahmet grabbed Hasan from the back, but with the strength of a lion, the young captain shook himself free, stabbing the admiral with his kinjal. He turned to shoot Raşid Pasha, just as Ahmet Ağa, a guard, rushed at him with a bayonet, wounding him in the side before Hasan could shoot.

Shouts could be heard in the corridors. The door burst open. Soldiers with guns at the ready surrounded the bloodied chamber. When he saw the troops, Hasan stopped shooting. He dropped his gun and kinjal.

"I surrender. I have no quarrel with you. The deaths of Sultan Abdülaziz and his wife, Neşerek Nesrin, my sister, have been avenged."

As he was being escorted out of the konak, an aide-de-camp to Ahmet Pasha spat on his face. Hasan jumped on the man, beating his head with fury until he was overcome and hand-cuffed.

The next morning Ayshe found her husband asleep in his clothes on the sofa. His face looked worn and strained even though his eyes were closed.

"Osman Ferid, wake up. Wake up."

Osman Ferid sat up. His head ached.

"You must dress quickly."

Ayshe wanted to give him time to recover before breaking the tragic news she had been told. She could not believe that Hasan, a favourite, charming and witty, was capable of such violence. They had visited his sister at Dolmabahçe Palace and had often been invited to receptions at Prince İzzettin Efendi's palace, not that Osman Ferid accepted, which had infuriated her. As her husband walked in, she rushed into his arms, tears streaming down her face as she poured out the horrendous news of Hasan's murderous rampage, shooting Hüseyin Avni and Raşid Pasha.

She felt his body tense as he stroked her hair absentminded-ly before turning to the window. He stood there motionless for a long time. She was about to touch him when he whipped around gripping her arms so tightly it hurt. He whispered in a strange, hoarse voice.

"Ayshe, I want you to promise to tell no one Hasan was here last night. Do you understand? No one! He was my beloved brother. May Allah bless and forgive him."

He walked into his room, locked the door and wept like a child.

The following day, stripped of his rank, a military court sentenced Circassian Hasan to death by public hanging. During the brief trial, Hasan appeared calm and controlled. He confessed that he and he alone was responsible for shooting Prime Minister Hüseyin Avni and Foreign Minister Raşid Pasha to avenge the deaths of his sister and the late Sultan Abdülaziz.

Cherkess Zish-Brakee Hasan was hanged in Beyazit Square on June 18, 1876, at the age of 26.

Months later, looking through a drawer in his desk Osman Ferid found a brown leather pouch containing a silver kinjal engraved with the letters Z. B. H.

CHAPTER 9

Russo-Turkish War

The coup d'etat brought a welcome change for the majority of citizens in Istanbul. A fresh-faced, young monarch known to support liberal and pro-Western views might use his power to elect a government that would lead the country towards constitutional reform. 'Murad, the Reformer' was the cry of the day as appointments were conferred on several Young Ottomans, including Namik Kemal, who returned from Cyprus to become Murad V's private secretary.

But the exhilaration was short-lived. Murad V was mentally impaired; his nervous disposition sank into confusion. He feared commitment and mistrusted the loyalty of those around him. Extremely excitable, he was unable to come to terms with the responsibilities of rule. He had lived in the enforced seclusion imposed upon heirs apparent to the Ottoman throne. Within his privately orchestrated world, he had been socially active and exceedingly popular, but it was soon evident that he lacked the mental stamina and physical strength to undertake the pressures, burdens and public exposure demanded of a reigning sultan. He was naturally highly strung and over-sensitive, given to swings of emotional instability which unwisely he fought to control with alcohol, especially champagne and cognac, tastes acquired on his tour to France.

Following the accession, and overcome by extreme anxiety and agitation his condition rapidly worsened. His dread of public appearances was so great that the ceremony to gird the sultan with the sword of Osman was postponed and later cancelled. Many people, mullahs and ministers in the government saw this as a bad omen. It was considered imperative that a sultan be girded with the historic sabre, the Sword of Osman, founder of the dynasty, a tradition belonging to the Caliph Omar and symbolizing the dignity of the Caliphate acquired by "Yavuz Selim," Sultan Selim I, the Resolute, in 1512. This ceremony, the Turkish equivalent of a coronation, was performed by the Çelebi, the head of the Mevlevi dervishes and carried deep religious significance, so long as the sultanate endured. One explanation was of a special connection between the Mevlevi dervish order and the imperial house, dating from the time of Ertuğrul, the Ottoman clan leader who frequently visited Jelal-ud-din Rumi, founder of the order. On one occasion the founder pronounced a still recorded blessing on Ertuğrul's son, Osman, the founder of the Ottoman dynasty.

The death of his uncle, Abdülaziz, combined with the murder of two ministers and the public hanging disturbed the sultan's already unbalanced mind with despair and fear. He fell into a deep depression. Foreign and Turkish doctors diagnosed him unfit to rule. Three months later, despite pleas from Namık Kemal and his liberal supporters for a postponement of the disposition, on August 31, 1876 a *fatwa* obtained from the Chief Mufti according to the laws of the sharia, deposed the sultan on the grounds of mental incapacity in favour of his unassuming brother, Abdülhamid.

Sultan Murad V was confined in the Cirağan Palace until his death in 1904.

1876 would be remembered as the year of the three sultans.

Osman Ferid was in a state of shock, numbed by the violence and public hanging. He retreated into a dark, desperate world. For the first time in his military career he became disinterested

166

in carrying out his duties; at home after a silent meal, he retired to his room. Ayshe was at her wits' end. She appealed to his brothers Mehmet, Ahmet and Ismael, who in turn attempted to address the matter, but they were unable to penetrate their brother's armour of grief and guilt.

Osman Ferid reproached himself over and over again for allowing Hasan to leave that night, knowing how hot-headed and fearless he was. Naively, he had thought he might persuade him to take a less dramatic course, legal action against the ministers who had organised the coup or a public appeal to Sultan Murad. How wrong he had been and how deeply he regretted the tragic outcome. Alone in his room he relived that night, desperately trying to remember every detail, but his memory was fogged by alcohol. Why had he drunk so much wine, when he knew one glass confused him? Could he have prevented this deed from happening? Would he truly have carried out his part as he had promised Hasan? Questions and more questions kept haunting him, giving him no peace.

The atmosphere in the barracks was tense, uncomfortable. The Circassian officers in the Royal Guards suffered from an identity crisis. They had not been part of the reform movement that had engulfed the city. Their loyalty was to Ottomanism and Islam and focused around the personage of the sultan, caliph and dynasty. They felt under threat. Their commanders, aware of Circassian Hasan's popularity, mistrusted their allegiance and judgment. Osman Ferid was too disconcerted to react.

One evening he returned home to find Zissi waiting for him. He hadn't seen her for some time so was pleased when Ayshe invited her to dine with them.

Zissi told them how she was helping her dearest friend prepare for her wedding feast and her latest project, dried sugared fruits.

"Ismail, Mehmet and Ahmet loathe the sweet smell of sugar so much they have sworn to lock me out of the kitchen next weekend unless I stop." As she rose to leave, she asked Osman

Ferid to walk her home. Ayshe insisted she spend the following weekend with them. "We might have a picnic at Therapia with Kazım," she suggested.

It was a clear, warm evening. Zissi took his arm as they walked home along the shore road, content to be together. Once in the family home, Osman Ferid sat in his old chair while Zissi prepared tea. He was happy to be there; he missed the noisy, boisterous evenings with his brothers. Zissi set the tray before him, pulled up a chair and took his hands in hers.

"I know you are suffering. We also suffer. We all loved Hasan. His sister was a very dear friend. This tragedy should never have happened; it has shocked and saddened the community. But you are wrong to torment yourself in this way. Hasan was set on revenge. He would not have allowed you or anyone else to stand in his way. No one could have stopped him from doing what he did. Grieve for him and the distressing consequences of his actions, as we all do. But you are drowning in self-pity, stagnating in a state of shock that is unbecoming. You are neglecting your responsibilities and duty.

"Have you forgotten you are a Shapli chieftain? Have you forgotten your duty to your family and the men in your company? You have closed your heart and mind to our problems. We—Ayshe, Kazım, your brothers, officers and soldiers and I—need you here now. We need your protection—we feel lost and alone. You cannot ignore us because you are filled with self-commiseration and remorse."

Zissi looked at her elder brother with clear, accusative eyes as she turned her back and walked to the window, tall and straight. Her words had fallen like the lash of a horse whip; she was the only one courageous enough to confront Osman Ferid with the truth.

She is so like mother, he thought, straightforward, unafraid and cruelly honest in her love. With his head cupped in his hands, Osman Ferid sat for an hour or more before he rose from his chair and walked towards her.

"Forgive me, Zissi, I have been obsessed by apathy and guilt. I am so confused. You are right. I apologize. I have been so wrapped up in my own bitter thoughts I forgot the people I love. I promise it shall never happen again. Thank you, my dearest, sweet sister, thank you."

She turned, her eyes shone, her face creased into smiles, Osman Ferid kissed her cheek as they held each other close.

"You remind me so much of Nan; never ever change."

To resolve the problem of unrest within the Royal Guards, the Ministry of War assigned Caucasians who might cause trouble to frontier posts throughout the Ottoman Empire. Osman Ferid was one of the first to receive his assignment. He was posted to Tripolitania in North Africa.

Tripolitania is situated at the northwestern tip of the kingdom of Libya, bounded by Tunisia on the west, the Mediterranean Sea on the north, Fezzan in the south and Cyrenaica in the east. Tripolitania and Cyrenaica were the only North African territories remaining under Ottoman rule. The last Karaman ruler, Ali, deposed by the Ottomans in 1835, had resumed direct rule, which met with strong local opposition from Arabic-speaking Semites and Berbers. The Senusi Order, a strict religious Muslim brotherhood founded in 1843, had spread like wildfire from Cyrenaica to Tripolitania.

When Osman Ferid arrived he found the garrison in a pitiful state. Dilapidated and dirty, the walls were partially covered with paint or left unpainted and rusty pipes dripped with brownish water. The Ottoman officials, officers and soldiers who met him did not look much better, thought Osman Ferid dryly. These remote garrisons were the last outposts of the once sprawling Ottoman Empire. The unfortunate souls appointed there were more or less forgotten, forced to spend their lives in exile. Salaries were rarely paid and months, sometimes years, would pass without leave as they settled to wait in vain for news, a telegram from the Porte or a rare visitor from the capital. They welcomed Osman Ferid halfheartedly. The head official, Ahmet Bey, invited him to dinner, plying him with questions about the city, mentioning names of relatives he might have met. Ahmet Bey collected taxes, kept accounts and wrote reports. He painted a gloomy picture of life at the garrison, the problems with brigands and rebels who stole their animals and attacked supply carriages crossing the desert.

The next morning, at dawn, Osman Ferid marched into the men's barracks and woke the sleeping soldiers with orders to follow him to his quarters with brooms and buckets of water. He had already thrown out the broken chairs and a stained wash bowl and torn down the grimy curtains. He provided them with paint and set them to work. He called an officers' meeting to outline the plan of action to be followed during his tenure of duty at Tripolitania. Murmurs of displeasure and plain cussedness were heard around the garrison but they all knew that "a new broom sweeps clean." They grinned, confident that the dry, desert heat, monotonous days and hot, dusty Ghibli winds would soon tire this new, young commander. How could they know Osman Ferid welcomed the challenge of "a chivalrous adventure" in hopes that it would lead him to shake off the lethargy and despair of the past months?

As time passed the garrison buildings were cleaned, repaired and painted and the water tanks and pipes renewed. The mess, kitchens, toilets, and stables were disinfected under the keen surveillance of the Major. Early morning roll-call, uniform and boot inspection improved personal appearances to some extent. Duties were pinned on a notice board each morning. The horses were groomed and the camels fed. He pored over the accounts with Ahmet Bey. Many of the older soldiers had not received pay for months and some had been at the post for years.

In order of precedence, officers, soldiers, non-commissioned officers and civilians working for the government were given leave to the nearest town. At night he studied the territory. Dividing his force into five patrol groups they headed for villages and tribal settlements to visit chiefs and local dignitaries, carrying greetings from the Sultan and Caliph with assurances of the Porte's continual protection with regular patrols around the territory.

Osman Ferid endured the hot, dry desert summers and cold winds that blew from the snow covered Alps of Europe in winter, when snowfall covered the high ground and temperatures dropped to 0° C (32° F) at night. The men under his command began to respond to his impassive day-to-day routine; much to their amusement, they watched him learn to ride and train a camel. When he wished to be alone he galloped out of the garrison before dawn towards the Jabal mountain district to spend the day riding to Al Hammadah al Hamra, the red stone plateau or along the plateau edge that dropped irregularly to the Mediterranean.

His pent-up passions found peace in the vast open spaces of the desert. It was here that Osman Ferid began to keep a log book on his life in the army. Every evening he wrote a detailed progress report with a list of projects and notes about the soldiers and officers in the garrison.

News from Turkey arrived by telegraph, usually official documents of state, warrants of arrests to be served or fines to be collected, until in early September when the lines buzzed with the news of the abdication of Sultan Murad Khan V on the grounds of illhealth and the succession of his younger brother, Sultan Abdülhamid II. Osman Ferid was relieved not to be in Istanbul during this change of royal power. Unsure of his future, he had put his military career in jeopardy and although this mission had forced him out of his depression, the thought of remaining at this remote desert fort forever filled him with dread.

On March 11, 1877 he received a telegraph ordering him to return to Turkey to take up a post at the War Ministry.

He was delighted. He missed his son, Ayshe and his family, the cool turquoise-blue of the Bosphorus and the bustling city. He had worked hard at the garrison to improve the conditions of the soldiers who served there. He looked forward to the new challenge in Istanbul.

Internal problems in the Balkans came to a head when the Christian subjects in Bosnia, Herzegovina and later Bulgaria rebelled against the harsh treatment dealt by the Ottomans over collection of taxes. The uprising was vigorously suppressed; even so the Great Powers, anxious to avoid a full-scale war, were reluctant to intervene. When Serbia and Montenegro declared war on Turkey in 1876, Russia felt obliged to defend the Slavic Christians.

In the hope of finding a peaceful settlement to the problem and to prevent further hostilities between Turkey and Russia, the British government called for a "Istanbul Conference" to assemble on December, 1876. Tentative steps towards substantial autonomy under a governor-general approved by the sultan and the European powers were about to be reached, when to everyone's astonishment, Abdülhamid declared the establishment of an Ottoman constitution, modelled on the French system, and prepared by his grand vizier, Midhat Pasha.

Midhat Pasha sympathized with the Young Ottomans who were angered by the blatant inequality suffered by the Muslim population against the privileges granted to the Europeans who lived in the country; his political vision was to establish a liberal constitutional regime. This announcement resulted in a complete defeat for the conference. Later Sultan Abdülhamid was to use the collapse of the conference to rid himself of Midhat Pasha, the man who had framed the constitution. Midhat Pasha was exiled in February, 1877. In March, with the control of parliament secured in his iron grip, the sultan decreed that Russian protection over Ottoman Christians was unnecessary. In exasperation, Alexander II declared war on Turkey on April 24, 1877.

The Russian army invaded the Ottoman Empire on two fronts: in Europe crossing the Pruth and in Asia from the Caucasus towards Kars, Ardahan and Erzurum. Ahmet Muhtar Pasha commanded the Eastern-Caucasus theatre; Abdülkerim Pasha commanded the western front. The Ottomans fought the joint forces of Russians, Romanians Montenegrin and Bulgarian insurgents.

Osman Ferid applied for active service on the Eastern Caucasus front but was ordered to join Abdülkerim Pasha's forces serving under Süleyman Pasha. By the time Osman Ferid's battalion reached the front, the Russian army had occupied Romania, crossed the Danube and established beachheads at Buchak with the intention of a rapid penetration to force the Ottomans into an early peace treaty. But as often happened in wars against the Turks, the Russians underestimated the formidable resistance of the Ottoman Army with its striking force of 800,000 and superior arms.

The Ottoman army spread out along the banks of the Danube from Montenegro in Serbia to Greece, counteracting surprise attacks by the Russians. Osman Ferid and his men made slow progress, marching in torrential rain on muddy roads, fighting along the river with bold attacks, camping at night under the windy Balkan skies. Their advance was frequently blocked and they suffered severe setbacks from lack of supplies and reinforcements which failed to arrive in time.

Joan Haslip describes the sad state of the Ottoman army in her book, *The Sultan, the life of Abdülhamid*.

"Mahmud Pasha, Abdülhamid's brother-in-law who was Grand Master of Artillery, exercised a fatal influence on the military councils of Yıldız. Time after time in these crucial months, when the Russians by the sheer weight of manpower were forcing their way through to the Danube, orders were issued and countermanned, incompetent generals put in command and able officers dismissed merely because they had failed to pay court to the sultan's brother-in-law. General Valentine Baker, a former English cavalry officer serving in the Ottoman Army, gives a heart-rending account of a war in which the uncom-plaining heroism of the soldiers who still gave thanks to their Padişah for the biscuits and water, which were sometimes their only rations, was offset by the criminal negligence of the gener-als in command and the intrigues and jealousies of the great pashas in the capital."

In June, the Russians entered Bulgaria from Zishtova, Nigbolu and Yantra. Crown Prince Grand Duke Nicholas Nikolaevich commanded the forces marching on Yantra while General I. V. Gurko commanded the forces that entered Zishtova to occupy Tirnova. On July 17, the Grand Duke ordered General Deroshinsky to the front and General Gurko to the rear to attack Shipka in full force. At first Hulusi Pasha's forces repulsed the Russian offensive, but without reinforcements, were soon over-powered by the sheer numbers of Russian troops.

The pasha realised the futility of attempting to break through the Russian lines under such conditions. To avoid com-plete surrender he ordered his troops to withdraw down the narrow paths and ravines that led away from the canyon. While they retreated, Hulusi Pasha, with a small force of volunteers, remained to defend the pass. These men fought to the end, defending the pass to save the lives of their compatriots as they made their way out of the fighting zone. None survived when the Russians broke through the entrance to the Shipka pass.

The role of a military leader with power over the Ottoman armies pleased Abdülhamid, but he lacked the character of a general at war. His reaction to the defeat of these brave men was impulsive and angry rather than tactical. Abdülkerim Pasha was dismissed from his post as Supreme Command of the west-ern theatre and replaced by Crimean war hero, Mehmet Ali Pasha, Governor of Crete.

Grand Duke Nicholas Nikolaevich marched to Ruschuk to

engage against the forces of Mehmet Ali Pasha but was repulsed and forced to retreat. He ordered General Gourko to capture Yenizagha, a station leading to the Edirne railroad.

Osman Ferid served under Süleyman Pasha, second-in-command to Mehmet Ali Pasha. There he met Colonel Valentine Baker, the English colonel from the 10th Hussars who had served in Crimea. In Britain he held a high reputation as a cavalry officer and strategist; later when he took up service with the sultan, he was placed under Süleyman Pasha. On June 27 they reached Karapınar by train with reinforcements. General Gourko, the Russian general, fought long and hard, but after suffering severe losses, outnumbered and outmanoeuvred by the Turkish forces, was forced to retreat. By August, the Ottomans had succeeded in recapturing the occupied area, except for the Shipka Pass, which remained in Russian hands.

On August 21, Süleyman Pasha ordered an offensive to recapture the last Russian pass, the Shipka Pass, but the Russians had brought in heavy reinforcements to fortify the pass against any offensive. At dawn the operation began in earnest. Turkish bombardment breached the Russian positions. Wave after wave of Turkish troops advanced in close formation into the Shipka Pass to the sound of the bugle and hoarse shouts of 'Allah, Allah'. The air was thick, clouded with smoke from cannon blasts and the whine of shrapnel.

Osman Ferid marched forward, uprooting Russians from their trenches, moving his troops towards the pass. He adapted mountain warfare tactics to protect his troops, fanning his company out into small groups, endeavouring to guide them as they rushed into bayonet charges through curtains of fire from Russian guns.

He led his force along the path towards the gun position that covered the lower entrance. Once he had mounted the gun position, to his dismay he saw cannons camouflaged on the ridges above pointing directly at his men as they rushed in. They had fallen into a deadly trap; retreat was impossible and heavy casualties inevitable. Osman Ferid did not hesitate. Flourishing his sword, he screamed "Advance, Advance," rousing the troops to move under the hailstorm of bullets, gesturing to the hidden cannons firing regular volleys of cannon balls.

"Advance, advance," he shouted, leading the charge fighting blindly, his troops responding faster and forward. They overpowered the Russian trench, providing a margin of safety for the men. Osman Ferid climbed out of the trench onto higher ground shouting, screaming above the ear-deafening rattle of guns to those who lagged behind, willing them on faster, covering their movements with his fire as he shot incessantly at the enemy hiding behind the curve of the ridge. Suddenly he was thrown against a rock as a bullet pierced his side. The burning pain spread through his body but he willed himself to move away from the rock. Lifting his sword, he kept shouting "Advance Advance,"as more troops ran for cover into the trench.

At that moment Osman Ferid was hit a second time in the chest and fell unconscious into the trench. The force and fury of the Turkish offensive lost its momentum. Süleyman Pasha had succeeded in recapturing part of the Shipka pass, which was a supreme victory against such a powerful force. Ottoman casualties amounted to approximately 13,000, while the Russians lost 6,000.

Osman Ferid opened his eyes to find himself on a rough stretcher moving in rhythm to the weary voices of troops singing a regimental marching song, as they made their way back to camp.

> Our army has taken an oath
> A fountain for history
> Our banner is our glory, our title Osmanlı
> Ours is this country, and ours the glory
> For which we gladly give our lives.

He was taken to a primitive field hospital. The doctor in charge looked at his wounds.

"These wounds are deep. There is nothing I can do except give him a morphine injection."

His orderly pleaded with the doctor to help him.

"This is Major Osman Ferid, one of the campaign heroes. He captured enemy trenches, two fortified gun positions, and forced his men to charge under fire to the safety of the trenches, saving them from certain slaughter. He kept on fighting, urging them to safety even after he was hit. He inspires his troops and we are proud to serve under him. You must help him."

The doctor shook his head doubtfully, but cleaned Osman Ferid's wounds as best he could for the long, painful train journey to the military hospital in Edirne.

Doctors were able to extract one of the bullets, but the other was lodged too close to the heart to be removed. Osman Ferid lived with a Russian bullet in his chest for the rest of his life. His convalescence was slow.

Being confined to bed for weeks made him impatient and irritable, continually demanding news of the progress of the war. The moment he felt well enough he crept out of bed to visit the sick and dying soldiers in their wards. He tried the patience of the young, overworked medics with suggestions they use natural recipes for poultices and painkilling cures he had learned in the Caucasus.

On, December 20, 1877, a telegram from the war ministry arrived with news of his decoration for bravery in battle, promotion to full colonel and commission as Commander of the 8th Regiment of the Guards.

Osman Ferid was finally declared well enough to be released from the hospital. Most of the hospital staff and patients gathered to say goodbye and wish him well. He had been a trying patient, a headache for the poor understaffed medical corps, but they could not but admire and smile at his enthusiasm and genuine concern for the troops and the hospital.

He returned home delighted to find a large party of family and friends waiting to welcome him. Tears, laughter, back-slapping, hugs of love and prayers to God, Thae, filled the room, as they congratulated his promotion and blessed his recovery.

His son, Kazım, now ten years old, had grown into a strapping young lad. Ayshe was relieved at her husband's safe return from the war and proud of his bravery and promotion. She forgot and forgave past disappointments as she looked forward to a happier future as wife of a colonel. She began to organise her life according to her husband's work schedule. She busied herself entertaining at home or visiting friends, shopping at the fashionable Rue de Pera, and then taking tea at the Lebon Café. Whatever her programme, Ayshe would be home in time to greet her husband. Osman Ferid was delighted to spend his evenings at home with Kazım, relating stories about his Caucasian heritage and the magnificence and magic of the Caucasus Mountains.

On August 18, 1878, Osman Ferid was appointed Assistant Commander and Aide-de-camp to the Commanding General at Taşkışla Barracks. A few months later on the sudden death of the Commander General, he was promoted Brigadier General, honoured with the title of pasha and given full command of the Taşkışla Barracks. He was 34 years old.

The Russian plan for advancement had received a setback. On July 20, Osman Pasha, veteran of the Crimea War and Turkish Commander-in-Chief, repulsed the Russians at Plevna and stemmed their advance. He dug his forces in around Plevna, building a strong military fortress that dominated the main routes into Bulgaria.

The first assault aimed at breaking Osman Pasha's hold failed, with severe Russian losses attributed to the Turkish army's modern breech-loading rifles that were superior to the Russian muzzle-loading muskets. Two days later a second assault with reinforcements from Prince Charles of Romania's army once more failed to rout the Turkish army. The Russians decided to besiege Plevna by encircling the fortress and starving the garrison. The hopes of the Ottoman army depended on Osman Pasha's decision. He received orders from Abdülhamid to stand firm against the Russian attacks with a promise of immediate reinforcements. The commander had serious doubts as to the wisdom of this military operation but withstood Russian attacks for five months from July 19th to December 10th without receiving any of the promised arms, ammunition or re-enforcements.

Aware of the hopelessness of his position, Osman Pasha decided to save the remaining force from starvation or worse by attempting to break through the Russian cordon, but was defeated and compelled to surrender. Russia was now able to execute its original plan of penetration into European Turkey by taking Adrianople on January 20, 1878. Osman Pasha, defender of Plevna, was hailed "Hero of Plevna." He was honoured by the Russian Tsar; on his return to Turkey he was promoted to Field Marshal and proclaimed Gazi by Sultan Abdülhamid.

At the time, Colonel Baker, known as Baker Pasha, had questioned Süleyman Pasha's strategy. He held that Gourko's advance could have been prevented had the Pasha not withdrawn into the mountains. He continued to voice his opinion after the war to anyone who listened.

Baker Pasha had settled on the island of Prinkipo, the largest in the archipelago of five islands in the Aegean Sea near the city. He spent his days at Yıldız Palace where he had become part of the sultan's elite circle of friends. Whenever he called on Osman Ferid at Taşkışla Barracks, he inevitably turned the conversation to limited strategic warfare as practiced in Britain, determined to argue his case and thus justifying his military viewpoint to gain Osman Ferid's approval as a comrade in arms.

Baker Pasha invited Osman Ferid and his wife to a reception at his residence on the island and placed his private launch at their disposal. Ayshe was thrilled; she had spent her summer vacations at one of the grand, wooden houses at Prinkipo as a child and looked forward to visiting old acquaintances. The island, famed for its pine trees, green lawns, and flower filled gardens was a lively, colourful mixture of British, German and Russians diplomats and businessmen who resided comfortably with their local Greek and Turkish neighbours. Osman Ferid and Ayshe took a horse-drawn carriage around the island, past the villa she had stayed as a child to the small home of her old Greek housekeeper. At the reception in Baker Pasha's elegant English garden she was delighted to meet friends who still spent summers on the island. As they boarded the launch in the evening watching the lights of the island fade, Ayshe took her husband's arm, "What a heavenly day; the island is as charming and enjoyable as I remember in my childhood. Oh Osman Ferid may we rent a villa and spend the summer season there next year?"

On January 27th, the British cabinet ordered its Mediterranean fleet to steam through the Dardanelles and for weeks it remained in the Gulf of Izmit, but when the Russian army advanced as far as San Stefano, the British Fleet steamed up to Prinkipo where its flagship, the *Alexandra*, anchored.

The Russians advanced as far as Çatalca before agreeing to a truce. On March 3 the Treaty of San Stefano was drawn up. Turkey was forced to accept concessions by which Romania and Montenegro were granted independence and Bulgaria, self-determination. The provisions of this treaty were later annulled by the Congress of Berlin.

PART THREE
ARABIA -MYTILENE- ISTANBUL
(1864-1878)

For your sake, I hurry over land and water
For your sake, I cross the desert and split the mountain in two
And turn my face from all things,
 Until the time I reach the place where I am alone with You.

                                                        –Al Hallaj

CHAPTER 10

Arabia - Mytilene - Istanbul
(1878-1912)

In her book, *Russia and Turkey in the Nineteenth Century*, Elizabeth Wormeley Latimer wrote:

"On August 31, 1876, Abdülhamid I was proclaimed sultan. He had been called to the throne in the darkest moment of Turkish history. The State had recently declared itself bankrupt; its finances were in a state of chaos; war was going on with Servia and was impending with Russia; besides which all Christian powers were exasperated by the outrages in Bulgaria. Eighteen months after Abdülhamid's accession, Russian troops had threatened his capital and extorted the treaty of San Stefano. The Congress of Berlin, while it tore up this treaty, consulted only the interests of Western Europe in the provisions that replaced it, and they greatly reduced the area of the sultan's dominions. Abdülhamid accepted the decision of the Congress - he could not do otherwise - but it taught him a policy to which he has strictly adhered. He dreads friends as much as enemies."

Abdülaziz had spent his time as heir apparent to the throne in a palace on the hills of Therapia, enjoying the jovial outdoor pursuits of a hunting, shooting country squire, while Murat V.

under the influence of his educated, sophisticated mother, had surrounded himself with a more liberal, cultured circle of friends.

Abdülhamid was an enigma. His mother, a Circassian dancer, died of consumption when he was just a child; his father, Abdülmecid, showed little sympathy for a son he did not particularly favour. Left to his own devices, he grew, without parental love, guidance or protection in the claustrophobic atmosphere of a harem of ladies from diverse backgrounds, where conspiracy and plotting were the only means to acquire personal power and safety.

He never forgot an incident that happened in his childhood. Sir Stratford Canning, then British Ambassador, was walking in the grounds of Topkapı Palace when he noticed a child sitting alone near a fountain; this must be a royal prince he thought. Greeting the child with a smile, he stopped to say a few friendly words to the lonely young prince. It was Abdülhamid. That simple gesture of kindness shown to him by the impressive figure of the ambassador in formal dress, years later influenced the sultan favourably to seek England as his ally.

Abdülhamid was slim, of medium height with dark complexion, a heavy black beard, sad expressive eyes, a prominent nose and large forehead. During those important formative years of living in constant fear for his safety, the need for self-protection was so strong that he became a shadow-like figure in the palace with few friends, suspicious of all men and their motives.

Lord Beaconsfield (Benjamin Disraeli), known for a strange sympathy he felt for Abdülhamid, was reported to have said, "He is not a tyrant; he is not dissolute; he is not a bigot or corrupt."

Another foreigner, Arminus Vambery, a Hungarian professor who had resided in Istanbul since 1860, became one of the few Europeans to win the sultan's favour and confidence, because perhaps it was said he acted as a spy amongst the dissidents. In his *Diversions of a Diploma* he quoted the sultan as saying:

"In Europe the soil was prepared centuries ago for liberal institutions and now I am asked to transplant a sapling to foreign, stony, rugged ground of Asiatic life. Let me clear away the thistles and stones and then we may transport the new plant; and believe me that nobody will be more delighted at its thriving than I."

Professor Vambery goes on:

"We need not shut our eyes to the deplorable conditions under which Turkey is labouring; we must not lose sight of ruined villages, neglected roads, decaying towns, choked harbours and an impoverished population; but we can, nay, we must be, indulgent and, instead of always finding fault with the Mohammedan Turk, we should begin to discard all political bias in our judgement of an Eastern Prince and of his people.

"In point of fact he (Abdülhamid) was neither as good as Beaconsfield's description nor as bad as the 'Adbul the Damned' of Watson's poems. The sultan's rule bore hard on the intelligentsia of all races, sometimes on non-Muslims minorities as such, but Turkey as a whole was not unprosperous and foreigners flourished under the protection of the Capitulations."

On August 31, 1876, following the girding ceremony with the sword of Osman, Abdülhamid II was proclaimed sultan. For security reasons he chose Yıldız garden with its vast park and forested hills surrounded by high walls as his home, for it had no connection to the city. Here he planned the Yıldız Palace complex with pavilions similar to Topkapı Palace, the Şale Köşkü, Malta Köşkü and the Çadır Köşkü, along with impressive royal stables which merged gently into the landscape. He designed a maze of secret passages and tunnels to be used as escape routes from ministers, staff or assassins.

Philip Mansel in his book *Constantinople* describes Yıldız Palace:

"Yıldız reverted to the traditional Ottoman palace pattern. Like Topkapı, and unlike Dolmabahçe and Çırağan, Yıldız was a mosaic of separate buildings—pavilions, kiosks and workshops—surrounded by gardens and a towering wall... Yıldız was a museum–complex and industrial park, as well as a palace and government compound. Within the grounds were a museum of natural history and another for the sultan's pictures and antiquities. A furniture factory with sixty workmen made the elaborate late Ottoman high-backed gilded or inlaid palace furniture. The sultan's personal photography laboratory, library and carpentry workshop revealed his favourite form of relaxation: he was a skilled carpenter who made desks for his daughters and walking sticks for his wounded soldiers. Yıldız also contained four hospitals, an observatory, a pharmaceutical laboratory, a printing press, an embroidery workshop and a zoo."

The gardens, 500,000 square metres planted with trees and flowers from all over the world, were the glory of Yıldız. According to a description of the inner garden behind the Küçük Mabeyn (small transitional space) by the wife of the Orientalist Max Mulle:

"'Exquisite shrubs and palms were planted in every direction, whilst the flower borders were a blaze of colour. The air was almost heavy with the scent of orange blossom and gardeners were busy at every turn sprinkling the turf, even the crisp gravel walks, with water."

Abdülhamid ruled for thirty-three years through a period of dramatic change in traditional Ottoman society. His reign was deeply controversial. An English magazine, named *Leisure Hour* wrote at the time:

"Few sultans have been so beloved by their subjects as Adbulhamid. Indeed he is to them quite a new type of sultan, and they do not fail to appreciate the novelty. He is a man who does not pass his days in his harem toying with slaves. He is a man who takes a real interest in public affairs, and who, far from following the example of his predecessors and leaving the reins of government in the hands of clever courtiers, insists on seeing and judging all things for himself."

Despite this, other articles and periodicals appeared within the empire and Europe decrying his autocratic rule and pretence that the country was governed by a constitutional regime. Abdülhamid had a deeply complex personality, as clever as he was cunning. His natural aptitude and hunger for learning had been encouraged early in his youth during visits to the money exchange and Turkish borsa, evenings spent with traders and businessmen, Christian and Muslim, at Galata and the Pera, but his judgment and reign were coloured by his paranoid distrust and fear of assassination. He maintained peaceful coexistence with the powers of Europe by holding his own in their political game of chess. He enforced the 1839 Tanzimat reforms and rebuilt the city on European lines. Although a constitutional parliament existed in name, it did not reconvene until 1908. The power and control of the empire lay firmly housed at Yıldız Palace. Determined to protect the rights of the sovereign, Abdülhamid stamped out any intellectual opposition or growth. He was devious and sly but, when it suited his purpose, his charm, wit and intelligence won over many allies. He worked long hours, reading every official paper before it was signed.

As long as governance remained under his iron-fisted control, with ministers demoted to that of bureaucrats, Abdülhamid welcomed change and carried out many reforms especially in education, reforms which would later undermine his own regime. He improved public education, enlarged the *Mülkiye*, a school for civil education, and the War College at Harbiye, adding naval and military engineering schools and medical schools for civilians and the military. Eighteen higher educational schools were opened covering subjects such as finance, fine arts, police and customs. The Franco-Turkish Galatasaray School became the Imperial Ottoman Lycée, an elite public school for the Turkish ruling classes.

In contrast, the sultan was known to generate a spirit of apprehension and distrust amongst those around him. His fears and suspicions developed into neurotic obsessions which he was unable to control.

As commander of Taşkışla Barracks, Osman Ferid had little personal contact with Abdülhamid except at formal occasions. One of his duties was to attend the Friday Selamlık, an elaborate public procession with an impressive military display attended by foreign dignitaries as well as the public. It was on these Fridays that the monumental gate of Yıldız Palace was thrown open and the sultan emerged in his carriage to ride to the Yıldız Hamidiye Mosque outside the palace gate on the hill of Beşiktaş. On holidays, Osman Ferid was part of the escort to follow the sultan to the Dolmabahçe Mosque or the Süleymaniye Mosque at Topkapı Palace.

It was just as well, for Osman Ferid doubted he would have been able to humour the sultan or survive the intrigues and secrecy of Yıldız Palace. It was rumoured that one half of the population in Istanbul spied on the other half and it was common knowledge that Abdülhamid's ring of spies reported daily to the sultan. At one reception after his return from war, Osman Ferid was surprised when Abdülhamid mentioned the incident in London concerning the photograph of Queen Victoria saying,

"One hopes, as your sultan, to inspire such loyalty and devotion."

Taşkışla Barracks in Taksim was an imposing neo-classic compound capable of housing two brigades. It stood as a landmark on a hill overlooking the Bosphorus. Nearby non-Muslim cemeteries had been relocated to Şişli and in their place, the first Ottoman park and gardens were opened to the public.

The barracks north of the park received continual complaints with pleas for protection against the danger of walking the short distance between Taksim Park and fashionable Pera at night. Osman Ferid discussed the matter with the Şehremini, Mayor of Istanbul, and it was agreed to build a Taksim Square Police Station.

On his first day as commander, Osman Ferid walked confidently through the grand rectangular building into the large open air courtyard. He had attended many official ceremonies at the barracks in the past and its vastness and splendour had impressed him as an Ottoman military establishment.

But such admiration also aroused envy and unease with many officials in high places; they feared the popular commander might become over-ambitious and set his sights on political power.

One day, Osman Ferid received a letter from one of the sultan's private chamberlains, a Caucasian friend, suggesting he purchase a konak about to be sold at Serencebey Yokuşu, the hill leading to Yıldız Palace.

Istanbul was a city in the throes of a construction boom. In 1839, the Anglo-Turkish Commercial Treaty granted foreigners trading rights equivalent to local traders. Years later this was extended to most European countries, making the empire a very desirable lucrative trade centre that attracted thousands of foreigners clamouring for business and a piece of the financial pie. The influx encouraged a building boom in especially areas around the palace and the Bosphorus and the embassies and business areas in and around the Pera. Unfortunately it emphasised the vast difference between European and Ottoman living standards.

Sultan Abdülhamid engaged architects to transform Istanbul into a European-like city. Foreign banks, hotels and office buildings mushroomed. Neighbourhoods damaged by fire were rebuilt in brick and stone on western lines. A network of roads stretched from the old city of Istanbul to new districts beyond Şişli and along the Bosphorus. Trains, tramlines, boat stations and even a short underground railway improved transport and communications. The wealthy and ruling classes followed the sultan, living in districts near royal residences and along the European shore of the Bosphorus. When Sultan Abdülhamid took up residence at Yıldız Palace, the district of Beşiktaş, the nearby hill of Serencebey, became an especially prestigious address.

Osman Ferid bought the konak situated below the royal gardens of Yıldız Park, overlooking the Bosphorus. The large stone building stood in a splendid garden with a large pool and stables surrounded by high walls. Its European exterior gave way to an Ottoman interior, a selamlık, harem quarters, servants' quarters and an exquisite marble hamam. Ayshe was enchanted with her new home, a grand, elegant house near Yıldız Palace. She entertained lavishly and within a short time became a frequent guest at the palace harem.

Osman Ferid adamantly refused to be drawn into the royal circle, preferring the company of his fellow Caucasian officers, especially Colonel Mehmet Fazıl Dağestanlı, second in command of the Caucasian Guards Brigade. They had become inseparable, spending afternoons at the sultan's stables at Yıldız or Therapia, galloping through the forest or dining with friends at Taşkışla Barracks. They enjoyed crossing from one shore to the other in their gilded pasha caique, stopping at the yalı of an acquaintance or sipping coffee in a café at a fishing village listening to the boatman's advice: "One has to accommodate oneself to soft water." According to Rüşen Eşref Ünaydın, "That's why those who wanted to cross from Emirgan to Çubuklu on the Asian shore had to follow the shore up to Yeniköy and allow themselves to be carried by the current from there."

Osman Ferid took Mehmet Fazıl to Yeşilköy to visit Hamid Bey's farm. Hamid Bey was pleased to see Osman Ferid and to meet a member of the Dağestanlı family, whom he had known in the Caucasus. They walked across the fields to the new extensively enlarged stables. Hamid Bey introduced his string of magnificent horses by name, selecting two fast, agile Moroccan Barbs for his guests. They galloped over the downs until sunset, the cool breeze of the sea fresh on their faces. Hamid Bey insisted they stay for dinner. Osman Ferid was gratified to find Hamid Bey in such good spirits, genial and relaxed; he talked about mutual family friends, recalling an amusing incident with Mehmet Fazil's father during the war. His amusing description of Osman Ferid when he first came to stay–young, gauche, desperately wanting to please but determined to win the Djighitovka tournament made them roar with laughter.

"Hamid Bey has mellowed with age," Osman Ferid noted as they climbed into their carriage.

One evening, Mehmet Fazıl invited Osman Ferid to Koska Konak to meet his brother-in-law, Ghazi Mohammed Şamil, second son of Imam Shamil. Ghazi Mohammed Şamil, a general in the Ottoman army and Commander of the Caucasian Guards, had been granted the title of *Rumeli-Beyler-Bey*, the highest appointments of the empire by the sultan. He had commanded the Caucasian Brigade in the Crimean war and been highly decorated for his gallant services in the Caucasian theatre during the Russo-Turkish war. Mehmet Fazıl served as his second-in-command.

Remembering the day Osman Ferid visited his father more than ten years ago, Ghazi Mohammed Pasha recalled how pleased his father had been to meet Shapli Bereketuko Hasan's son.

"Your father was loyal to my father and the Circassian cause; he was brave enough to give his life in that last desperate stand. One of our many misfortunes were the betrayals—who would have imagined the taste of Russian gold would prove more powerful that their bullets."

Ahmed Vefik Pasha, an intellectual, outspoken diplomat and ambassador, was a frequent visitor. Although not Caucasian by birth, he had married a Circassian and had played a leading role in the relocation of refugees to villages around Balıkesir and Bursa. Often guest of honour at Circassian community soireés, Ahmed Vekif's sympathy for the plight of the Circassians began when he served as embassy secretary in London. There he became acquainted with the fervent English group of supporters who wrote articles in the London press and held meetings defending the Caucasian mountaineers. Osman Ferid looked forward to the Pasha's visits to Koska Konak, plying him with questions about his term in England. He invited Ahmet Vefik Pasha to meet his brothers. Ayshe prepared an elegant dinner and when the pasha mentioned his fondness for Caucasian dances Zissi and Ahmet jumped to perform their favourite dance, much to the Pasha's delight.

Field Marshal Fuad Pasha was a Circassian who had served Abdülhamid as aide-de-camp when the latter was an imperial prince. He had accompanied the sultan on the European tour; his loyalty and devotion to his master, now sultan, were unquestionable.

In the world of suspicion, distrust and insincerity that pervaded the palace, Fuad Pasha had become quite unscrupulous, full of intrigue and mischief. Many of his Circassian friends called him Deli Fuad (mad Fuad). Jealous of the sultan's affections, he would stop at nothing to gain his master's approval. For a long time Fuad Pasha had secretly envied Mehmet Fazıl's popularity at court and within the Caucasian society. An incident at the palace ignited darker feelings of resentment and malice towards his one time friend.

Georges Dorys wrote:

"The sultan has a distinct liking for animals, and at Yıldız Palace he keeps a mini zoo, including wild beasts and a wide variety of tame and trained ones. During his walks he feeds fruit and other delicacies with his own hands to gazelles, highland goats, mouflons and chamois. The sultan also greatly enjoys fights between rams just as Abdülaziz liked cock-fights. A special place in the park has been set aside for a dog's hospital and splendid kennels. The most handsome species of every dog are comfortably installed there in stark contrast to their wretched cousins in the streets of Istanbul."

Late one afternoon as Abdülhamid and his guests strolled

through Yıldız garden, one of his small dogs ran ahead barking and jumping in front of a lion's cage. The lion paced slowly back and forth, until to everyone's horror, the cage door suddenly opened and the lion sprang out of the cage to chase the dog. The keeper had fed the lion, but had failed to bolt the door of the cage properly. The horrified guests scattered behind shrubs and trees as the dog raced towards its owner with the lion in hot pursuit. Abdülhamid froze. Mehmet Fazıl, standing close by, ran in front of the sultan. Jumping on the lion's back, he locked his arms around its neck in a vicious grip. They fell rolling on the ground as Mehmet Fazıl pressed the lion's hind legs with his own.

"Get ropes," he shouted.

No one moved.

"Shoot the lion," ordered the sultan.

But no one took out his revolver for fear of hitting the major. Keeping an iron grip on the lion's neck from behind, Mehmet Fazıl pressed his body weight on the animal's back leg then dragged him towards the cage. With super human strength he pushed the lion into the cage and locked the iron door tightly.

Mehmet Fazıl fell to the ground, badly wounded with deep scratches on his face, arms and legs, too exhausted to rise as Abdülhamid walked towards him. The sultan thanked him warmly, congratulating him on his quick action and bravery. Ordering a doctor to attend to Mehmet Fazıl's wounds, he cast a withering look of disgust at his guests and retainers as he walked quickly back to the palace.

The lion incident became a joke at Koska Konak.

They teased Mehmet Fazıl.

"Where did you learn to fight lions?"

Mehmet Fazıl admitted the truth.

"It was only after I stepped in front of His Majesty that I realised I would have to wrestle with the beast. Then I remembered that royal lions are well-fed, which helped."

He recalled one occasion when he was eight years old in

Daghestan; he and his father went hunting in the mountains. He shot what he thought was a large cat, only to find on closer inspection that it was a mountain lion. His father gave him a fine rifle as a reward, a reward that still stood in his cabinet.

A deep bond of trust grew between these three extraordinary Caucasian men. Habibet Hanım, Gazi Pasha's devoted wife, adored her brother, Mehmet Fazıl, and welcomed Osman Ferid into the intimacy of the harem, insisting he dine with the family. According to Caucasian custom, Sofiate, their elder, served coffee while Nefiset, aged five, sat quietly next to her mother.

The Taşkışla Barracks became a military centre for the modernization of the Turkish Army where officers and soldiers loyal to the sultan gathered. Life at the Beşiktaş konak ran smoothly under Ayshe's watchful eye; while enjoying an active social life, she was a devoted wife and conscientious mother. She deferred to her husband's every wish, prepared Kazım to enter military school and, now that relations had improved, welcomed her in-laws and their families. Osman Ferid's desire for a peaceful life at home led him to take the line of least resistance in domestic matters by allowing Ayshe the freedom to enjoy her social activities and surround herself with friends.

Early in the morning, before setting off to the barracks, Osman Ferid gazed at the silent waters of the Bosphorus and prayed to Thae, god of the mountains, thanking him for his blessings. Remembering his mother, he whispered to the wind.

"I kept my promise, Nan. Rest in peace."

With the blessings of her brothers, Zissi finally succumbed to the charms of a handsome Circassian officer she had met at her best friend's wedding. The young brides squealed with joy when told their husbands were to be stationed in Adapazar, an Anatolian town with a thriving Circassian society. Ayshe insisted the couple stay at the Beşiktaş home whenever Zissi and her husband visited Istanbul.

One evening Mehmet, Ahmet and Ismail marched into the

house in obvious good humour. Mehmet saluted his brother, "Brigardier Shapli at your service," he laughed,

"Osman Ferid, I have come to ask for your blessing. Sultana Naile, Sultan Abdülmecid's daughter, has agreed to become my wife."

"At ease, Officer." Osman Ferid grinned as he embraced his brother. "I am very happy for you. I cannot imagine a better person, a finer officer to become a royal *damat* (son-in-law). May Allah bless your marriage."

Ayshe was thrilled, delighted at the prospect of a royal wedding in the family.

Besides a love for money, a well-stocked library of books and photographs of the city and an insatiable curiosity for knowledge, the sultan had no interest outside ruling his empire. He did not have a intimate circle of friends; he surrounded himself with financiers, bankers, bureaucrats, Germans, (who were said to run his spy ring), ambassadors and diplomats (depending on his interest and their politics), heads of the military forces and religious leaders.

His sudden interest and open admiration for the dashing young Circassian officer who had saved him from the lion aroused envy and irritation, especially when Mehmet Fazıl was treated as guest of honour at palace receptions. At a special presentation ceremony, Mehmet Fazıl was awarded the Order for Exceptional Merit and promoted to colonel. Osman Ferid sensed the envy and ill-will of Fuad Pasha and his cronies, as Abdülhamid honoured and praised his bravery. He mistrusted Fuad Pasha and thought the presentation would bring nothing but trouble.

After the ceremony the two friends walked down the hill to the Beşiktaş house, instead of taking a carriage. It was a clear, fresh evening and Mehmet Fazıl was in great spirits, talking about his promotion.

"All you have to do is fight with a royal lion," he joked caricaturing the seriousness of the ceremony.

They retired to the "den," a large basement room Osman Ferid had converted into a comfortable games room with ample space for fencing and boxing. The walls were hung with memorabilia, the coat of arms for his father, trophies and medieval armoury acquired from visiting Circassians, a gun cupboard filled with valuable weapons, guns swords, jewelled kinjals and magnificent swords and a library filled with titles concerning the Caucasus.

When Osman Ferid voiced his concern about the dangers of palace intrigues Mehmet Fazıl laughed.

"Osman Ferid, you worry too much. We are soldiers in the Ottoman army, not courtiers; a brush of royal approval cannot harm us surely. We use His Majesty's magnificent stables and now we'll be invited to hunting parties and evening soirée at that delightful theatre at Yıldız Kiosk. Don't worry about palace conspiracies, my friend. That has nothing to do with us."

Mehmet Fazıl grinned as he envisioned an attack with the sword in his hand, but his noble bearing, courtly manners and personal bravery attracted too much attention for the likes of Deli Fuad and his friends, twisted by fear and jealous at the thought of losing the sultan's trust and interest.

One evening, Ghazi Mohammed Pasha was surprised to hear Fuad Pasha announced at a late hour. The two were not friends and had little in common. Even though he was well established and influential at the palace, Fuad Pasha was not popular within the Caucasian community for he had ignored all appeals to support their cause.

Ghazi Mohammed Pasha greeted his guest cordially, as Fuad Pasha apologized and immediately explained the reason for his late visit. In a low, conspiratorial voice he said he had come on a secret and dangerous mission. A group of influential officers were planning to overthrow the sultan and establish a constitutional government. He said he had been instructed to approach Ghazi Mohammed Pasha and the Caucasian Brigade to join them in the coup.

Ghazi Mohammed Pasha was appalled, repelled at the audacity of a man who dared present such a proposal to him. He looked at Fuad Pasha with revulsion. In a cold, authoritative voice, he reproached the field marshal for having the insolence to suggest such an ignominious plan. He avowed the Caucasian Brigade's loyalty and alliance to the Caliph of Islam and the Ottoman Empire and ordered him to leave the house.

Fuad Pasha had not expected such an outburst of fury; he had miscalculated the pasha's ethical code of honour. He sat in the hall at the palace full of apprehension and misgivings, not knowing how to resolve the situation, when he noticed two officials he knew reported daily events and gossip to the sultan. He joined them for dinner and during the evening, knowing any breath of suspicion sent the sultan into a state of agitation, he casually insinuated that Mehmet Fazıl had more than once spoken of the dedication and loyalty the Caucasian Brigade held towards their commander and that should Ghazi Mohammed Şamil be appointed Caliph, peace and prosperity would reign throughout the Empire.

As Fuad Pasha had foreseen, his words were reported to Abdülhamid, whose instinctive fearful and suspicious character did not allow him to consider the absurdity of the scenario presented him. The sultan's obsession with assassination and being overthrown, no matter how unfounded, was enough to ignite his suspicion, which in turn forced him to think and act in a certain way for his self preservation at any cost. That Ghazi Mohammed and Mehmet Fazıl were loyal and devoted officers made no impression on him when he summoned them to the palace for a private interview. After questioning them over and over and finding no validity for the aspersions, he denounced them for their failure to report Fuad Pasa's visit.

Ghazi Mohammed Pasha responded to the sultan respectfully but firmly:

197

"Your Majesty, I am a soldier not a spy. I was insulted and angered but later thought he might have been ordered to test my loyalty."

The sultan looked surprised.

"Perhaps so, perhaps so, but you should have informed me."

He seemed deeply disturbed and anxious.

"I am surrounded by enemies who wish me harm".

Ghazi Mohammed and Mehmet Fazıl glanced at each other. The pasha replied gently.

"Your Majesty, we are here as your guests. We have sworn allegiance to you as Sultan and Caliph of the Ottoman Empire. We serve you with loyalty and devotion, values my father, Imam Shamil, demanded from all Caucasians warriors. Palace intrigues and corruption are alien to us; our word is our honour."

Although the words soothed the sultan's vanity and no proof of the slightest trace of disloyalty was found, his anxiety and gnawing doubts continued to cause him sleepless nights.

After weeks of indecision he decided the only possible solution to regain his peace of mind was to disband the Caucasian Brigade and exile its commanders. Ghazi Mohammed was granted the rank and title of Field Marshal, without command, and exiled to Medina in Arabia. Mehmet Fazıl was promoted Brigadier-General with orders to serve as commander of the Baghdad garrison in Iraq. They were prohibited from ever meeting in Arabia. Meanwhile, Fuad Pasha smooth-talked Abdülhamid into believing he had acted on behalf of the sultan to check the loyalties of those powerful commanders.

Hadduc Fazıl Dağistanlı, Dağistanlı Muhammed (Mehmet) Fazıl's daughter, in her book *Bir Kahramanın Hayatı* (The Life of a Warrior) relates many charming stories about her father and his fondness for animals.

"Every morning when he was in exile in Baghdad he would ride to his farm where he kept most domestic animals, trained thorough-bred Arab and English horses, lions and camels, and even hunting birds."

Hadduc Dağistanlı wrote that her father had been given 5,000 pieces of gold by the sultan before his exile, which he distributed to the civil servants working at the palace. In 1882, he and Ghazi Mohammed Pasha were taken under guard escort to board a ship into exile.

Osman Ferid was left lonely and despondent as his two friends departed on their separate journeys. Once more he was to suffer the separation from those he loved; ironically he thought his love and devotion never seemed strong enough to overcome the forces of war, death, politics or intrigues.

Secret police began collecting evidence against those who had been regular visitors to the Koska Konak. Files of incriminating evidence, unbelievable accusations, the simplest remark or action took on twisted treasonous implications. Osman Ferid realised he was under suspicion, but ignored his brother's warnings to protect himself.

He had made friends and enemies during his command at Taşkışla Barracks. His enemies worked secretly for his downfall, while his friends gathered to protect him. Mehmet begged him to allow his wife, Naile Sultana, to speak with Abdülhamid, but Osman Ferid refused. He was past caring; that such honourable officers as Ghazi Mohammed and Mehmet Fazıl had been treated with such disrespect was intolerable.

Abdülhamid found no justification for the accusations against Osman Ferid, but spiteful insinuations whispered in his ears were never forgotten.

"Your Majesty," whispered the snake-like spy, "Osman Ferid Pasha is commander of Taşkışla barracks, the most powerful, well trained army in the country. Whoever controls the barracks controls the fate of Ottoman military power. It is well known that the pasha sympathizes with his exiled friends. His position could prove a threat to Your Majesty and the country."

On May 7, 1887, Osman Ferid was promoted to major-general, named an honorary aide-de-camp to Sultan Abdülhamid, and assigned to command the Medina Garrison in Arabia. The decree gave him authority over the North of Najd, including the autonomous Shammer tribes of Central Arabia. It also conveniently removed him from the Taşkışla Barracks and Istanbul.

Taşkışla Barracks prepared a rousing military ceremonial parade. The military band played; soldiers and officers marched and saluted their commander with a three cheer farewell to show their respect and appreciation. Osman Ferid knew he would never again command such an elite force. In his speech he thanked them for their participation: "It has been an honour to serve for so many years as commander to the finest force in the land." He encouraged them to continue with plans for modernization, to remain loyal to the sultan and the empire. The wave of affection was almost palpable as Osman Ferid saluted the company for the last time.

Ayshe was aware of her husband's predicament, but chose to remain silent. She prayed his brothers and friends might persuade him to resolve this appalling situation, the threat of exile to Arabia, by appealing to the good will of the sultan; if not, she thought he should resign from the military service.

She had spoken to Mehmet's wife, Naile Sultan, who assured her she would gladly speak to the sultan on his behalf, but Osman Ferid had forbidden Mehmet to interfere under any circumstances. That evening Osman Ferid dined with his brothers in the garden.

Once again they begged him to allow them to speak on his behalf, but Osman Ferid was adamant. After they departed, he sent a servant to ask his wife to join him for coffee. He stood up as she walked into the garden.

"Ayshe, come sit here."

He offered her his chair, drawing one closer for himself. He looked at his wife. The years had treated her kindly; she had changed very little during their twenty years of marriage. She was still a beautiful woman, more mature and calmer. He needed her loving support and understanding now more than any time in his life. He took her hands in his, caressed them as he spoke of his assignment to Arabia.

She pulled her hands free, her eyes glistened with tears; she looked like a captured gazelle as she drew away from him.

"Ayshe," he said softly.

She loved her husband, but the thought of leaving Istanbul, her father and friends for a life in the desert, in hot, primitive conditions, perhaps for years, was beyond her.

When he called her name again she silenced him.

"Osman Ferid, many influential people wish to help you— my father, your family, friends, but you refuse their offers. You prevent Naile Sultan from approaching her brother, Abdülhamid. If only you were not so proud and stubborn we could resolve this intolerable situation. Hand in your resignation. Please, Osman Ferid, consider my position, consider your son."

Osman Ferid looked at her for a long time, then sighed.

"No Ayshe, there is no way out, I shall go to Medina."

He turned and walked into the house.

Long before dawn Osman Ferid walked through the garden; the sun was a red ball of fire filtering through the heavy mist hanging over the Bosphorus, the eerie, black outlines of motionless boats on its dark waters were framed by the green, wooded hills. Seagulls swooped from one roof top to another in silent flight. It was a moment of utter beauty and tranquillity, before the beginning of another day with its hopes, expectations, disappointments and heartbreaks. Osman Ferid looked around for the last time hoping to preserve and cherish this moment before walking to his waiting carriage.

He never returned to the Beşiktaş home and never saw Ayshe again.

CHAPTER 11

Medina- Marriage to Nefiset

The following day Osman Ferid set off for Adapazar to visit his sister. Zissi's family resided in a large wooden house set back in a vast garden of wild flowers, fruit trees and animals. It was a noisy, happy home full with children or guests from Istanbul. Zissi, as high-spirited as ever, chattered away as she took his arm to walk around the neighbourhood or sit under a cypress tree taking tea. She was fiercely loyal. Glancing at Osman Ferid, she dared criticise her sister-in-law's behaviour but Osman Ferid placed his finger to his lips and shook his head, silencing her childish outburst.

They shared a deeply loving relationship; she promised to keep in touch with Ayshe and Kazım and send him news. Zissi gave a splendid farewell reception in his honour; friends and officers from her husband's regiment were impressed to meet the handsome, but reserved pasha.

On his return to Istanbul, Osman Ferid was met by Mehmet's aide-de-camp with a letter from his sister-in-law, Princess Naile. It was an invitation to stay at the residence, a magnificent yalı at Ortaköy, until his departure.

Princess Naile was frail and shy with the exquisite manners of the royal court. She adored her dashingly handsome husband and it had saddened her to see him so despondent, knowing he was unable to prevent his brother's departure to Medina. One evening she suggested that Osman Ferid, Ahmet and Ismail stay with them until the time of his departure. Mehmed was so grateful he lifted her in his arms and danced her around the room.

During the day the brothers would ride out to Therapia to lunch with friends or take a royal caique along the Bosphorus; sometimes they simply lounged in the selamlık or walked in the garden, thankful for the peace and intimacy of those precious days together. The princess joined them for dinner, but retired to her quarters when friends from the Caucasian community or the army paid a call. She sympathized with their concern for their brother; Arabia was a dangerous assignment. They might never see him again.

One evening after supper Princess Naile remained beside her husband.

'Osman Ferid, the princess has something she wishes to say."

She smiled as she turned to face her brother-in-law.

"I admire my husband's loyalty and close ties to his family. After so many years of being kept apart, my relations with my brother, Sultan Abdülhamid are, at last, amiable and courteous; he invites us to receptions at the palace and has been gracious enough to visit us. When I was a child I rarely saw him. We had different mothers and were not allowed to play together. I believe he is quite fond of me. Dear Osman Ferid, my husband and I have discussed the reasons behind the sultan's decision to exile you to Medina; they are quite trivial. With your permission, it would be a pleasure for me to address the sultan on your behalf. I will arrange an audience. I am sure he will respond to my request favourably with a pardon."

Osman Ferid rose, kissed the princess's hand lovingly and then placed his hands on Mehmet's shoulders.

"My dearest Princess, I am deeply touched and appreciate your concern more than I can say, but I must refuse your gracious offer most emphatically and ask you to promise never, never to request anything from the sultan on my behalf. I have accepted my post and will perform my duties to the best of my ability. I will not allow you to undermine your relationship with the sultan or arouse his displeasure. Ayshe and Kazım, Ahmet, Ismail, Zissi and her family need your royal support and protection, dear Princess. All I ask is that you and Mehmet protect my family."

Mehmet embraced his brother.

"Your family will be in save hands. Have no fear. Your son is our son."

On May 15, 1887, Osman Ferid embarked on a French steamer for the first leg of his journey to Beirut. There were few passengers aboard: a large Armenian family, two or three Greek merchants and some government officials. Part of the ship had been appropriated for soldiers. The first stop was Smyrna (Izmir), a prosperous, harbour town in the Aegean with a large Greek population. White stone houses with wooden shuttered windows lined the promenade; the harbour was crowded with boats from every part of the world, large and small, flying colourful flags, creaking as they bobbed in the calm, blue sea.

More passengers embarked as the ship sailed on through the Mediterranean to Alexandretta (Iskenderun). The weather was warm. At night a soft breeze blew over the blue sky and sea. As the ship moored at Alexandretta, barefooted workers clambered up to lower a wide platform onto the pier to allow carriages, horses and goods to disembark.

Osman Ferid took a stroll along the pier while the ship was being refuelled. The harbour was a hub of noise, smells and dirt. Porters bent under huge loads moved slowly with animal-like rhythm; veiled women in long black gowns scurried through narrow streets. Levantine merchants stood in front of overfilled warehouses, bartering over prices. It was a lively port for commerce with Arabs from all over Arabia buying, selling or haggling in loud voices.

As the ship steamed on, keeping close to the sandy bays and low cliffs of the Syrian coast, the days became unpleasantly hot. Passengers remained in their cabins waiting for the cool evening breeze before venturing on deck. Osman Ferid found the monotonous days soothing; he spent time reading reports and working on a rough strategy plan for the garrison, but most of the time he lay on his berth reflecting on the traumatic circumstances of the last few months, experiences which would leave an indelible mark on him for the remainder of his life.

He had been disappointed, hurt, but not overly surprised at Ayshe's refusal to accompany him. He had not been a good husband. They had little in common from the very beginning of their marriage; that it had lasted twenty years was due to his wife's efforts and patience. His military career had been the focus of his life, his tenure at Taşkışla Barracks its glorious peak. The violence and horror of Circassian Hasan's actions and public hanging had shocked him so deeply; he had been unable to function for a long time. His senses had closed into a shell of emotional and physical numbness, unbalanced by guilt and regret.

He would miss his friends dearly, especially Mehmed Fazıl and his brothers, favourite haunts and evenings spent with the Caucasian community. He reminisced on his past, its journey from the snowy, cold, Caucasian mountains to this steamboat on its journey to Medina and the desert. Perhaps he should have taken Zissi's suggestion of retirement more seriously. He could have bought a horse farm, enjoyed breeding a string of thoroughbreds, rather than spend an indefinite number of years in a dry Arabian desert. He gave a rueful grin; sea voyages seem to trigger philosophic moods.

He dined at the captain's table where the conversation inevitably turned to politics, religion or the state of the Empire, becoming quite heated at times and leaving the captain with no choice but to interfere rather strongly. One hot, humid morning, the steamer moored at St George's bay on the northern side of the Lebanese ranges. The city spread over the wooded hillsides to the east and west, its fertile plains, sandy beaches and rocky headlands dominated by Mount Lebanon.

Osman Ferid fought his way through the noisy crowd to a waiting carriage which would take him to the governor's official residence where he was to present his credentials before joining the camel train to Damascus, which would take another four days.

It followed the well-travelled route used by military and civilian merchants. Oases, guest houses and inns provided food, water and rest at regular intervals on the journey.

In his evocative book, *Mirror to Damascus*, Colin Thubron describes Damascus in particular;

"Damascus, always fiercely political—I rarely met a Damascene who was not prepared to take over the reins of government instantly—remains a scorpion's nest of nationalism."

The same applied throughout the Arab territories for decades before and during the last years of Ottoman sovereignty.

The governor of Damascus invited Osman Ferid to stay at his sumptuous residence. At one reception, he was introduced to Abdul Mejuel, Bedouin sheikh of a tribe of nearly three hundred Bedouins. The sheikh was a man of great intelligence and capacity, extremely forthright when discussions turned to the problems caused by differing Bedouin tribes in Arabia. Abdul Mejuel emphasized the importance Bedouins gave to the "first meeting," advising him on how he should conduct himself.

"You will be judged by the first impression you make on a Bedouin tribe. You must win their respect. Approach with confidence and trust no matter what the situation or their initial reaction may be; a Bedouin knows instinctively if you are apprehensive or fearful and will not respect you if you are."

Osman Ferid never forgot the good sheikh's wise words; his advice helped him achieve respectful relationships with most of the tribes throughout his career in Arabia. He learned that years earlier Sheikh Abdul Mejuel had married a beautiful English lady, Jane Digby, wife of Lord Ellenborough until her divorce. Although much older than the sheikh, they had had a close and lasting relationship. She lived in Damascus and was said to have influenced the sheikh and won the devotion of his Bedouin tribe until her death in 1881.

Osman Ferid and his caravan began the next step of the journey at sunrise, passing through the Great Rift Valley along Jabal'Ajlun with its rugged landscape, salt marshes and valleys choked with sand dunes. They travelled by day under the blistering sun, their heads wrapped in white, cotton cloth pulled over the face to protect the nose and mouth from the sun and sand, stopping at nightfall at an oasis to rest and replenish supplies.

"The dogs bark but the caravan moves on."

The camel is king of the desert and dictates the movement of the camel trains, which can be as long as six miles. They are capable of staying two weeks without water, carrying 500 pounds, and feeding on the dry, prickly leaves of oasis trees. Supper often walked with the train in the form of goats, sheep and cows. At sunset when the camel train came to a halt at an oasis or camp, the camel keepers would slaughter a lamb or sheep, stew it over an open fire, and bake flat bread with a hard thick crust while everyone gathered around to eat and warm themselves from the bitter, desert cold. Osman Ferid realized that survival in the desert depended on knowledge and respect for the environment, as it did in the Caucasus. It took six days to reach Amman.

Amman was a small Ottoman district under the command of an army major who welcomed Osman Ferid. Refreshed after a night in a comfortable bed, he set off to the port of Al-Aquabah on the Red Sea with a new military escort, giving a sigh of relief when he saw the narrow strip of water. The commander of Aquabad had placed a gun boat at his disposal to cross the Red Sea to Yanbu Bahr, the last port of call for Medina.

Yanbu, protected by an Ottoman garrison, was a small but significant port of entry for overland journeys to Medina and the interior of Hejaz. Osman Ferid received a military welcome from the commander of the garrison, a colonel from Istanbul. On his first evening he dined with the officers, Turkish officials, and wealthy merchants. They painted a dismal picture of life in Medina, of the desert, the problems with Bedouin tribes and taxes.

"Come, Sirs," Osman Ferid answered, "this holy place is blessed, surely that must give one satisfaction."

The evening before they were to leave on the final lap of their journey, Osman Ferid dined with the colonel at his quarters. Over coffee, the colonel said,

"Pasha, I must warn you of the dangers you may encounter crossing the desert. The Shammar and Wahhabi tribes who dwell in and around Al Hejaz are hostile to any authority other than their own sheikhs. They resent subjugation by the Ottoman sultan and are known to attack whenever the occasion arises. There are Bedouins who roam the desert, ravaging caravans and camel trains. News of your arrival has spread like a sand storm. I fear they might attack your train to demonstrate their hostility and defiance against Ottoman rule. As a precaution I suggest a military force accompany your caravan across the desert to Medina. Once you are settled and in command, you will be in a stronger position to control the insurgency and their trouble-making sheikhs."

Until the early hours of morning they discussed the best policy to address a consensus between the tribal chiefs, Bedouins and Ottoman soldiers based in Arabia.

The camel train with its military escort left Yanbu for its final destination, Medina.

The tribal structure of Arab society, which had remained unchanged throughout its history, had influenced its horizons

and limited its loyalties. Rule by a central authority from a remote capital was contrary to the Arab way of life and tolerated only under compulsion. Stubborn resistance to the Ottomans had existed since the reign of Suleyman I, the Magnificent. The Wahhabi Empire had spread with the help of a religious movement based on puritanical reforms. Established in 1703, the religion had gradually disappeared from view, but "its scattered embers of puritan fire smouldered on in the desert spaces in defiance of new rulers."

Northern Arabia was controlled by Jabal Shammar, fief of the Rashidis, while Al Hasa, Hejaz and Yemen remained under Turkish rule until the revival of the Wahhabi movement under Ibn Sa'ud after 1912.

The camel train moved with slow monotonous rhythm. Osman Ferid, sweating in the stifling mid-day heat rebounding from the soft sand, welcomed the cold nights spent huddled around a fire. Soldiers, suffering in silence in their uniforms, were told to suck on small stones like desert nomads to keep the saliva flowing; water rations were given in the morning and evening. Osman Ferid, like other travellers on their first journey through the desert, was fascinated by its beauty, its unbelievable silence and extreme climate, its arid landscape forming differing shapes and horizons and the sudden appearance of cactus and shrubs and acacia trees. At night the sunset turned tall, palm trees into shadowy minarets under a sky filled with billions of stars, brighter than the sun.

On the third day Bedouins were sighted in the distance riding parallel to the camel train. Throughout the day their numbers increased as they rode at a safe distance from the military escort. As dusk drew, they began to close in, silent and menacing, their black robes flying, as their camels moved swiftly and surely over the sands. The camel train halted for the night at an oasis; the camel tenders went about their business, unloading camels, setting up tents, lighting fires to prepare the evening meal.

The Bedouins, keeping a safe distance, began circling the camp, breaking the stillness of the night with wild howls and screams. Osman Ferid stood outside his tent looking at the volatile hosts raising clouds of sand as they galloped around.

"Is there anyone here who understands what they are shouting?" he asked an orderly." Yes, Pasha, there is a sergeant-major, a Bedouin loyal to the sultan."

"Bring him to me."

Osman Ferid invited the soldier inside his tent.

"Sit down," he said, pointing to a chair.

"Tell me, what this is all about?"

The soldier looked uncomfortable.

"Pasha they are wild, primitive nomads incited by their chiefs against the rule of the foreigner. They have been paid to intimidate and scare you, upset your arrival to Medina. They say you will not find the comforts of Istanbul here because they, like the sands of the desert, swallow their enemy without leaving a trace. Tomorrow they will return for a handsome baksheesh (bribe) in gold. Then they will leave you in peace."

With the first rays of light, the lieutenant standing guard outside Osman Ferid's tent, hearing movements from within, called out to his commander in a loud voice.

"Pasha, the Bedouins are moving towards the caravan. We are ready to make a stand, Sir"

Osman Ferid appeared, dressed in the military uniform of a major-general of the Imperial Ottoman Army with a display of medals and decorations on his chest. His belt held a sword and revolver and on his head he wore a red fez. The lieutenant looked at him in amazement.

"I do not want any unnecessary bloodshed. I shall approach alone to speak to them. They might allow us to continue in peace."

The young man couldn't believe his ears; the pasha has gone mad, he thought.

"But Pasha, you do not know how dangerous these nomad are. They are thieves who will kill for your medals, sword, even your boots. They do not care who you are. Sir, it is my duty to protect you, I beg you, Sir."

Osman Ferid gave the lieutenant a withering look as he dismissed him.

"You are relieved of your duty, Sir. Bring me a white stallion."

Once mounted, he called the young man and spoke to him in a kinder tone.

"I do not wish to enter Medina with blood on my hands or relieved of my gold by Bedouin nomads. Should anything happen to me, ride to Medina and report to the governor."

The military escort presented arms as Osman Ferid rode out of camp towards the Bedouins waiting behind the sand dunes, their black hooded jellabas and headdresses tied tightly with long scarves against the morning cold. When they saw a figure approach on horseback, they began to shriek and scream in expectation, waiting to measure the strength of the troops. As the lone rider drew closer, their screams petered out in disbelief; there was but one rider. Out of sight, the military escort watched with rifles at the ready in attack formation.

Osman Ferid, erect and imposing, rode slowly towards the Bedouins, his body as taut as a spring, ready to react at the slightest movement. He narrowed his eyes searching for the chieftain wearing a white jellaba astride the finest stallion. Osman Ferid rode straight up to him aware that the Bedouins were closing ranks around him. He raised his left hand which held the royal edict, the Imperial *Firman*.

"Allah Akbar, as Salem-in Aleikum."

He bowed his head to the chieftain speaking with a slow, authoritative voice.

"I carry the Imperial Firman of our all powerful and illustrious Caliph, descendant of the beloved Prophet –may His soul be forever blessed– Sultan Abdülhamid Khan II. "His Imperial Majesty has sent me to bring order, peace and justice to you, our

Majesty has sent me to bring order, peace and justice to you, our brothers in Islam. As long as I carry this Firman no one can touch or harm me. Disobedience is punishable by death by the sword."

As he spoke he raised his sword dramatically into the air. The Bedouins watched Osman Ferid's commanding performance with unease. Unsure of his words or intention, they hesitated and began to mumble. Some began to move backwards, while others stood defiantly.

Osman Ferid lowered his sword to address the chieftain.

"Translate what I said to your people."

The chieftain scowled, repeating Osman Ferid's words with bad grace.

There was a long, uncomfortable silence. Suddenly a Bedouin, shouting in Arabic, lifted his musket and aimed. Osman Ferid felt the hot air as the ball whizzed passed, ripping the epaulette on his left shoulder. He dug his heels into the belly of the stallion. Charging with a mighty swipe from the side of his sword, he threw his attacker onto the sand pinning him down with the point of his sword pressed on his heart. The boy squirmed, crying for mercy.

No one moved except the chieftain, who his eyes wide with fear, cried,

"Oğlum, Oğlum (my son, my son)."

"You were warned." Osman Ferid replied sternly, "Disobedience is death by the sword. I am sent by the Caliph to bring peace, order and justice, not war. If you give me your word to obey, I will spare this boy's life in the name of the merciful and powerful Sultan of the Ottoman Empire."

The chieftain shouted,

"Praise be the Caliph. Praise to the Sultan."

With a dramatic gesture Osman Ferid lifted the sword, swinging it in its sheath. The chieftain fell on his knees, mumbling his gratitude. His followers threw themselves onto the sands, shouting,

Praise be to Allah
Praise be the Prophet
Praise be the Caliph Sultan.

Osman Ferid pulled out a leather pouch and emptied the gold coins in front of the chief. He bowed his head in salute before turning his stallion and riding towards the military escort. The troops presented arms and the camel train cheered as he approached with three loud shouts.

"Osman Ferid Pasha cok yaşa - Long live Osman Ferid Pasha."

They moved on past Badr Hunayn, famed for its "singing sands," Ain-i Hamra and Bir-i Abbas until on the seventh day, the camel tenders pointed to the gates of Medina on the horizon. Osman Ferid gave a deep sigh of relief and thanked God. The journey from Istanbul, by sea and overland, had taken forty hot, dusty, sandy, uncomfortable days.

He realized he had much to learn on how to survive in the parching stifling heat of the desert as he had learned to survive the blistering cold blizzards and snows of the mountains. He called for a stop at Ayn al Zarya, the blue spring, ordering troops to bathe, animals to be brushed and fed and uniforms and appearances smartened before they entered the city.

The camel train headed by the major general immaculately dressed in full parade uniform entered Medina through the Bab-i Ambariah Gate. The streets were deserted except for a few old men in long hooded jellabas sitting on stools at open-air coffee houses or ambling along the dusty streets staring at the camel caravan as it passed. Some waved, some shouted, "Hoş geldiniz, hoş geldiniz. Welcome, welcome." Barefoot boys ran beside the camel train, hands outstretched, shouting, begging and pleading for baksheesh or sweets. As he rode to the residence of the governor of Medina, Osman Ferid felt the heat, sand and dust intensified by the sacred air of mystic spirituality and peace which permeated this hallowed ground.

The governor greeted him warmly as he presented his credentials, congratulating him on his brave stance against the Bedouin tribe.

"Word travels fast in the desert. I shall write an official report to the sultan and despatch it to Amman so that it can be telegraphed via Damascus to Istanbul.

"The telegraph has made communication so much easier and faster; the sultan will be pleased by your courageous act in his name."

The Governor accompanied him to the Medina Barracks where he was greeted by a military guard of honour. Osman Ferid inspected two infantry battalions, a Turkish unit of horse-drawn artillery and a cavalry of 2,500 Arab irregulars under the command of a Rashidi sheikh. A military landing ground with a regular infantry company was stationed south of the town at Sultanah.

Eager to retire to his quarters after such a long and traumatic journey, Osman Ferid was surprised to discover a letter from Ghazi Mohammed on his desk.

"My Dear Friend, Welcome to Medina. I prayed for your safe journey and wish to congratulate you on your courageous stand against the Bedouin tribe. I look forward to welcoming you as an honoured guest at our humble home. May Allah be with you."

The letter was signed with the seal of Ghazi Mohammed Şamil. Osman Ferid had been so wrapped up in his own thoughts he had completely forgotten his dear friend, Ghazi Mohammed Pasha and his family resided in Medina.

He replied with a quick note.

"My Esteemed and Dear Pasha, it will be an honour and pleasure to visit your home."

The letter, accompanied by a gift, a fine set of Circassian silver desert spoons, was delivered by his aide to the pasha's residence immediately.

Aware of the political power Arabia commanded as a religious and spiritual centre in the Middle East, imperialist interests began to show more than a healthy interest in the area. Even so, Osman Ferid found the garrison ill-kept and undisciplined. The size or place of a garrison was of no consequence to him, small or large, a forgotten border outpost or desert, if a garrison flew the Ottoman flag, it represented the military might of the Ottoman Empire demanding the same care and military administration given to Taşkışla barracks.

Immediately Osman Ferid put into action the strategy he had used in every new post to overcome former administrative defects. As a boy soldier in the Caucasus he had been taught that the safety and wellbeing of every soldier was the first priority in military training. Janbolat words echoed in his brain, "A leader is as good or as bad as the soldiers under his command." Military reform was expensive and unavailable in this desert outpost but Osman Ferid was practical; he knew how to utilize existing resources and materials for the better.

He chaired meeting after meeting with senior officers discussing ways to implement change. He improved and widened the recruiting grounds, organized timetables for regular inspections and early morning rollcalls, supervised exercise and organised mock patrols.

Kitchens, mess and sleeping quarters, stables and artillery depots were cleaned and whitewashed with orders to be maintained in prime condition. Gardeners were employed to clear the undergrowth, attend the parade grounds and plant local fruit-bearing trees and vegetables. The clinic and medical services were updated and tailors mandated to repair uniforms. Osman Ferid was the first on parade in the morning and the last to blow out his lamp in the evening. His insistence on cleanliness and hygiene for men and animals soon began to take shape. The officers responded, appreciating the personal sense of value and comfort it afforded them. He kept a log book of daily activities and programmes with the names of officers, soldiers or civilians of merit who lived or worked at the garrison. With time he set up salary systems and a rotation system for off-duty leave. Once a week with a platoon, he visited chieftains and Bedouin camps. Within the garrison, he was known as a hard task master setting standards by example, but the Arab community felt intimidated and looked upon the new commander with caution. They saw him as an obstacle rather than a friend.

Many evenings, before he retired, he would stop at the Shamil residence where he was warmly received, a long lost dear friend and fellow Caucasian, as Habibet Hanım put it,

"Dear Osman Ferid you are a most welcomed addition to our small family."

He was sad to hear that Sofiate, the Pasha's elder daughter had died so young.

Ghazi Mohammed Pasha held the rank of Field Marshal without portfolio. He had been brought up under the stern traditions of Islam. At the age of six, during his father's escape from Akhulgo under Russian fire, he had been wounded in the leg. Following his elder brother's capture by the Russians in 1855, Shamil proclaimed him heir and successor. He was respected as one of the ablest and most courageous commanders. A fine horseman and marksman, he had served his father with unquestioning devotion accompanying him into exile to Russia. After Shamil's death, he was proclaimed 4th Imam of Daghestan in 1873. He and his family returned to Istanbul; in 1877 he led a Daghestani regiment against the Russians in the Russo-Turkish war.

He lived in a large residence surrounded by an oasis of lush, green gardens, shady trees and lakes. He seemed resigned to his exile and confided to Osman Ferid.

"'All I ask from Allah is to end my days here in peace with my family."

He owned a large farm on the outskirts of the city where he bred magnificent Arab and English horses, camels, and domestic animals, planted acres of fruit trees and seasonal vegetables.

"It reminds me of the aoul at Vedeno," he told Osman Ferid on their first visit.

"The farm produces more than enough for our needs. We gather fruit, vegetables, eggs, meat, and bake bread and distribute the rest among my people and the school at the mosque.

"Nefiset comes here every day to ride her favourite horse and supervise the farm. She is a very keen gardener and is learning to bake bread."

There was little or no social life in the holy city, yet Ghazi Mohammed's fame as Shamil's son, his quiet assurance, humility and deep knowledge of Islam attracted a following of like-minded people who came to pay their respects. Arabs, Circassian officers, Imams, Bedouin chieftains and important visitors from every corner of the Muslim world were welcomed at the residence, spending evenings discussing politics, the finer points of religion, the Quran, world events and their affect on Islam, these meetings were a tribute to his powers of diplomacy in itself.

Ghazi Mohammed wrote poetry in fine Arabic calligraphy.

"Cease five before five

Your youth before your old age

Your health before your illness

Your richness before your poverty

Your leisure before your occupation and your life before your death.."

When he failed to appear for dinner, Osman Ferid received a gentle scolding from Habibet Hanım.

"Habibet, Habibet Hanım," said the Pasha defending his friend.

"Osman Ferid does have a garrison to run."

Habibet was devoted to her husband, attending to his needs and filling his days with quiet pleasures and comfort; she knew he enjoyed Osman Ferid's company and he reminded her of her beloved brother, Mehmet Fazıl, exiled commander of the Baghdad garrison, so she delighted in his visits.

After dinner their daughter, Emine Nefiset, served tea from a magnificent silver Russian samovar while her mother sang French, Russian and Caucasian songs to entertain them. Habibet Hanım ran her household as her ancestors had in the Caucasus, a comfortable haven of well being and continuity, sufficient unto themselves. Home was their world.

Emine Nefiset had grown into a charming, young girl. She reminded Osman Ferid of his mother, slim, fine featured with long dark hair under her white veil. She was reserved but poised for her age; her eyes and face would suddenly crinkle as she giggled then just as suddenly revert back to its usual calm expression. She was extremely observant, which might account for her gift as an impersonator. She claimed it was the result of sitting at her father's side listening and watching his guests when he entertained at home.

Osman Ferid's hard work and consistent efforts towards attainable goals within the barracks began to produce results. His aim was to establish a basic system which might improve the Ottoman military position in Medina, then throughout his domain. Duties completed, the officers and soldiers enjoyed organised sports and competitions amongst themselves, showing refreshing enthusiasm and a changed attitude. The troops began to enjoy patrolling the provinces in clean uniforms on healthy, well-kept horses or camels. Osman Ferid believed promotion a positive incentive. His monthly report to Yıldız Palace frequently included the names and progress of outstanding officers.

The first year passed quickly. He proved he had the capability to lead those under his command and win the respect of the leading elite in a foreign country His days were busy and challenging but the nights, in his bare quarters at the barracks, were lonely.

When he returned from Ghazi Mohammed's residence he began to think more and more of Nefiset, as they called her. She was so well-mannered, quiet but spirited; she filled his thoughts on lonely nights. Feeling uncomfortably embarrassed and quite distracted, he decided not visit the residence for a while; he managed to invent plausible excuses whenever Habibet Hanım sent a servant to enquire after his health.

A month passed; one day he received an official invitation from Ghazi Mohammed Pasha to attend a reception for the governor of Medina. Arab officials in long white robes, Turkish officers in uniforms, imams and visiting bureaucrats and merchants from Turkey crowded the garden. Ghazi Mohammed Pasha welcomed him warmly.

"We missed you Osman Ferid, I hope you are well?"

After supper, a servant whispered into his ear; Habibet Hanım wished to speak to him in the harem. Osman Ferid went to her quarters. She smiled as he kissed her hand.

"Osman Ferid, come, sit next to me. How are you? I hope your health is well. We have missed you at our little gatherings. I hope we have not offended or done anything to displease you?"

That she should think they had offended him unnerved Osman Ferid. He could not lie or find an excuse; he decided to confide in her. Awkwardly he admitted the reason for his absence was his deepening feelings for Nefiset. Habibet Hanım smiled, taking his hands in hers she gently kissed his cheek.

"Osman Ferid why do you suffer so? We are delighted. Nefiset adores you."

"Nefiset and I have often spoken of ways to help you overcome your reserve and shyness." she said laughingly as she told a servant to call the pasha.

Ghazi Mohammed Pasha's respect for his wife caused him to excuse himself from his guests immediately. Habibet Hanım met him at the door with the news. He walked towards Osman Ferid, his arms outstretched.

"My dear friend, I am delighted you wish to ask for my daughter's hand in marriage. Nefiset is my beloved daughter; you will be my son. I bless you both. You have made us very

happy. Come let us share this glorious news with my distinguished guests."

Osman Ferid was elated; he gave thanks for his good fortune. To be received with such affection and sincerity by the
parents of the woman he loved was more than he could ever
have dreamed.

Osman Ferid and Emire Nefiset were married in a modest,
Muslim wedding ceremony on November 12, 1888. The bride
was sixteen years old; the groom forty-four.

CHAPTER 12

The Struggle in Arabia

Look at the camel
And how it is created
Look at the sky and how it is raised
Look at the mountains and how they are set
Look at the earth and how it is spread.

> Muhammad, Prophet for our Time, Karen Armstrong

After the death of his father, Imam Shamil in Medina in 1871, Ghazi Mohammed returned to Istanbul to settle at Koska Konak, where in 1872, Emire Nefiset was born. She had delicate cheek bones, dark hair and deep brown eyes that looked almost black next to her white, porcelain-like complexion. Her calm and pleasing disposition, sensitivity and intelligence led many to believe her older than her years.

She grew up in the closeted world of an exiled family. She was taught Russian and Turkish and the skills and etiquette of a noble Circassian family. She was surprisingly observant and beneath a quiet demeanour lurked an infectious girlish giggle ready to surface at any moment. The death of her sister Sofiate had been a great tragedy for the family.

Her father had found solace in his younger daughter, often

calling her to sit near him when he entertained. She had been weaned on the drama and colourful history of her ancestors. She remembered Osman Ferid's visits to the Koska Konak. He had been kind and friendly and when he appeared at Medina, Nefiset began to look forward to his visits. She had fallen in love with him long before he noticed her. As her mother had said laughingly, they had often discussed ways to overcome the pasha's natural reserve and shyness.

Ghazi Mohammed suggested the new couple live in one of his residences within the compound. It was a spacious, comfortable villa with a garden shaded by tall date palms and a stream that meandered into a marble pool. The fatigue of a day at the barracks disappeared as his young wife led him into the harem, smiling, teasing and full of loving enthusiasm; her vast knowledge and deep insight of the Caucasus never failed to surprise him.

With the aid of Hood Lala, her personal servant, she ran her household with a kind, but firm hand, no easy task with such indifferent, lazy servants. Hood Lala's mother was a Nubian slave whom Ghazi Mohammed had bought when he saw her being beaten in the slave market. Mother and son had served the family faithfully ever since. When his mother died, Hood Lala became Nefiset's houseboy and guard

On weekends Osman Ferid and Nefiset drove to the farm to ride across the dunes and sands, her veil flying in the winds, her eyes sparkling with happiness. He told her about life at the Shapli aoul, his father, Janbolat and his beautiful mother whose sense of humour, intuition and courage never failed her even in the most difficult moments. Osman Ferid felt rejuvenated, full of energy. For the first time since he had left the Caucasus, he felt young at heart, mentally, and physically capable of enjoying Nefiset's youth and unconditional adoration. Each day he fell more and more in love with his young bride, calling for her as soon as he entered the house. When they heard him calling, "Nefiset Hanim, Nefiset Hanim" the servants scurried off to tell their mistress the pasha had returned.

The two families lived in close harmony. Osman Ferid would call on his friend and father-in-law for an hour of quiet conversation before they walked across the garden to the Shapli residence to join his wife and her mother for dinner. In 1891, Nefiset gave birth to her first child, a son named Şamil, after her grandfather, Imam Shamil. Within five years, she gave birth to three more sons, Bereket, Arif and Gazi.

The history of Arabia, for centuries, had been a hotbed of intrigue and desert warfare. Tribal war was peculiar to the existing social order. Since the tribe was the basic political unit in Arabia, wars took the form of raids: mainly for robbery or vendetta. This developed a spirit of self-reliance, courage and co-operation among the members of a single tribe, but intensified warfare and rivalry among differing tribes, creating a state of instability and unrest and the reason for the power struggle between the House of Rashid, the House of Wahhabi-Saud and the Ottoman Empire.

The pilgrimage to the holy cities of Mecca and Medina—known as the Hajj—is one of the principal articles of Islamic belief.

"It is the duty of every person who has the requisite means, to undertake a pilgrimage to the house of God (*Quran*, Chapter III, Verse 96)."

The pilgrimage includes sacred acts carried out at the Kaaba in Mecca and a visit to the second holy city of Medina to pray at the Prophet's tomb and mausoleum.

Medina lies in a prosperous oasis bounded by lava fields with a number of wadies (water-courses) in which mechanical pumps built by the Ottomans irrigate the surrounding lands. Ottoman control of Medina had weakened before the Wahhabis took the city in 1804.

A Turko-Egyptian force re-took the city and was able to sustain effective control for a period of time. This resulted in a favourable consensus for the Ottomans and Rashidis, who—

loyal to the sultan—imposed peaceful co-existence in matters of local control until the revival of the Wahhabi movement under Ibn Saud continually stirred unrest, inciting rebel bandits to attack in large wild groups.

Having established friendly relations with the Rashidi Sheikhs, Osman Ferid and the governor of Medina organized a meeting with the sheikhs to discuss an agenda and strategy for the maintenance of peace and security in the area, but all attempts to befriend the Wahhabis tribes failed to overcome their deep-seated distrust of the Turkish administration. The situation was further ignited by a growing conflict between Osman Ferid and Ahmed Ratip Pasha, the governor of Hejaz. Differences came to a head between these two strong-willed men when Ahmed Ratip Pasha sent word that, as the city of Medina lay within his juris-diction, henceforth all decisions pertaining to the city were to be made by the office of the governor of Hijaz, by-passing the authority entitled to the office of the governor of Medina.

As commander of the Medina garrison, Osman Ferid con-sidered it his duty to report directly to the governor of Medina. Should the situation necessitate further authorization, then and only then, should it be reported to the governor of Hejaz. The governor of Medina was an amiable man but Ahmed Ratip Pasha exercised his official powers to the limit, brushing aside opposition to his authority. This attitude led to greater friction between these three men. At one meeting Osman Ferid present-ed a plan for a joint military operation against a certain rebel-lious Bedouin tribe but Ahmed Ratip dismissed them as incon-sequential. A few weeks later, a fierce Bedouin attack against a platoon of soldiers resulted in serious loss of lives. Osman Ferid was beside himself. Furious and deeply upset, he held that if his plan had been carried out, these deaths could have been avoid-ed. Communication between the governor and commander completely broke down. As it was impossible to avoid meeting at official functions in such a tightly structured society, a frosty greeting sufficed.

The governor of Hejaz, enraged by Osman Ferid's behaviour wrote an official letter of complaint to Abdülhamid, accusing the commander of the Medina garrison of disrespect to his position and authority.

This unpleasant situation coincided with Abdülhamid's growing interest and attention in Middle Eastern politics. He was about to sign an agreement to link Medina to the telegraph system and construct an extension of the Anatolian railway from Konya to Baghdad and the Persian Gulf as far as Hejaz. Security and safety from rebellious nomads in the area for the construction work was of the utmost precedence. Abdülhamid was aware of Osman Ferid's control, discipline and power within the Arab territories and had no intention of seeing his plans jeopardized because of a misunderstanding between his subjects. He sent the governor of Hejaz a sharp answer, emphasizing the need for peaceful collaboration.

To maintain continual vigilance along the route, Osman Ferid increased the number of troops and daily patrols. He regularly visited Bedouin chiefs, appealing for their coordinated efforts to restrain the skirmishes so that work on the telegraph poles could be completed on time, something unheard of in the sandy deserts of Arabia. Turks and Arabs who came into contact with Osman Ferid could not but admire his energetic and responsible approach to the task at hand. At the same time he also attracted dangerous enemies, angered by his interference and unbending rule of law on behalf of an absent sultan. That he was less than generous with his baksheesh displeased the corrupt.

In 1893, an official ceremony was held to celebrate the telegraph line connection from Damascus to Medina. The honour of sending the first telegram from the Holy City to the sultan in Istanbul was conferred on the commander of the Medina garrison for his invaluable participation. The sultan sent a gracious telegram of congratulations to everyone concerned, including the Bedouin chieftains for their cooperation. Osman Ferid was promoted to lieutenant general. The telegram was signed, Abdülhamid.

At home, Osman Ferid wore the cool, comfortable Arab jellabas, while Nefiset favoured white, loose robes. She wore her hair plaited and braided in Circassian fashion, or hanging loose over her shoulders under a fine white veil. As he entered the nursery she rose to welcome him and then, before they retired to their quarters, sat at his side while he played with the children. When alone with her husband, Nefiset was an intelligent, witty conversationalist. Osman Ferid had come to rely on her judgment; she listened attentively and was more tolerant of human weaknesses than her husband. She often scolded him for his unbending, stubborn attitude.

"Paşam, Paşam, your stubbornness will bring serious trouble one day; try to be more flexible and patient. There are times when it is wise to compromise for the sake of peace."

Nefiset had been weaned on Caucasian affairs, military life and politics. Osman Ferid respected his remarkable young wife's opinions; for one who had lived such a sheltered limited life, she had acute powers of observation and a surprisingly broad, even liberal, understanding of humanity.

Nefiset's marriage and the birth of her children brought joy and great pleasure into the lives of her parents, who embraced this loving family scene as a gift from Allah. Habibet Hanım supervised the nursery, training bemused slaves from Nubia in the art of raising children according to Circassian customs. On September 27, 1897, Nefiset gave birth to their fifth son, Hamza Osman. Her father would find an excuse to pop into the nursery to play or tell stories to his grandchildren about the Caucasus, to which they listened with wide-eyed pleasure and squeals. When Osman Ferid appeared he threw up his hands.

"Ah, save me from these little warriors." Their father joined in the games until planting kisses on their foreheads, both men escaped to the selamlik.

Osman Ferid had not received any formal religious training, except from the old village imam who had preferred the ancient teachings of the Adat to the strict code of Islam. During those quiet hours with his father-in-law, before their wives appeared, Osman Ferid learned the religious and political power of Islam and Islamic societies. The pasha explained the chief duty of a Muslim was to create a just community in which all members, even the weak and vulnerable, were treated with respect. The political well-being of a Muslim community was of extreme importance. Ghazi Muhammed believed a purely political program would be superficial in social reform without spiritual transformation.

Ghazi Muhammed explained the rights commanded by the sultan as Caliph of Islam, the rise of Muradism, and the reason his father, Imam Shamil, had preached and fought a holy war campaigning against the Russians for more than twenty-five years. He spoke of his personal frustration in Russia, his surprise and disappointment at his father's acceptance of his exile, adding that he believed his father had lived his life according to the Islamic philosophers who divided man's life into three periods: a time for learning, a time for action and a time for contemplation.

After his exile, Shamil had devoted his life to prayer and meditation, attempting to build better understanding and relations between the two nations. Ghazi Muhammed Pasha was a mine of knowledge; it gratified him to share his experiences with his son-in-law, to help him address the subtle diplomatic, as well as the military, problems he faced in Arabia. Habibet Hanım often scolded her husband for his sobriety and seriousness.

In the evening, behind the thick walls of the harem Habibet Hanım played the piano and sang Russian songs while Nefiset recited poetry or impersonated a guest or an incident in the nursery. The ladies brought warmth and colour into the sober lives of their husbands. Habibet Hanım had spent ten years in Russia with her husband at the Shamil residence, moving from Kaluga to Moscow and then St Petersburg. She spoke Russian and French, had visited the royal court of the Tsarina of Russia and had accompanied Imam Shamil to the Opera House. There were times when duty demanded Osman Ferid address foreign visitors; he would greet them with a few words in French or English before calling his translator. Nefiset took great delight in imitating her husband at these receptions, "mumbling in a language no one understands." Her parents tried not to laugh, but Osman Ferid laughed even louder, promising dire revenge!

When Osman Ferid and Ghazi Mohammed Pasha entertained at the residence, Nefiset and her mother dined with the children and then, following the tradition set by Imam Shamil, should the guests be family friends, the ladies would join them for coffee.

Every morning Osman Ferid's desk was piled high with telegraphs, letters and official papers. He read each piece of correspondence carefully before attending to the pressing issues of the day. Nothing was too trivial; nothing was overlooked.

One day he received a telegram from his brother, Mehmet. Mehmet's wife, Naile Sultan, had died and his brother was bereft with grief. Osman Ferid replied at once, recalling her kindness and generosity in his darkest days. Nefiset wrote a loving letter of condolences.

In 1896, he received a telegraph from Istanbul expressing concern in the growing interest of the Russian government in Arabia and their subversive infiltration into Arab tribes.

The steady increase of Russian visitors to Arabia had already caught Osman Ferid's attention causing him to set up an investigation. During that time, the Ottoman Embassy at St. Petersburg had granted a Russian officer of Turkish origin, Abdülaziz Devletshin Kenaz, permission to travel throughout the country. Osman Ferid monitored his travel details from

Damascus through Palestine to Hejaz and Medina before continuing to Mecca. On his arrival at Medina, he was escorted to the garrison to be interviewed by the commander.

Osman Ferid doubted the true purpose of his pilgrimage, finding him a suspicious and untrustworthy character. Much to Kenaz Bey's indignation, his permit to travel was cancelled and he was escorted from the garrison to the border. Later it came to light that Kenaz Bey had compiled a detailed report of 460 pages about Arabia for the department of Arab-Middle Eastern affairs in Moscow.

Another incident involved a Cossack cavalry officer, David Ivan Lifkin, a spy who visited Arabia under the pseudonym of Mehmet Hasanoğlu. He spoke fluent Arabic, Persian and Hindu and had travelled extensively throughout Egypt and Afghanistan. By the time Osman Ferid's intelligence sources learned of his presence in the country, he had disappeared. On his return to Russia he compiled a comprehensive report on the topography, route maps and guides of the Arabian Peninsula, adding that one million rubles would buy the friendship of certain influential sheikhs and emphasizing the wisdom of placing Arab speaking bureaucrats in Russian embassies, consulates and businesses in major cities to win over Arab communities.

The most notable spy to operate in Arabia on behalf of the Russians was the mufti of Orenburg's Islamic community, Sadik Efendi.

The mufti, a devout Muslim leader, had received an audience with the sultan at Yıldız Palace and had received gifts from the caliph. Under the guise of a religious pilgrimage through the Hejaz to Medina and Mecca, the mufti's true mission was to bribe, offer baksheesh and supply arms to dissident Arab sheikhs in return for their loyalty to Russia. When the mufti arrived at Medina, Osman Ferid held a reception attended by the governor of Medina, Ghazi Mohammed Pasha, officers from the garrison and many powerful Arab sheikhs in the province.

Osman Ferid and the pasha found the mufti devious and

secretive. On the following day an influential sheikh and friend related the disturbing conversation he had with the mufti, thus confirming Osman Ferid's suspicions. He consulted Ghazi Mohammed Pasha, who urged extreme caution; the mufti was a powerful religious leader with diplomatic immunity. Should his suspicions be unfounded, Osman Ferid would have the might of Islam on his head.

Weeks of painstaking intelligence-gathering activities on the part of his most trusted officers produced a detailed report of the mufti's movements and meetings, which proved beyond doubt that Osman Ferid's suspicions were justified. The mufti was spying and gathering material for the Russian Intelligence Service. His briefing to the Russians included the suggestion that the Russians would be wise to monitor British activities in Arabia. To promote their interests in Arabia, the British were using missionaries and business companies as channels to lavish baksheesh on various sheikhs; the British were extremely active in Yemen, Hejaz and Muscat. The mufti reported the need for urgent action to prevent British dominance in the area.

In 1899, undeniable proof of active treason by Sheikh Sayyed Abdulkader, a powerful Arab sheikh, was brought to Osman Ferid. He had been suspicious of the sheikh for many months but had been unable to prove the depth of the charges. The documents, which were up for sale to the highest foreign bidder, included confidential information about Turkish military units, with details of their strength and firepower in Arabia. Osman Ferid led a unit of troops and intelligence officers on a surprise search of the sheikh's residence, where incriminating evidence of treason was uncovered. He placed the sheikh under house arrest, with Turkish troops guarding the confines of the property. A detailed report was sent to Abdülhamid at Yıldız Palace, with copies to the governor of Medina and the governor of Hejaz.

Sheikh Adbulkader was a powerful leader with a large and loyal following. He wrote a letter to Sultan Abdülhamid protesting against the arrogance and disrespect to which he had been subjected by the commander of the Medina garrison, accusing him of slander, bigotry and prejudice against his person and demanding his immediate recall from Arabia. Ghazi Muhammed Pasha thought it prudent to guard their own residences and begged Osman Ferid to keep alert. Sheikh Adbulkader was a powerful enemy and had friends throughout the province.

Abdülhamid read the report and letter with great care, aware of the nest of intrigues, spying and power struggles within Arabia between the sheikhs and the foreign powers, especially England and Russia and the Ottoman Empire. He knew Osman Ferid's judgment and integrity were above question, but he was shrewd and experienced enough not to condemn, or make an enemy of such a powerful Arab leader. He decided to play for time.

"The devil's work is done in haste," was his usual motto.

Osman Ferid was summoned to Istanbul.

Considering the enormity of the charge, the sultan's decision did not surprise Osman Ferid. On the contrary, he was thrilled; not only could he present his case in person but it afforded an occasion to return to Istanbul with Nefiset. He rushed to the residence to share the good news with his wife. To visit Istanbul with Nefiset and to introduce her to his family after an absence of 13 years would be well worth any decision made by the sultan.

Nefiset was working in the garden with the children and nannies, supervising rows of plants and flowers for planting. When she saw Osman Ferid approaching, she looked up questioningly. Something important must have occurred to bring her husband home in the afternoon. He took her hand and led her into the harem, handing her the telegraph.

"We're going to Istanbul," he smiled planting a kiss on her forehead.

"You will meet my family, my sister Zissi, my brothers. We shall take a caique across the Bosphorus, shop in the Rue de Pera."

Hearing Osman Ferid's voice, Habibet Hanım went off to find her husband.

"I must tell the pasha."

Ghazi Mohammed Pasha's reaction was one of caution, "It will not be the first time the sultan sacrifices a commander in his service to appease a powerful sheikh."

"I have considered that option," replied Osman Ferid quite happily:

"If that happens I shall tender my resignation. I can occupy myself with the farm and breed Arab horses, perhaps racing camels, until the children are old enough to attend school. At that time Nefiset and I will take them to Istanbul and leave them in the care of my family and then we shall return to Medina. Our home, our life is here with you, dear Pasha. I will not allow anything or anyone, not even the sultan of the Ottoman Empire, to interfere with my family. It is too precious; nothing, no one is powerful enough to part us."

Ghazi Pasha rose to embrace his son-in-law. Habibet Hanım wiped away her tears and Nefiset beamed with pleasure at the prospect of seeing Istanbul, the city she had left as a child never to return.

CHAPTER 13

Istanbul

On November 19, 1900, amid tears, smiles, hugs and kisses, Nefiset left her young children in the capable hands of her parents. Accompanied by their eldest son, Şamil, aged nine, she and Osman Ferid set off on the camel train to Yanbu. His entourage was made up of two aides-de-camp, fifteen army officers, four civilian officers, three loyal Rashidi Sheikhs, the two intelligence officers who had uncovered the Sheikhs documents, three personal servants and a unit of troops to accompany them to Yanbu. Whenever Nefiset left the compound of her home, she wore a belt with a dagger and pistol under her white Arab garb as protection from attack or kidnapping.

The camels bound with their heavy loads set the pace as the camel drivers, on foot or donkey, led the train through the blasting desert lands. Osman Ferid had adapted well to the changeable desert climate after spending days, and even weeks, on grim camels under the scorching sun riding to every corner of the Hejaz province. The desert's mystic power, its ever-changing landscape, wind whipped rocks and mountains, gorges and hot, savage winds, its clouds of dust and endless sands, its cloudless skies, intense sunlight and chilly nights with heavy dew, luscious green vegetation and date palms surrounding the welcomed oases had cast its spell on him. Its vastness, desolation and silence had fascinated him as he grew to respect the sober countenance of the desert nomads' lined, leathery faces reflecting their harsh existence in the desert.

Two days into their journey, an officer pointed to a sand cloud rising in the distance. Riding towards them was a tribe of Bedouins belonging to Sheikh Abdulkader's tribe. Osman Ferid monitored their movements throughout the day, ordering his men not to react.

"I think they want to frighten us, but will not attack."

That night everyone remained awake and alert, listening to their fierce yells and charges as the Bedouins circled the oasis from a distance. Next day they set off at dawn as planned with the Bedouins still following, taunting and shouting, until dusk when they retreated, as Osman Ferid had assumed, back to Medina.

The travellers broke their journey at Jerusalem to visit his eldest son, Kazım, now first secretary to the governor of Jerusalem in the employ of the Ottoman Foreign Office. They shook hands, at first stiff and formal, feeling slightly awkward after a separation of thirteen years. Kazım was pleased to welcome his father as a senior Ottoman official. He was tall and well-built and had his mother's dark handsomeness.

He greeted his brother, Shamil, warmly and kissed Nefiset's hand respectfully. As he showed them to their quarters, Nefiset took his arm.

"You cannot imagine how excited and happy I am to meet you and to go to Istanbul with your father; he has often spoken about you. I always wished for an 'Ağabey' (elder brother) and now I have one."

As Osman Ferid and his sons visited the historical sites and prayed at the mosque, they talked about the past. Osman Ferid was pleased when Kazım spoke of how his aunt and uncle had been involved in his education, attending school functions and insisting he spend part of his holidays with them. He had attended the formal funeral of Sultana Naile and been saddened to see his uncle, Mehmet, overcome with grief.

Kazım introduced his father to his colleagues and friends and on their last evening he hosted a magnificent reception in their honour, inviting the governor of Jerusalem and leading military and civil and religious officials.

Osman Ferid was in great spirits as they made their way towards Istanbul, stopping at archaeological and religious sites, visiting prominent Ottoman dignitaries and military friends. Two months later they arrived at the Istanbul home of Nefiset's parents, Koska Konak.

Nefiset set about preparing the house, unlocking cupboards and trunks and taking out family silver to be polished. The windows were thrown open, rooms dusted, kitchen cupboards cleaned and filled. She did not accept incompetence; gently but firmly she trained her small staff to be efficient and respectful, especially when it concerned her husband's comfort. She tidied the garden, sweeping leaves and collecting broken twigs into bundles even though it was quite cold and windy. One morning Shamil ran into their room.

"Pasha Baba, it's snowing," he shouted in surprise.

They rushed into the garden, which was blanketed in snow. Osman Ferid shook the branches of a tree, showering his son and wife with snow. They played like children, laughing and throwing snow balls until, flushed, cold but exhilarated, they rushed indoors for a hot drink. Nefiset gave a reception for Osman Ferid's family and friends when Zissi came to stay with them. Nefiset was blissfully happy, delighted to make the acquaintance of her husband's family and to have returned to this beautiful city once more.

Two weeks later, Osman Ferid was summoned to Yıldız Palace for an audience with Sultan Abdülhamid. The sultan was in conversation with his ministers, but received him graciously. After the initial cordial greetings, the sultan invited him into his private chamber. He enquired by name of the Arab princes, leaders and sheikhs, and the imams and mullahs who had visited Istanbul as his guests. He questioned the political and military situation in Hejaz, Medina and Mecca, Osman Ferid's sources concerning the subversive activities, and the infiltration of the British and Russians into Arab tribes.

Then Abdülhamid turned to the events that had led to the house arrest of Sheikh Abdulkader. He listened without comment, looking at the papers on his desk. Now and then he fired a question in a sharp voice, raising his eyes. As he replied Osman Ferid felt the sultan's eyes penetrating his very soul.

After a while the sultan closed the folder, thanked and dismissed him with a polite bow of his head, wishing him a pleasant stay. Osman Ferid walked out of Yıldız Palace with a deep sense of relief. He thought how fortunate he was to serve in the desert rather than as aide-de-camp to the sultan. He would not have lasted very long here, he thought ruefully.

He recounted the audience to Nefiset. He had found the sultan aged: his shoulders more bent and his skin pallid and drawn against its grey beard. The sultan seemed even more suspicious and uneasy than ever. Osman Ferid doubted he had satisfied the sultan with his answers concerning the political situation and His Majesty's position as Caliph and Protector of Islam over the Arab provinces.

Abdülhamid preferred the smooth praises and flowery words of royal courtiers to the impersonal and factual report Osman Ferid had presented. Nevertheless, Osman Ferid was not overly concerned. He had discussed early retirement with his wife; the thought of spending more time with his young family appealed to him.

By royal decree, attempts to modernize and rebuild Istanbul into a European city had only succeeded in emphasising the difference between the residential areas on either side of the Golden Horn. The district of Pera was modern and prosperous, with impressive European buildings lining newly-built, wide roads stretching from Karaköy to Ortaköy along the Bosphorus shore-line; residential areas had spread along the Taksim-Şişli road, which connected the city to the north. The new Pera Palace Hotel and Yıldız Palace blazed with electric light. Shops along the Rue de Pera offered trailing tea-gowns from Paris and Vienna, while the old city, even though the royal avenue, the Divanyolu, had been extended, remained a maze of irregular, narrow, badly lit streets, its wooden houses set against the unique, breathtaking skyline of mosques and palaces. Most areas of the town remained dimly lit and dangerous at night, with wild dogs and gypsies scavenging the streets.

Accompanied by Zissi, Nefiset delighted in visiting the beautiful white, wooden waterside mansions, the *yalis*, set in their green, shaded gardens. Sometimes early in the morning, Osman Ferid and his brothers rode over the hills to lunch at the Maslak hunting lodge, their old haunt. One day his brother, Ahmet Pasha, commander of the Cavalry Brigade at Selimiye Barracks, accompanied him to Taşkışla Barracks where he was welcomed with a military parade and given a personal tour by the commander. He was gratified to see that many of his innovations had been improved.

In the evenings, a stream of visitors, family and friends came to pay their respects. Members of the Caucasian community brought news from the Caucasus. Osman Ferid was pleased to welcome fellow officers with whom he had served in the war. But news in the city was alarmingly similar to the unrest and dissatisfaction that had plagued those dark days prior to the overthrow of Sultan Abdülaziz, except this time, it was cloaked with fear and mistrust against the sultan and his network of spies.

Osman Ferid was disappointed to learn that the promised military reforms had been put on hold; the powerful ironclad ships bought at such enormous expense from England had not empowered the naval forces, but had been allowed to rust.

Nefiset charmed everyone with her quiet manner and graciousness for one so young. Osman Ferid's family and friends rejoiced in his happiness; they had never seen him look so well, so relaxed and content in his marriage to this delightful, young mother of his children.

Shamil and his parents walked from Beyazit along the shore road, past the Sirkeci train station to the Galata Bridge to watch the crowds, as de Amicis wrote:

"A hurrying, pushing throng of foot-passengers comes and goes all day long, now and then crowding to right and left to make room in the middle of the street for porters, carriages donkeys or omnibuses. Almost all the business conducted in Istanbul flows through this quarter."

On, September 12, 1901, Osman Ferid, his wife and family attended Mehmet's lavish wedding to his second royal bride, Esma Sultan, daughter of Sultan Abdülaziz. Mehmet (Seryarver Damat, Mehmet Paşa bin Hassan) had been promoted to field marshal with the title of pasha and he served as chief aide-de-camp to Sultan Abdülhamid.

The family prayed for his happiness, for a long and fruitful marriage after the tragic death of his first wife, Naile Sultan, youngest of Sultan Abdülhamid's eight sisters, whose death a few years after their marriage had left her husband and the royal court in deep mourning.

Osman Ferid was summoned three times to Yıldız Palace for more gruelling audiences with the sultan. At the last interview Abdülhamid thanked him for his loyalty and assiduity in Arabia.

Before orders for his return to Medina arrived, Osman Ferid and Nefiset, along with his brother Mehmet and his wife Esma Sultan, were invited to a royal reception at Yıldız Palace. Before leaving Istanbul, they decided that Şamil should attend the French Lycée at Istanbul under the guardianship of Kazım, his eldest son, who had returned from Jerusalem.

On November 1, 1901, Osman Ferid, his wife and retinue began the return journey by boat, then overland by camel train to Medina. They had thoroughly enjoyed every moment of their stay in Istanbul, but it had taken longer than they had anticipated, nearly a year, and they missed the children, Ghazi Mohammed Pasha and Habibet Hanım. It was time to return home.

On April 7, 1902, Osman Ferid was honoured with the title of Sheikh-ul-Haram, Keeper of the Prophet's Tomb in Medina (Harim-i-Sherif), promoted to General of the Army (1st. Ferik) with command over the vast territory that spanned all the lands from the Hejiz to Najd.

Osman Ferid was 58 years old.

CHAPTER 14

Visit of the H. H The Nawab Sultan Jahan, Begam of Bhopal

On his return Osman Ferid handed over the daily duties of the garrison to his trusted second-in-command in order to concentrate on the responsibilities of Sheikh-ul-Haram. Officers led patrols, travelling the length and breadth of the Hejaz, keeping a watchful eye on unruly Bedouin tribes, troublesome Arab chiefs, and foreign insurgents. Osman Ferid, known to be restless sitting behind a desk, was not beyond inventing an excuse to lead a patrol on its ride through the desert to visit an influential sheikh.

Much of his time and energy was spent addressing the political and religious problems brought on by the insurgency of foreign powers, especially the British, who were infiltrating and causing serious unrest amongst the Arab people. When faced by an issue of particular sensitivity he would invite Ghazi Muhammed Pasha, who was deeply respected and welcomed by powerful chieftains and princes throughout Arabia, as an ambassador of peace to accompany him.

The *Milliyet Newspaper* wrote on July 16, 1933:

"Yıldız Palace sent a dispatch to the army regarding the British intelligence in Mecca, which read, 'British espionage and intelligence activity are increasing in South Arabia every pass-

Osman Ferid Pasha: 1st. Ferik Sheikh-ul-Haram, Guardian of the Holy Shrine of Medina, Protector and Keeper of the Prophet's Tomb.

Emine Nefiset.
Osman Ferid Pasha's wife (1873-1959).

Kaaba, Mecca, Saudi Arabia.

حرم بيت الله

Harem Mecca, Kaba Sharif

Osman Ferid Pasha's sons: Şamil, Bereket, Arif, Hamza Osman.

Ghazi Mohammed Pasha with his grandsons Şamil, Arif, Bereket and
Hamza Osman (1898-99 Medina).

Osman Ferid Pasha's children (Medina 1907).

Osman Ferid Pasha
attends a tribal meeting
(Medina 1902).

A religious
gathering.

شريف امحمد علي شيخ عثمان باشا
علي ضابط
شي
شيخ
جلابغث

Osman Ferid Pasha with Şamilzade Ghazi Mohammed Pasha at a ceremony in Medina (1902).

Tribal meeting.

Osman Ferid Pasha with friends.

Pera palace Hotel
Constantinople.
August 7th 1911

My esteemed Friend
I am obliged to you
for your favour & in reply
hereto write to say that I
am going to Summer Palace
Hotel at Therapia today &
shall be living there till
the 17th of this month. I

shall be only too delighted
to see the ladies at any
time at the hotel that may
be convenient to them. I
hope you'll kindly let
me know in advance at
whattime the ladies would
be coming.

With kindest regards
Your sincere friend

Sultan Jahan
Ruler of Bhopal

Hand written letter from ruler
of Bhopal.

Osman Ferid's children: Saadet, Şamil, Habibe and Melek (Mytilene 1910).

Bekir, Bereket, Gazi, Şamil, Hamza Osman, Arif, sons of Osman Ferid, (Mytilene 1911).

Şamil, Saadet, Sait Şamil (a cousin), Habibe Hamza Osman and his wife Melike (Istanbul 1932).

Family photo with visiting relative, Ubih-Aziz el Masne Pasha, military advisor to King Faruk.

Hamza Osman Erkan with his son Aydın Osman Erkan, the author.

Nefiset with two of her daughters, Zübeyde and Saadet.

Şeyh Şâmil'in Torunu

Semih Mümtaz S.

Kısacık bir hastalığı müteakip hemen iki gün içinde ve geçende iki gün evvel âzimi darı cinan olan (Nefise Hanımefendi) mücahidi muhterem Şeyh Şâmil merhumun oğlu Mehmed Paşanın kerimesi ve Şeyhülharem Osman Ferid Paşanın refikası idi. Medinei Münevverede evlendi ve Arslanlar gibi evlâdlar yetiştirdi. Bir çok acı da gördü. Zevcini ve evlâdlarından birkaçını kaybetti. Fakat tevekkülünü biran kaybetmedi. Tahammülünün asîl teznzhürlerini göstermekten bir dakika fariğ olmadı. Daima güler, daima tertipli, emsali nadir terbiyeli, fartı ıhlâs ile hayırhah, fukaraperver, hasenatın âşıkı, dostlarına, evlâdlarına dost ve arkadaşlarına muhabbetli, onları evlâdlarından ayırmıyacak kadar şefkatli bir hanımefendi idi. Güzel menkıbeleri saymakla bitmez.

Birinci Harbi Umumî sıralarında Cenevrede oğullarile beraber ikamet etmekteler iken kendilerini tanımış, ellerinden öpmüştüm. Onun elini öpmenin başka bir zevki ve inşirahını tatmıştım. Gayet mültefit, inşirah verircesine mültefit bir hanımefendi idi. Ömrünün sonuna kadar da öyle kaldı. Vekar ve şerefinden bir habbe eksiltmedi.

Hayırhahlığından bir nebze kaybetmedi. Vefalılıkta da emsalsiz, herkesin iyiliğine dua etmekte, hattâ delâlet etmekte cidden vakur idi. Yaptıkları iyilikleri göstermek şöyle dursun zedildiğini, görüldüğünü görmek istemezdi. Başörtüsüz belki onu öz evlâtları da göremezlerdi. Kıskıvrak, tertemiz, bembeyaz, berrak ve her mânada nûr-efşan bir kadındı; hem ihtiyarladıkça güzelleşen bir nur parçasıydı. Vefatından mütevellid hüznü ve kederi,, onun nurlar misali uçup gitmesinden hâsıl olan itmi'nan ile tesliye ediyorum ve müşarünileyhaya Cenâbı Haktan rahmet ve mağfiret temenni ediyorum. Şuna da eminim ki merhumeyi tanıyanlar hiç şüphe etmem benimle yekzebandırlar. Allah rahmet eylesin; Nefise Hanımefendiye.

S. M. Ş.

Semih Mumtas' commemoration of Nefise Hanimefendi on her death.

Hamza Osman Erkan.

Şamil with his sister Saadet Shapli at the Konak at Serencebey, Beşiktaş.

"BEŞİKTAŞ KULÜBÜ.
9 MAYIS 1950.

Hamza Osman Erkan.

Hamza Osman in practice.

ing day. The sultan has appointed General Osman Ferid Pasha as Sheihk-ul Haram (Protector of the Prophet's Tomb) and sent him to Medina with the specific duty of combating foreign espionage. It is indeed difficult for General Osman Ferid to combat efficiently with such a wide network of spies and their subversive activity.

"According to official records of Ottoman counterespionage networks, four missionaries, Mr Glasers, Mr Fortlemontes, Mr Thomas Horewins and Mr Dogitts, attempted to enter the sacred city of Mecca disguised as Arab sheikhs.

"On hearing this, Commander General Osman Ferid Pasha immediately organized his officers and gave strict orders for their arrest. Three were detained before they entered the sacred grounds and were escorted under guard to the borders. Mr Fortlemontes managed to escape and was able to travel freely about the country for two months until he was captured, put under custody and then handed over to the British Consulate at Jeddah. General Osman Ferid is the son-in-law of the second son of Shamil, national hero and liberation leader of North Caucasus. Following the coup of 1908, I visited him many times at his father-in-law's konak at Koska. He described the extent of intrigue that took place between the foreign powers and local Arab Sheiks against the established order of the Ottoman Government."

Final work for the installation of electricity in Medina with generators to light the Prophet's Tomb and Mosque was completed. Inviting a large audience of religious leaders, Arabs, Turks, Bedouins, civilian and military personnel, Osman Ferid turned the switch. Gasps of disbelief and cries of wonder filled the air at the awesome sight of the magnificent religious monuments, the Prophet's Tomb and Mosque, illuminated and blazing with light in the vast, dark desert. The introduction of electricity had caused controversy amongst the people of Medina and its surroundings. While the majority welcomed the comfort and social implications modern technology in the form of electric energy provided, just as they had welcomed the telegram, the powerful reactionary mullahs vigorously rejected its introduction as an invention of the infidel.

One evening as Osman Ferid was about to lock the heavy door of the Harim-i-Sherif, he caught the glimpse of a shadow hiding behind a tree on the pathway in front of him. He walked slowly past the tree, then—with the agility of a panther—turned in time to catch the raised arm in an iron grip, twisting it until the dagger fell and the assailant screamed out in pain. Osman Ferid hit him with such force that the assailant fell unconscious on the ground. Guards arrived to carry him off to prison.

The assailant was young, just a boy, a devout Muslim. His attitude, however, was defiant and unrepentant. He shouted prayers, accusing the Sheikh-ul-Haram of violating the laws of the Holy Quran, of sacrilege, by installing electricity, an invention of the unbeliever, the infidel. He ranted and raved, then fell on his knees sobbing. Osman Ferid ordered him to stand, putting his revolver on the desk. When the boy saw the gun he fell silent.

"You have lost your dagger. What would you do if I offered you this revolver?" asked the pasha.

The boy looked puzzled; then with inbred cunning and quick wit, he responded with deference.

"'Efendi, if I am pardoned and given a revolver, I will serve you for the rest of my life."

He moved towards the table to take the gun, but Osman Ferid was too quick; he picked it up and pointed it at the boy's heart.

"My son, you are young, foolhardy and confused. The gun you desire is made by the same foreigners, the infidels, who invented electricity. These inventions are not against religion; they are products of modern technology. Electricity is a source

242

of energy used by every progressive and modern country. The Sultan and Caliph of all Islam has accepted electricity and ordered his followers to benefit from its power.

"Islam is not against progress. It will bring light and comfort to the darkest corners of our cities in Arabia. You have been wrongly instructed by fanatic and ignorant men and should pay for your action with your life. But I, by the power of the Caliph, have decided to pardon you. You will remain in the garrison, attending prayers, performing menial duties under supervision until you learn that Medina is a sacred, but progressive city."

There were other incidents of attempted violence against the Sheikh-ul-Haram. The guard watch was increased and every precaution taken until the furore slowly died. Osman Ferid believed the attacks and demonstrations were instigated by foreign powers using fanatic fundamentalists to undermine his authority and the power of the Ottoman Empire.

The capital, Riyadh, had fallen into the hands of the House of Saudi after they defeated the Rashidis in a daring, dramatic coup. Abd-al-Aziz, later King Ibn Saud, was twenty-two years old when, on January 15, 1902, he arrived at the outskirts of Riyadh with 200 men gathered from wandering tribes as he rode through the desert. Accompanied by fifteen warriors, he scaled the walls of the capital, overpowering the Rashid governor and his escort in a surprise attack at the gate of Mismak fort. The oppressed population hailed Abd-al-Aziz as their leader and liberator.

1902 ended in grief for the Shapli family. Ghazi Mohammed Pasha suffered a sudden heart attack and died peacefully in bed within a few days. Letters and telegraphs of condolence arrived from many parts of the world, including an elegantly handwritten letter of condolences from the sultan delivered personally by the governor of the Hijaz. He was remembered and mourned by Caucasians throughout the Caucasus and the Middle East, especially by those who had fought and served with him in the army. Some had shared his exile in Russia and Arabia and had been friends in Istanbul. He was deeply mourned by his loving family, whom he had protected and guided throughout his life. He had been a staunch defender of liberty, a devout Muslim, and an inspiring teacher eager to share his experience and knowledge.

Habibet Hanım was plunged into grief, unable to share her hopelessness and pain even with her beloved daughter and grandchildren. Osman Ferid received a telegram from Mehmed Fazıl Daghestani, Habibet Hanım's brother, whom she hadn't seen since his banishment to Iraq, begging that he persuade her to visit him in Baghdad, but she refused; she had lost the will to live. The love, respect, faith and companionship they shared had not diminished with years; it had brought stability and meaning to their wandering existence. She died quietly, three months after her husband's death.

The house was silent, washed with death and sadness. Except for her sojourn to Istanbul, Nefiset had never been separated from her parents. She was crushed, lost without their constant love, closeness and encouragement. She shed no tears in front of the children, turning away in despair.

"Sunt lacrimae rerum," Virgil wrote, "there are tears in the nature of things, but mortal things touch the mind."

Her husband's love and tenderness were her only solace. The prayers and funeral arrangements were subdued. Osman Ferid received guests in the selamlık; few ladies ventured into the harem. Nefiset was too unwell to receive visitors. The couple spent their days walking in the garden, visiting the nursery in the afternoon so that Osman Ferid could tell stories about the great Caucasian heroes in place of their beloved grandfather, retiring into the privacy of the harem to spend quiet evenings in prayer. Osman Ferid remained at Nefiset's side until she regained her strength and peace.

In October, 1903, Osman Ferid received an official letter from Mr C. P. Dewey, British consul-general in Jeddah, informing the Sheikh-ul-Haram of the forthcoming visit to Mecca of Her Highness, The Nawab Sultan Jahan Begam— Ruler of Bhopal in India. It included a letter written by the Begam to the Sheikh-ul-Haram:

'The idea to visit the angel-cradled portal of the Light of the World, the Master of the Universe, the Intercessor for Sinners, the Medium of the Faith, our Prophet –on whom descend the Blessings of God– has long been fixed in my mind. This year I decided, God willing, to pay homage to the heaven-domed shrine at Medina, to have the honour of kissing Your Excellency's hands during the blessed month of Ramadan prior to the performance of the sacred Hadj. I will be accompanied by my followers and kafila as necessity demands:

"Your Excellency's fame as a kind dispenser of justice and generosity to the pilgrims resorting to the hallowed Tomb of our Holy Prophet, and as commander under whose administration peace and safety have been secured and turbulence and rapacity and suppressed, has confirmed and accelerated my resolve to undertake the holy journey long contemplated. I have accordingly decided to present myself first at the Prophet's Holy Tomb at Medina where after invoking the blessings of God upon the Holy Spirit of the Master of the Universe I propose to spend some time under the shadow of your protection. It is accepted that "a traveller is a stranger even though he be a king," as it is also well known that "every newcomer is a danger." For a stranger to travel in an unknown country without a proper escort would be unwise and imprudent. I trust Your Excellency will be pleased to make the necessary arrangements regarding the safe escort of myself and my followers from Yanbu to the Blessed City on our journeys. I beg an escort of 100 Turkish soldiers to be placed at my disposal on my arrival at Yanbu.

"God willing I shall soon have the honour of paying my

respects to Your Excellency. I sincerely hope that this humble expression of the profound respect and goodwill which I entertain for Your Excellency will find favour in your eyes. My trustworthy delegates who will precede my visit are instructed to explain the details of my visit."

The Nawab, Sultan Jahan Begam, G. C. I. E

Ruler of Bhopal

The steamer moored at Yanbu on November 21, 1903. The Begam and her entourage were greeted with a military welcome by Ferhat Pasha, the governor of Yanbu, Turkish and Arabian dignitaries and representatives of the British government. After resting at the governor's mansion for a week, the ruler of Bhopal, accompanied by 300 followers, began the camel train journey to Medina with 200 camels, escorted by 132 private guards and 100 Turkish soldiers and officers. Bedouin bands were sighted around the Khil hill. They followed the caravan train in the hope of baksheesh, but fearing the Turkish soldiers, kept their distance. Osman Ferid ordered an attachment of 300 troops to ride out to Bir-i-Abbas to escort the Begam and her party to Medina.

On December 2, at the gate of Bab-i-Ambariah, the governor, sheikh-ul-haram, the mufti, Arab sheikhs, military and civilian staff welcomed their royal guest with a 21 gun salute. A mansion had been prepared for the Begam close to the Medjidye Gate of Bab-i-Ambariah. Women were not permitted to enter the tomb of the Prophet, but a royal edict granted by Sultan Abdülhamid, the Caliph, allowed the sole female ruler of a Muslim state to visit the Prophet's tomb. To everyone's relief, arrangements were carried out with military precision.

On December 8, 1903, the Begam wrote a letter to Major Impay.

"According to the advice of the Sheikh-ul-Haram, I have sent a telegram conveying my deepest gratitude to the Sultan and

Caliph of the Ottoman Empire. The Sheikhs of this place compel me to act as they dictate. I fear that in a case of non-compliance, they may disturb me and put obstacles in my way."

The Begam and her party proved colourful distraction in the sober month of Ramadan, the holy month of fasting, a month of prayers and meditation. During her stay the Begam was invited by the wives of the governors and leading Turkish and Arab dignitaries to a series of *iftar sofra*, a sumptuous feast served at sunset after a day of fasting. These meals were prepared with great care; they began with a prayer, a sip of water, an olive, salt or a date followed by appetizing courses of soup, meats, pilaf, olive-oil vegetables, *böreks* and pastries with tray upon tray of delicious sweets, baklava filled with nuts and oozing with honey, succulent dates and fruits and milk puddings all washed down with a small cup of thick, black sweet coffee or tea. Competition between the kitchens in the grand houses to present the finest table were fierce.

The ruler of Bhopal was dark-skinned, small, intelligent and very brave. Nefiset paid an official call, inviting the Begam to dine at the harem. After supper, Osman Ferid joined the ladies for coffee, a Caucasian custom the Begam found most amusing.

In her book, *The Story of a Pilgramage to Hijaz*, the Begam wrote:

"The Sahabzadas Ubaidullah and Hamidullah then proceeded, on my behalf, by way of a return visit, to the Government House where the Sheikh-ul Haram and the Muhafiz Paşa (Governor) were present. The Turkish garrison were drawn up and as the Sahibzadas arrived the troops presented arms. The Band at the same time played the national anthem 'God save the Sultan.' They then returned to their houses, and after the noon-day service the Sahibzadas paid an 'Id' visit to the Sheikh-ul-Haram, at his house, and were treated to tea, coffee, Turkish sweets and sharbat. The wife of the Sheikh-ul-Haram, the daughter of the Governor and the wife of the Treasurer-General called on me. I treated them to refreshments as required by custom and, having ceremoniously partaken of them, they took their leave."

Osman Ferid uncovered rumours of a planned raid by the Hamidah clan on the Sultan Jahan Begam's return caravan train. For her own safety and that of her people, he advised her to delay her return for a few weeks so that she might be accompanied by the Syrian Mahmel (sacred carpet for the Kaaba) caravan and travel in safety.

A letter addressed to Usman (Osman) Pasha, the Sheikh-ul-Haram read:

"I shall be very glad to you if you will kindly convey to H. I. M. the Sultan on my behalf my sincere thanks for the kind attention and protection which His Majesty has been graciously pleased to extend to me, for detailing troops to escort me, and for enabling us to reach Medina in peace and safety and to encamp close to the holy shrine. Kindly at the same time express my gratitude to His Majesty for the fact that both the Muhafiz and the Sheikh-ul-Haram Pashas, as well as all the officials in the holy city, have accorded me more than customary honour and courtesy. It is now my intention to prolong my stay at Medina and then to proceed to Mecca with the caravan from Syria. Therefore I venture to hope that you will, on your part, show the courtesy in making the necessary arrangements; moreover H. I. M the sultan's uniform kindness gives me full confidence that His Majesty will be graciously pleased to issue the requisite orders and command the officer in charge of the caravan to take me safely from Medina to Mecca."

The active opposition to his authority in Arabia by Ibn Saud's bold expansion activities including a religious pan-tribal organisation known as Ikhwan (Brethren), plus the British policy of maintaining its status quo in the Persian Gulf, stirred Abdülhamid, as Caliph of All Islam, into action. He proclaimed his intention of constructing the Hejaz railway with an initial personal donation of 50,000 pounds. He believed it was his moral obligation as caliph to undertake this huge venture to protect the lands under his domain.

Response to his appeal that the project be financed by Muslim countries was encouraging, as funds poured in from Muslim states in the Middle East and India. The Hejaz railway project from Damascus to Medina and Mecca would be a symbol of the sultan's good will and interest in the holy places in Hejaz. The arduous journey to Medina and Mecca would be more comfortable and safer for the hundreds of thousands of pilgrims who travel to the Hadj from all over the world. It was to be constructed by foreign engineers using the most modern technology to demonstrate the strength and collaboration (brotherhood) of Muslim countries to the western world.

It was imperative to sustain safety and security for the construction from raiding Bedouins, and to protect the shiny raillines crossing the sandy desert from acts of sabotage and theft.

Joan Haslip in her book, *The Sultan the Life of Abdülhamid II* wrote:

"...the bulk of the work was done by the Army and the Muslim peasantry who worked with enthusiasm on a job which would ensure them a place in the Prophet's paradise. The success of the Hedjaz railway was to prove to the outside world that, given an impelling force, the Turks were capable on their own initiative of carrying out a successful enterprise entirely free from graft. In spite of the enormous difficulties encountered by the climate, the terrain and the raids of marauding Bedouins, work proceeded so smoothly and efficiently that only eight years after the sultan had launched his first appeal for funds the railway had already reached the outskirts of Medina."

Osman Ferid worked tirelessly, riding across the length of the desert encouraging, cajoling, and even bribing tribal and

Bedouin chieftains to join him in this huge venture. Surveillance patrols kept a twenty-four hour vigilant watch along the lines to ensure work could proceed safely. Even so, skirmishes continued: one day, as he was riding back to camp, Osman Ferid's horse was shot and fell under him. He leapt on an aide's horse, galloping after the attackers, shooting wildly to disperse the group and chasing them until he captured three Bedouins.

In 1899 Nefiset gave birth to their sixth son, Bekir, who was followed in subsequent years by four girls, Saadet, Habibe, Safiye and Zübeyde. Nefiset was exceptionally well organized, with ten children, along with servants and nannies to supervise and a large household to run. She personally attended to her husband's every need and found time to enjoy an hour or so each day in the garden. With each birth she seemed to gain confidence and inner strength; she grew with each of her children, while Osman Ferid relived his lost childhood. He was the axis of her life. They enjoyed picnics at the farm where the children learned to ride at the early age of three. The boys were taught to shoot and fence by their father; the girls filled baskets with fruit and vegetables and planted trees under their mother's diligent eye, while the babies slept in the arms of their nannies under the shade of the fruit trees. At the end of the day the Shapli family with their sleeping babies and exhausted children piled into carriages between the fruits and vegetable baskets for the homeward journey.

Nefiset was content within the limitations of a deeply Muslim society; she valued those private moments of love and intimacy with her family. Her mother had been especially lively and entertaining. Habibet Hanım's harem had been happy, full of laughter. Nefiset, although less gregarious, entertained her family by reading in Turkish and Arabic or performing hilarious impersonations of her husband and his sober friends with great gusto.

Osman Ferid shared his workload with Nefiset, for he trusted her judgment, knowledge and refreshing approach.

His evenings began with a visit to the nursery, taking over the role of their grandfather. He told the children stories of Shamil, of their grandfather and the Caucasus.

"Pasha Baba, one more please about the wild Cossacks or Narts," they would beg, until he answered:

"Enough of your noise, you little Moscovites; it's time for bed," as he kissed each child good night.

On formal occasions and religious holidays, the boys were called to the selamlık dressed in specially designed Ottoman military uniforms. They were taught to shake, rather than kiss hands. Years later, in Istanbul, when a child kissed Nefiset's hand, she would clasp their hands in hers and kiss the child's cheeks.

One evening, Osman Ferid was cleaning his pistol in the lower garden for target practice. As he took aim a cat walked into sight and fell. At that moment, Nefiset appeared.

"You have shot a cat!"

He was about to say it was an accident, but his wife was angry and upset.

"How could you be so cruel? It could have been one of my cats. Pasham you have killed many men to defend yourself and your country. You do not have to defend yourself against animals, especially a cat; you should protect them, not shoot them."

His darling Nefiset was quite capable of showing her displeasure and putting her husband in his place. That evening when the servant announced that *Hanimefendi* (my lady) would dine with the children, he knew he had not been forgiven.

The cat was buried in the garden. Nefiset remained in the nursery. Whenever he came to say good night to the children, their mother would tell them to love and protect animals. Baskets of flowers and fruits did not help. Three days later Osman Ferid, full of regrets, had an idea. He ordered his aide to find the prettiest cat in Medina. It arrived in a basket, a heavenly ball of white fluff guaranteed to soften the steeliest of hearts. That evening Osman Ferid, wearing a sheepish expression, presented the basket to his wife in front of the children. He was forgiven amongst squeals of delight.

Turkish soldiers in far outposts in the empire served for years without pay or recall. Osman Ferid had initiated a system of discharge for the soldiers who had completed ten to fifteen years of service. The first detachment of two dozen left to join the camel train to Damascus. Within a few days, news of a bloody massacre by a Bedouin tribe reached Medina. The Bedouins had attacked the unarmed men for loot. When they found nothing they had ripped open their stomachs looking for gold.

Osman Ferid was beside himself with rage. It was a brutal and defiant insult against his authority and troops. He led a large force into the desert, pursuing the attackers for days, spending nights at oases and gathering information against those who had committed these atrocities. On the tenth day, they sighted the tribe at a wateringhole. After a fierce skirmish they captured five leaders and many Bedouins.

The trial was held in the public square in Medina. Osman Ferid, with military and Turkish officials, sat in judgment. He showed no sign of mercy; the murders had appalled him. He held the leaders responsible and sentenced them to death by public execution. Their severed heads were placed on spikes on iron railings in the square.

[This incident was watched from a small window at the top of the barracks by my father, Hamza Osman Erkan, Osman Ferid's son, who was eight at the time. He often told us how frightened he had been and how he would never forget the horror of what he had seen.]

In 1904, Ibn Saud defeated a combined Rashidi and Turkish force of eight regular battalions at the Battle of Bukairiya. The

Turkish government withdrew all its troops from Central Arabia. Ibn Rashid continued the struggle alone, but was killed in 1906, leaving Ibn Saud the undisputed leader of Arabia, except for the Jabal Shammar, fief of the Rashidis and the Turkish provinces of Al Hasa, Hejaz and Yemen. Encouraged by Saudi victories, the tribes in Yemen and Jeddah began a revolt in 1906. The Ottoman governor in Yemen approached Osman Ferid for assistance and it was decided to meet in Jeddah. Osman Ferid was against military force.

"Either way we have little to gain. If we are successful, so much blood will be shed that any future reconciliation will be out of question. If we are defeated it will be the end of Ottoman rule in Arabia." Osman Ferid was a unifying force in the region, a person whose name evoked consensus and reconciliation in a country of unrest.

Finally after hours of discussion it was decided to invite the sheikhs to a peace conference. Invitations were stamped with the seal of the Sheikh-ul-Haram of Medina. Mahmut Nedim Pasha, the last governor of Yemen wrote in his memoirs, *Arabistanda Osmanlı İmparatorluğu Nasıl Yıkıldı?* (The Fall of Ottoman Rule in Arabia):

"I consulted with His Excellency, Osman Ferid, commander of Medina concerning the situation of the Bedouin rebels. He agreed on a peaceful approach without unnecessary bloodshed. He then suggested we send news to the desert to call in the Arab sheikhs. Strange are the customs and state of mind of these desert people; those brutal sheikhs began to arrive peacefully like cats out of the desert the next day. One name was enough, one name the Bedouin trusts, respects and fears. When that name sounded, the desert yielded and was silent. That name was Osman Ferid Pasha – the Commander.

"The sheikhs respected and trusted the Pasha; they knelt in his presence and kissed his knee. Osman Ferid understood the power of traditional councils. He addressed them with authority, emphasizing that rebellions were unacceptable and against the rule of the Sultan and Caliph. Hours of diplomatic discussions resulted in a begrudging show of loyalty and allegiance, sworn on the Quran, to the caliph and his representative in Medina. Prisoners were exchanged and the sheikhs returned to their tribes. This meeting, presided over by the presence and personality of Osman Ferid Pasha, prevented a worsening of the situation and the subversive activities of the British Consulate in Yemen.

"A year later, I spoke to Hakkı Pasha about the critical situation in Arabia. He was desperate. I said mark my words, Pasha, you can do but one thing, there is only one solution. Somehow you have to arrange for Osman Ferid to come from Medina. Osman Pasha had a great and much respected reputation in the whole of south Arabia. For it was a fact that the pasha's power and respect in the year 1900 was as much as the Saudi Kings today."

CHAPTER 15

Retirement and Exile

Educational reforms encouraged by Abdülhamid had established public schools, universities, military and religious schools, which in time gave rise to a new intelligentsia, an educated middle class. This new educated class blamed the Tanzimat reforms for the deterioration of the empire and sought to reassert the principles of Ottomanism. Lord Palmerston, British politician and ambassador, had called the reforms "a grand stroke of policy" for having opened the doors of the Islamic state to Christian Ottomans within the empire, at the same time attracting an influx of foreigners eager to reap financial benefits from foreign concessionaires.

In 1875, the Porte was declared bankrupt. At her death in 1880 a royal princess left the empire with a debt of 16,000 gold liras. The widening gap between the lifestyle of Christians and Muslims subjects was not merely financial, but social as well. Pera had been transformed into a modern, cosmopolitan area, favourably comparing with the capitals of Europe, Paris and Vienna, while the old city remained neglected and dangerous without electricity, its dark, dimly-lit winding streets and wooden houses torched by frequent fires, their occupants oppressed and angry.

The Ottoman Empire had lost Bulgaria, Bosnia-Herzegovina

and Crete. The Committee of Union and Progress, (C. U. P) had risen from the embers of the exiled Young Turk movement in Salonica (which had set the seeds for constitutional monarchy, opposing the sultan's absolute rule and attacking Tanzimat reforms as an erosion of Islamic values).

Having suspended the first Ottoman parliament in 1878, Sultan Abdülhamid reigned supreme until 1908. He excelled at the art of political chess, playing one nation against another for his own benefit. In many ways a period of controlled progress, it was overshadowed by political frustration and unrest that affected both Muslim and non-Muslim subjects within the empire and the international communities as well. Concerned for the plight of non-Muslim communities in the Balkans, foreign powers demanded further reforms; these mandatory demands angered Abdülhamid. Irritated by the continual interference of the European powers, the sultan decided to turn his attention to the Middle East. With the ultimate power as Caliph of All Islam, the sultan chose to support the cause of Islam against Christian intervention in the Middle East by encouraging the pan-Islamic movement. Uprisings occurred in Mesopotamia and Yemen.

In 1908, military disturbances spread through the Third Army Corps in Macedonia. Empowered with funds, arms and troops, two young Turkish majors, Enver Bey and Niyazi Bey, followers of the Committee of Union and Progress Party, demanded a revival of the constitution of 1876. In *The Ottoman* Lord Kinross wrote:

"On December 17, Sultan Abdülhamid drove through the streets, a bent, huddled figure in an overcoat, with an ashen complexion, to open the new Turkish Parliament, convened in its original meeting place, the Foundation of Learning, on the site of the old Byzantine Senate House."

On April 13, 1908, a counterrevolution by the First Army Corps in Istanbul, supported by a large crowd of religious extremists, crowded into the square in front of the Chamber of

Deputies crying 'Down with the Constitution, Down with the Committee!' but it was to be short-lived.

The army of liberation, the Third Army, marched through the streets of Istanbul restoring calm and order. Political power lay in the hands of the Committee of Union and Progress backed by the military power of Mahmut Şevket Pasha, the commander of the Third Army in Thessalonica (Mustafa Kemal, later President and Father of the Turkish Republic, served as his chief of staff). Şevket Pasha proclaimed a state of siege and enforced martial law for two years. As the old regime collapsed, there was a breakdown in law and order and the C. U. P, without any experience in the rule of law, took control of the country.

Joan Haslip in her book, *The Sultan* writes:

"On Sunday, April 25, the Sheikh ul Islam gave his answer to the fateful question, 'If an Imam of the Muslims appropriates public monies; if after killing, imprisoning and exiling his subjects unjustly, he swears to amend his ways and then perjures himself.... if he causes civil war and bloodshed amongst his own people; if it is shown that his country will gain peace by his removal, and if it is considered by those who have power, that this Imam should abdicate or be deposed, is it lawful that one of these alternatives should be adopted?

"In his white gold robes and yellow turban, the Sheikh ul Islam, representing the highest dignity of the Mohommedan faith, was called upon to depose Sultan Abdülhamid. Aware that he himself was as much in the power of the Committee as the sultan, he answered:

'It is permissible'"

Sultan Abdülhamid, absolute ruler for decades, was deposed in favour of his younger brother, Crown Prince Reşat Efendi, who was girded with the historic sabre and proclaimed Sultan Reşat, Mehmed V, Caliph of All Islam.

On May 12, 1909, Osman Ferid, General, Sheikh–ul-Haram of Medina, received a telegraph confirming his retirement, after 45 years of active service in the Ottoman Army. He was 65 years old and had served 22 years of his military career in Arabia. They had been stimulating, active but strenuous years; he had survived disappointment, overcome challenges and achieved many of his goals and now it was time to enjoy his family, return to Istanbul, close to his brothers and friends. The wording of the telegraph had not surprised him; he had expected it for weeks. Waving the telegraph with a smile at his aide-de-camps, he set off to find Nefiset.

For the first time in the history of the Ottoman Empire, the oath of loyalty to the Sultan and Caliph included an oath of allegiance to the Union and Progress Party. Telegrams were sent to Ottoman subjects in command positions throughout the empire. When he received the telegraph, Osman Ferid read it carefully; the implication was clear. It stated that refusal to take the oath meant at best retirement, at worst a dishonourable discharge.

Osman Ferid's reply was polite and honest. He would be honoured to swear an oath of loyalty to Sultan Reşat Mehmed V, to serve him as a faithful servant, an officer of the Ottoman army and Sheikh–ul-Haram under the Caliph of all Islam, but it was against his principles, as an officer in the Ottoman Army, to swear an oath of allegiance to any political party.

Osman Ferid belonged to a generation that upheld the concept of Ottomanism; they saw themselves as Ottoman citizens in the service of the Sultan of the Ottoman Empire and Caliph of all Islam. He had never thought of himself as a Turk, nor had he supported the national movement or Turkish state. He was an officer in the Ottoman army. The military forces remained above politics.

Now that Nefiset's parents had died, there was no longer any reason to remain in Medina. Preparations for the journey to Istanbul began in earnest. The house was closed; the farm and stables left in the capable hands of their Bedouin farm manager and trusted friend.

Their personal belongings, boxes upon boxes of gifts and precious heirlooms Nefiset chose to keep, were packed with care. The residence was a beehive of activity; Arabs, Turks, Bedouins and foreigners from all over the Hejaz called to pay their respects and wish Osman Ferid farewell. Many expressed concern for the prospect of peace and stability after his departure. An old friend, a Shammer sheikh, as he opened his arms to envelope him in a farewell embrace whispered in his ear, "Beware of desert rats."

The new commander of the Medina garrison held a farewell ceremony in the pasha's honour. In front of a large audience, a military band played Ottoman and Arab marches as Osman Ferid reviewed the parade of troops for the last time. By the end of the month, the Shapli family was ready for their journey to Yanbu.

Osman Ferid's last act as Sheikh-ul-Haram was to pray at the Prophet's Tomb and Mosque.

Trains had not begun to operate on the Hejaz railway so they were obliged to join the camel train at the Bab-i Ambariah Gate. Osman Ferid, his family, a large military escort, and a mile long string of camels carrying their heavy loads, began the tedious trek through the desert. At night they rested near the cool waters of an oasis, shaded with palm trees; soldiers squatted around the campfire while the caravan protectors prepared the meal, watered and fed the animals.

On the third day, a scout reported large bands of Bedouins riding towards them from behind the sand hills. Osman Ferid halted the camel train. Having heeded the advice of his friend, Osman Ferid was prepared for an attack. With Hood Lala standing on guard, the younger children jumped into empty chests brought specially for the purpose. Troops were issued with Winchester repeating carbines with seven shot cartridge magazines far superior to the single muzzle loading muskets or breach loaders used by Bedouins. They were ordered to aim at every third man at regular intervals, a deadly strategy against chaotic, frenzied desert attacks.

Osman Ferid handed guns to his sons, including Hamza Osman, aged 12,

"At your age I fought side by side with my father; now it is your turn to fight by my side. Keep close to this officer."

Nefiset, having taken out her gun and kinjal, kept close to her officer as she took up her position.

The Bedouins circled the caravan at a distance and then began to move in closer and closer, screaming and shouting as they galloped, causing sand storms of dust. Osman Ferid waited for the belligerent, aggressive hordes to get close enough before giving the signal.

The surprise attack of the Turkish troops unnerved the Bedouin onslaught; still they fought in chaotic circles against the fierce charge until dusk, when, energy spent, they galloped off leaving their dead sprawled in the sand. The rest of the journey passed peacefully. At Yanbu, Osman Ferid thanked and saluted his military escort as they boarded the ship to sail to Istanbul.

Osman Ferid had asked his brother, Mehmet, to buy an appropriate residence on his behalf for his family. Mehmet chose a delightful, white yalı on the Asiatic shore of the Bosphorus in the Şemsi Paşa district of Scutari, (Uskudar) in a large tree-shaded garden, which led down to a private quay and boathouse which housed an elegant pasha caique, a gift from his sister-in-law.

"The caique is the essence of the joy of the Bosphorus," wrote Abdülhak Şinasi Hisar.

The Shapli family were charmed by their new home sandwiched between the green, wooded hills and winding Bosphorus, its turquoise water lapping against the quay and the refreshing, crisp breeze from the Black Sea. After years in the dry, hot desert, it was a dream house for Nefiset and the children. The boys enrolled at the French Lycée; the girls were taught by governesses at home.

Osman Ferid welcomed a constant stream of visitors, while

Nefiset trained her new household and worked in the garden. His brothers called every day, often staying for jolly family dinners.

Osman Ferid was content, pleased to have resigned from official duties after so many years and able to spend his days with his family, brothers and friends in a beautiful yalı in Istanbul. He looked back over his life with satisfaction, a successful, fulfilling military career, a happy marriage in which he had fathered ten children and thanked Allah and Thae. He was proud of his brothers' achievements; they too had surpassed their youthful aspirations, had led interesting, productive careers in the army, surviving the bizarre atmosphere at the Ottoman court, the turmoil of Abdülaziz' reign and the intrigues at Yıldız Palace. During Sultan Abdülhamid's reign, Colonel Ismael, the youngest brother, had been exiled to Aleppo in Syria where his nephew, Osman Ferid's son, Kazım, was governor. Ahmet Pasha, Cavalry Commander at Selimiye, had taken early retirement. Field Marshal Mehmet Pasha retired after the death of his second wife, Esma Sultan, to care for his two children in a graceful mansion at Ortaköy. Zissi, as lively as ever, was overjoyed with her brother's happy family and retirement. Whenever she and her husband, a retired colonel, came to Istanbul to visit their sons at the military academy, they stayed in a private quarter at the yalı that Nefiset had prepared for them. "This is your home in Istanbul with us."

Mehmet, twice royal damat, (son-in-law), higher in military rank than his elder brother, accorded Osman Ferid the traditional Circassian respect to an elder brother by standing with his brothers until Osman Ferid sat. They had aged well, were still active, healthy and good-looking. Osman Ferid suffered from diabetes, but Nefiset's splendid but strict care, a healthy diet and enforced rest kept it under control. After supper, she poured tea from her mother's magnificent Russian Samovar while servants passed around black, sweet coffee with baklava, dates and desserts from Arabia.

Years of hardship, exile, success and failure, love, sorrow and death had not dampened the spontaneous pleasure the Shapli family enjoyed as they gathered in the privacy of their home. Mehmet, Ahmed and Zissi needed no persuasion to jump into a Circassian dance; Nefiset's impersonations of the family, Arab friends or Osman Ferid sheepishly speaking English or French, sent them into peels of laughter. Ismail, in his quiet, elegant manner told of his adventures in Syria and Iraq, and throughout the Middle East, where, thanks to his influential, young nephew, he was able to travel and enjoy his exile. In Baghdad, he had stayed with Mehmed Fazıl Daghestanli, Nefiset's uncle and Osman Ferid's dear friend.

In *The Near East from Within* the anonymous author writes:

"Life in Turkey is always interesting, even in its moments of supreme idleness. One finds continually something to see and something to observe or to admire, and to any student of human nature it affords sources of enjoyment such as he meets nowhere else in the world. For one thing it is so totally different from what one sees generally...

"...I left Istanbul for a considerable time returned again for a few months stay in the latter half of 1908 and the opening months of the following year and after another long interval found myself for the third time entrusted with a mission to Stamboul during 1913 in the closing days of the Balkan wars. To my astonishment Turkey was a changed country.

" ...A certain spirit of independence had replaced the abject submission prevalent during the reign of Abdülhamid..... varying political parties had sprung into existence and were struggling for notoriety and predominance, a certain freedom of thought had established itself.

"...It is undeniable that, in a powerful degree, this rejuvenation was due to the exertions of the Young Turk party and especially to the personality of Ender Bey (more recently a Pasha)."

Osman Ferid found himself in a similar position. Since he had left Istanbul for Arabia, most of his correspondence had been official telegraphs concerning military or religious orders, financial or security problems, and supervision of the rail works constructed through the desert; his own writing was about his efforts to suppress skirmishes, ensure peaceful and friendly relations with the sheiks of the Hejaz or minister to the Holy Prophet's Tomb and Mosque. Except for hearsay from guests and visitors, who used caution when conversing with the Sheikh-ul-Haram, he had been unaware of the political and social changes and the growing discontent that had spread throughout Turkey.

One hot, day in August of the same year, a servant announced two officers at the gate requesting to see the pasha. They introduced themselves as officers from the investigation committee of the Union and Progress Party, sent to accompany Osman Ferid to the military headquarters. It seemed a strange request, but Osman Ferid consented with good grace. As they drove in the carriage the officers informed him that he had been summoned for questioning. He was surprised.

"Questioning" he asked, "whatever for and by whom?"

They walked up the wide stairs, through corridors into a large room where he was asked to wait. A colonel, followed by six officers, entered the room. They introduced themselves and invited him to sit. He was asked to identify himself. He answered in an authoritative voice.

"First Ferik, Sheikh–ul-Haram Osman Ferid, retired Pasha of the Imperial Ottoman Army, former Commander of Medina and the Hejaz."

The colonel studied the notes in front of him.

"Osman Ferid Pasha, we represent the first investigation committee of the Union and Progress Party. Your name is mentioned in a report presented to the committee by Sheikh Sayyed Adbulkader. He states that as a prominent sheikh in the Hejaz,

he was unjustly persecuted when you were commander of the
Medina Barracks. He accuses you of abusing your power and
position to gain favour with the sultan.

"He says he was victimised and pronounced guilty by Sultan
Abdülhamid on the strength of your accusations. We are here to
investigate every case of persecution brought against the
deposed sultan. Sheikh Sayyed Abdulkader has claimed indem-
nity against his unjust prosecution and charges you with slander. What do you have to say?"

Osman Ferid was quite unprepared for the shocking accusations thrown at him in such a curt manner, but he made no out-
ward sign. After a few minutes of silence, looking at the faces of
officers in front of him and choosing his words with great care,
he related the incident as it happened, how he with his trusted
officers had searched and found confirmation of subversive
activities and receipts for payments of large sums of money
from foreign sources.

He had presented a formal report with the incriminating
documents in person to Sultan Abdülhamid. Osman Ferid was
informed the sultan intended to deal with the matter himself.
Since then he had heard nothing of the case except that Sheikh
Sayyad Abdulkader had left the province of Hijaz. When asked
if he possessed written evidence, he shook his head. He had
handed all the documents to the sultan; it was not for him to
retain any information. The colonel and officers thanked him for
his cooperation.

That evening he told Nefiset how degrading it had been to
witness military personnel belittling their position and power,
behaving in the same suspicious manner as the old regime at
Yıldız Palace to conspire against their own officers and superiors.

Two weeks later Osman Ferid was recalled to the military
headquarters to appear before the investigation committee. The
colonel looked ill at ease as he asked Osman Ferid to sit. The
colonel did not look at him as he spoke.

"Osman Ferid Pasha, a thorough search has been made in the offices at Yıldız Palace and the Porte but no papers or documents were found to incriminate Sheikh Sayyed Abdulkader. What we did find among the sultan's papers was a *firman*, a royal decree, signed by Abdülhamid and dated a week before his deposition promoting you to field marshal. You are entitled to retire as field marshal because the firman was signed by a reigning sultan, but it will be opposed by the military court. What it does prove is that you were amongst those favoured by the sultan.

"Is that the reason you refused to sign allegiance to the Union and Progress Party?" Shaking his head in disbelief, Osman Ferid rose to his full height.

"Colonel, I have served as a loyal and faithful officer in the Ottoman Army for more than 45 years under three reigning Sultans and Caliphs of the Empire. My ancestors are simple but proud warriors from the Caucasus. I was never part of the web of intrigues and political scheming that stifled the Palace or Porte. I did not understand it then and I do not understand it today. I am a soldier. My duty was to serve and obey, and Allah knows that is what I did."

He bowed his head and walked towards the door.

"You know where to find me. Good day gentlemen."

Osman Ferid walked out of the military headquarters.

At the end of the month, Osman Ferid was tried by a military tribunal, accused of being loyal to the deposed sultan and hostile to the Union and Progress Party. He was exiled for an indefinite period to the island of Mytilene and stripped of rank and titles. The world of rules and orders he knew and understood had collapsed around him. His brothers, Field Marshal Mehmet Pasha, Ahmet Pasha and Colonel Ismail sat at the back of the court.

At the time of the trial, the grand vizier was Hüseyin Hilmi Pasha, ex -governor of Yemen in 1898, an experienced politician and intimate friend of Osman Ferid. They had met officially many times, had even discussed the activities of Sheik Sayyed Abdulkader. Osman Ferid wrote a letter appealing for his intervention against these unjust accusations, reminded him of their conversations on the subject of the sheikh in Yemen, adding his only wish was to retire in peace at Scutari. He received no reply.

One evening, the Grand Vizier's private chamberlain visited the yalı. He apologized for the late hour and the inconvenience. He had come to express Hüseyin Pasha's regrets and apologies at the decision of the military court, adding that the grand vizier himself was powerless in the hands of the Unionists. The country, said the chamberlain, was going through an evolution. Only time would heal and correct the misdeeds of justice due to misrule.

Many innocent people caught up in the evolving political and historical change of ideology taking place within the Empire suffered similar injustices. The concept of Ottomanism/Islam was giving way to Turkism and the idea of liberty, equality and justice and national sentiments

Hüseyin Hilmi Pasha was a just and proud man with an unblemished service record. As grand vizier under the Union and Progress Party, he found it impossible to remain impartial or accept the edicts being carried out. On December 28, 1909, he handed his resignation to Sultan Reşat Mehmed V and retired from politics.

Nefiset was outraged, appalled at the miscarriage of justice and the treatment accorded to her husband in his retirement. It was beyond belief to imagine that a man who had been a consistent example of unstinting duty with 45 years of loyal service to the Ottoman Empire should be condemned and exiled by a military court. The children, wondering what had happened, crept around the house in silence not to disturb their beloved Pasha Baba. Visitors, except his brothers, were politely turned away.

Every day his brothers came to sit with Osman Ferid in the garden, discussing ways and means to rescind the military decision. They wondered whether they should appeal to the Ministry of War, to a civil court, or write letters to influential friends and newspapers, but Osman Ferid simply listened, shaking his head with a weary smile until the cool, crisp Bosphorus air forced them indoors.

He tried, but was unable, to understand the reason and events that led to the predicament into which he had been drawn. His unswerving faith in the truth and loyalty of the Ottoman Army and to its officers had been swept aside with the stroke of a pen. He and his Turkish and Circassian friends had often discussed the future of the Empire and the military services. They recognized and supported the necessity for change within the government but had remained detached. "The army is above politics," they would insist in the hope that a satisfactory outcome for a more liberal constitutional monarchy be achieved. After all, he was a Circassian in the service of the Empire, a faithful practitioner of Ottomanism. His loyalty was to the "Empire, Sultan and Caliph." Not having been born a Turk, he had never felt the necessity to identify himself with nationalism and the movement for a new identity that had risen within the crumbling empire as it was being replaced by the state of Turkey and other states based on principles related to ethnic identifications. He had frequently sympathized with, and voiced his concerns to, his fellow Turkish officer friends at the dilemma and difficult choices with which they were confronted, but at no time and under no circumstances, would he have considered being involved.

Again he was driven into exile, again forced to leave his home and friends for a strange land. It was too much to bear at his age, too heavy a burden to carry, his weary heart cried more out of sadness than anger as he watched his beloved wife pack her shattered dreams neatly into trucks in preparation for the journey.

On August 30, Osman Ferid, his wife, children, three maids, a French governess and Hood Lala arrived on the island of

Mytilene to be welcomed by the governor of the island, Faik Ali Bey, the younger brother of one of Osman Ferid's closest friends. The governor had prepared a charming villa for the Shapli family in a well kept garden, within walking distance to the sea. Arif, Gazi, Hamza and Bekir attended the local school while the girls were taught by their governesses.

Mytilene, a sanjak under Ottoman rule, was the largest island in the archipelago of islands in the Aegean Sea, with a land area of 630 sq. miles. In those years the island had a small, mainly Greek, population of 50,000. Dominated by a medieval fortress, the rugged coast line protected the rich vineyards on its fertile plains. Most of the islanders were fishermen or farmers, simple, hospitable people who welcomed their illustrious guests by leaving baskets of grapes and fresh fish at the gate of the villa; later they presented the children with a small boat.

These friendly gestures slowly overcame the natural reserve of the Shapli family. After breakfast, the children, with their governess in tow, would explore the island, often lunching at one of the village cottages. On April 7, 1910, Nefiset gave birth to their last and eleventh child, a girl. Osman Ferid named her Melek (Angel). When he held her in his arms and her tiny hand grasped his finger, he smiled saying she was a gift of love and hope, born to heal their troubled life.

It saddened Osman Ferid to know his wife suffered; he knew she missed the yalı, the garden she had tended with such loving care, and the Bosphorus. She was shocked and angered by his conviction and exile. He admired her indefatigable spirit and resilience, the energy she spent for the sake of the children, and the effort she made to console him.

"How fortunate we are to have come to this lovely island. This is our first holiday by the sea ever; the children will learn how to swim and take sailing lessons."

Her husband smiled; she was so like his mother and Zissi, determined to make the best of any situation in order to keep the family safe and happy. In the afternoons they walked by the sea, grateful for the fresh air and warm Aegean sun. Nefiset delighted in the unfamiliar but welcoming culture of the Christian Greeks. Wrapped in a white gown and shawl she greeted the locals as she walked with her tall, handsome husband in civilian clothes through the village. The villagers were amused to see the Shapli family pass by their cottages on their early morning ride. Osman Ferid and his wife rode sedately, leading the boys and girls on horseback, while the youngsters clung on to their ponies under the watchful eyes of Hood Lala, who rode at the end of the crocodile line. Osman Ferid tried to control his ill-humour, joining in family outings and playing with the children in the nursery before he retired, but he was full of resentment and indignation.

Nefiset felt his need for space; she sympathized with his dilemma, knowing how much he hated disorder and irresponsibility and how he flared up with anger when confronted with injustice. She watched from her window as he walked to the edge of a cliff to sit staring out at sea for hours; although she was deeply concerned for his health, she dare not disturb him.

Throughout his long career he had distanced himself from the intrigues and politics of the Porte and Palace; now at this time in his life, to suffer the humiliation of a military court accusing him of a crime he had not committed, to be stripped of military rank and banished from his home was mortifying, unprecedented and utterly unacceptable.

One evening, the governor called with a telegraph from Süleyman Nazif, which said he was about to arrange a meeting with leading members of the party to review Osman Ferid's case. Suleyman Nazif was a highly respected newspaper editor and poet with a degree of influence among military leaders of the Union and Progress Party. He had requested Osman Ferid's brothers to attend. The governor handed the telegraph to Osman Ferid; it extended greetings to the pasha and his family with the hope, Allah permitting, of good news in the near future.

Life on the island was pleasant, with the long, hot summer days cooled by fresh breezes from the Aegean. The green olive trees on the sloping hills blended with the purple of the luscious grape vineyards spread on the flat plains. Villagers passing by would stop to enquire after the pasha's health or –if he were sitting in the garden– be invited to join him for a glass of tea or lemonade. Weeks passed; Osman Ferid's health continued to trouble him, but Nefiset was relieved to see her husband responding to the simple, quiet beauty of the island, its peaceful atmosphere and friendly people. He appeared less agitated, more relaxed, joking with the children that they should never forget this long holiday treat by the sea.

Chapter 16

Turn My Head to the Caucasus

Early one morning, a messenger from Government House arrived with a letter asking if the governor might visit that afternoon. Osman Ferid greeted Faik Ali Bey in the garden; the governor seemed quite flurried and could hardly wait for the servant to fill his glass with cool lemonade and take his leave before he took an official looking letter out of his pocket.

"Dear Pasha, good news at last. This is a special pardon signed by the Union and Progress Committee with the seal of Sultan Reşat Mehmed V, which declares the charges brought against you have been rescinded. Your honour and rank have been restored; you are a free man. I wanted to be the first to congratulate you."

"Thank God, Thank Thae, and thank you, my dear friend. I am deeply grateful and indebted to you, your brother and everyone who worked so diligently on my behalf. I shall never forget your generosity, the kindness you have shown to my family during our sojourn on the island, and now this noble act, to bring this welcomed news yourself. How can I express my appreciation?"

Osman Ferid insisted the governor stay for dinner to share the family's celebration. Nefiset wept for joy, the children and staff danced, shouting.

"Osman Ferid Pasha, çok yaşa Osman Ferid Pasha, çok yaşa Faik Ali Bey, çok yaşa Faik Ali Bey."

Dinner was a feast worthy of a king. After one year and ten months, Osman Ferid and his family returned to their yalı at Şemsi Paşa in Scutari, Istanbul.

On August 4, 1911, the Nawab, Sultan Jahan Begam arrived in Istanbul. Andrew Ryan in *The Last of the Dragomans* describes her visit:

"We had an interesting visitor in the person of the Begam of Bhopal, the fourth woman in succession to rule that state. She too had been in London for the coronation (the coronation of King George V) and took in Istanbul on her way back to India. I met her at the station and was in attendance on her much of the time during her stay. Our relations were most affable, although I never saw her face, so strictly did she veil from top to toe. She was devoted to the Caliphate as a Muslim, and equally devoted, as an Indian ruler, to the King-Emperor. She insisted that no one but the British Ambassador should present her to the sultan.

"...When I thought that I had settled everything with the master of ceremonies, she sent a message on the morning of the day to ask whether Eastern or Western etiquette was to be observed. That question was unanswerable, as the occasion was without precedent.

"...The Begam stumped me once again by asking whether she should kiss His Majesty's hand. I rapidly ascertained that this was customary for princesses of Turkish blood. I told her this, but said that she must choose for herself, remembering that she was a sovereign. We entered the presence. The Begam retained her veil. The sultan said how pleased he was to see her. She said how honoured she was to be received. The same formula was exchanged with the elder son, with the younger son and with the minister of state. It was comically monotonous, but it was at least conversation..

"...It was suggested the Begam visit with the sultan's ladies."

The Begam inquired about the whereabouts of Osman Ferid Pasha and expressed her desire to visit her old friend.

Nefiset and Zissi prepared a magnificent luncheon party, inviting his brothers and son, Kazım, with their wives. The Begam arrived in an imperial caique accompanied by two of her sons and four attendants. It was a lovely, warm afternoon; they sat in the garden and reminisced about their days in Medina. The Begam expressed the pleasure and sense of fulfilment she had experienced as the first women to visit the Prophet Muhammed's Tomb, her deep gratitude to the former sultan, Abdülhamid and the Sheikh-ul-Haram, Osman Ferid Pasha. She talked about her audience with Sultan Mehmed Reşat and her pleasure at having the opportunity to meet the Sheikh-ul-Haram's family from the Caucasus. Before her departure she graciously presented the Shapli family with valuable gifts from India.

A few days later a letter arrived from the Begam addressed to Osman Ferid Pasha.

Pera Palace Hotel
Istanbul
August 7, 1911.

My Esteemed Friend, I am obliged to you for your favour and in reply thereto write to say I am moving to the Summer Palace Hotel at Therapia and shall reside there until the 17th of this month. I shall be delighted to accept the ladies as my guests at a time convenient for them. I hope you will let me know in advance when the ladies wish to visit me.

With kindest regards, your sincere friend,
Sultan Jahan, Ruler of Bhopal

Meanwhile, in the empire there was a thirst for revenge. Even so, while struggling to solve questions of responsibility for past miscarriages of justice in the old regime, the Committee of Union and Progress introduced a series of reform bills. A commission of enquiry began to examine the contents of Yıldız Palace and a military court was established; mistakes took place, but many laws and changes were undertaken at the same time. Squads were sent to clear the streets of the roaming wild dogs attacking in packs. Vigorous action against fires in the old city was greeted with relief by the poor citizens living in wooden houses. A general plan for a drainage system was drawn and discussed. Reforms in the customs house, attempts at decentralisation and the development of the gendarme were all on the agenda.

When permission was given by the C.U.P. to form private societies and foundations, Osman Ferid and his Circassian friends established the Circassian Relief Society in Istanbul in August, 1908. Meetings were held at the yalı; funds were appropriated to educate Circassian boys and girls in Turkey and the Caucasus; sponsorship was found for cultural and relief programmes throughout the country. The group established and published *Qhuaze*, the first Circassian newspaper. When the Russian Embassy allowed travellers to visit Circassia, the Circassian Relief Society, in an effort to promote Adyghe culture and language, set up an exchange system for visiting folklore groups, teachers and students, an effort that continued with great success until the outbreak of the First World War.

The stress of the last two years, especially the humiliating ordeal of the military court, had taken a heavy toll on Osman Ferid's health; his diabetes worsened and the pain in his chest, partly due to the Russian bullet embedded close to his heart, increased. He put on a brave face and was an obedient patient for the sake of his dear wife, but much as he tried he could not rid himself of a feeling of betrayal by the establishment to which he had dedicated his life. To serve in the Ottoman Army had been the driving force of his life. He had so looked forward to his retirement with his wife and young family in Istanbul, close to his brothers and sister, but contrary to his expectations, the joy and pleasure of his retirement had been scarred; crushed, he had lost the will to overcome this last ordeal.

By June he was confined to bed with swelling in his right foot. Nefiset personally attended to her husband's needs. She cooked his food, prepared his medicine, washed and bathed him. Each morning, she cut fresh flowers from the garden for his room, brought the daily newspapers, changed his books and checked his writing material. He continued to write articles for newspapers and magazines, which were published in Istanbul, Egypt and Arabia. He wrote articles on travel, especially in Arabia, encouraging Muslims to make the pilgrimage to Medina and Mecca now that the Hejaz railway ran scheduled trains during the month of Ramadan. He also wrote and published poetry.

His large room was sunny and welcoming, with chairs arranged around his bedside to seat the constant flow of visitors and well-wishers, retired officers, old Caucasian friends, many of whom he hardly knew but had met on his travels After the children bade goodnight to their father, Nefiset and her husband would eat their supper on trays in his room; his brothers often came to share these quiet, intimate evenings.

He wrote a letter to each of his children, to his brothers, to Zissi, and to his wife, arranged his private papers and financial accounts, instructing Hood Lala to keep them safe until his death. He did not fear death, but hated the thought of a long, drawn-out illness. Alone, even for a moment, he would attempt to lift himself, but the slightest exertion left him breathless and in pain.

Soon visitors, other than the family, were forbidden. Nefiset moved into his room and a few days later he fell into a coma. The house was silent, heavy with grief; the blinds drawn to keep out the sun's rays. Nefiset moved like a ghost, preparing trays he did not eat, arranging fresh flowers he did not see on his bedside table. Zissi stayed at the yalı caring for the children while her brothers did their utmost to ease Nefiset's burden. On the fifth day of the coma, Şamil, his elder son was sitting next to his bed when he saw his father's eyes flutter and open.

"Pasha Baba, how do you feel, Sir?'

Osman Ferid nodded, in a weak voice asked, 'Nefiset?'

She walked to his side and sat on her chair.

"I am here Pasham, at your side."

Osman Ferid smiled as she held his hand, in a whisper,

"Thank you, my love. May Allah, may Thae, bless you and the children."

Osman Ferid closed his eyes; silent tears ran unheeded down Nefiset's cheeks as she held his hand for what seemed an eternity to young Shamil. Slowly Osman Ferid raised Nefiset's hand to his lips and uttered his last words,

"My love, turn my head to the Caucasus."

With his head turned to the Caucasus, Osman Ferid died peacefully on July 19, 1912, at the age of 68.

EPILOGUE

–by Joan Kim Erkan

Osman Ferid was buried at Eyub Sultan ceremony. His tomb stands high on the highest hilltop overlooking the curving waters of the Golden Horn. Several months after his death, Kazım Pasha, Osman Ferid's elder son, invited Nefiset and her family to join him at Geneva, Switzerland. They lived in a charming villa named Chalet d'ermitage; the boys attended college and the girls studied at the Institude de Jeune Filles.

On November 11, 1914, the Ottoman Empire entered the World War I.

Gazi, aged 18, Hamza Osman, 17, and Arif returned to Istanbul as volunteers to fight against Russia on the Caucasian front, but were sent to fight in the southern theatre in Mesopotamia. They fought in the battle of Shaiba in Iraq in April 1915. Gazi and Arif were wounded; Gazi and Hamza Osman were decorated.

At the end of the war Nefiset and her family returned to Istanbul. The yalı at Scutari had burned in a fire during the war, so they settled at the Beşiktaş Konak. Of the eleven children, only four married: Hamza Osman, Bekir, Saadet and Zübeyde.

Nefiset lived with her unmarried children, Şamil, Bereket, Gazi, Arif, Habibe, Safiye and Melek at the Besiktaş Konak until she died on November 2, 1950 at the age of 77. She was buried next to her husband at Eyub Sultan cemetery. She suffered the deaths of three of her children: Melek died at twenty of tuberculosis, Arif and Gazi from wounds suffered in World War I.

After watching a gymnastic display 'Idman Müsameresi'at the Tepebaşi Theatre Osman Ferid's children, Hüseyin Bereket and Mehmet Shamil, along with twenty four young sportsmen, founded the Beşiktaş Bereket Gymnastic Club at the Beşiktaş Konak at Serencebey. This club later became the Beşiktaş Football Club. Meetings were arranged, and trees cut in the garden, much to the gardener's dismay, to install equipment for fencing, wrestling, boxing, gymnastics and other sports. Shamil was elected president while Bereket was general secretary. They decided the colour of the club should be red and white, the colour of the national flag. At that time, gatherings especially of young men were frowned upon by the government. The club was fortunate in that two of its founding members were the sons of Osman Ferid Pasha, Guardian of the Holy Shrine of Medina and General of the Imperial Ottoman Army, a distinguished family above reproach.

The Beşiktaş konak was sold in 1970.

Hamza Osman Erkan spent two years as a trainee banker at the Ottoman bank in Paris before returning to work for the bank in Istanbul. In 1929, he became General Director of Iş Bankası, a Turkish bank, first at Mersin then Afyon. He served as Afyon Member of Parliament in the Cumhuriyet Party until 1950. Later he joined Adnan Menderes' Democrat Party as Member of Parliament from Adapazaar, an Anatolian town with a large Circassian population. His fate was similar to that of his father. Although innocent of any misdoings, he, along with Members of Parliament from the Democrat Party, were imprisoned during the 1960 military coup. He was sentenced to five years imprisonment at Kayseri prison in Anatolia and released after three years for reasons of health. He married Melek Çiftçi, the daughter of a wealthy landowner from Aydın and had four children Aydın Osman, Guneş, Osman and Akın. His brother-in-law was General Kazım Karabekir. Akın Erkan died in 1980, Osman Erkan in 2009. The author, Aydın Osman Erkan, died in 1998.

Bibliography

Aracı Emre, *Istanbul to London music text*, Kalan Müzik Yapım Ltd Şti, Istanbul, 2005.

Bell James Stanıslaus, *Residence in Circassia*, vol 1, Edward Moxon, London 1840

Blanche Lesley, *Sabres of Paradise*, Butler & Butler Ltd, London, 1960.

Chenciner Robert, *Dagestan, Tradition & Survival*, Curzon Press, 1997.

Dagistanlı Hadduc Fazil, *Bir Kahramanın Hayatı*, Doğan Kardeş Istanbul, 1969.

Erkan Hamza Osman, *Bir Avuç Kahraman*, İnkilap Kitabevı, Istanbul, 1946

Freely John, *Istanbul*, Penguin Books, London, 1996.

Gammer Moshe, *Muslim Resistance to the Tsar*, Frank Cass & Co Ltd, London, 1994.

Göztepe Tarik Mümtaz, *İmam Şamil Dağıstan Aslanı*, Gün Basımevı, Istanbul,1950

Haslip Joan, *The Sultan, The Life of Abdulhamid*, The History Book Club, London, 1958.

Jahan Sultan, *The Nawab Begam, Ruler of Bhopal, Story of a Pilgrimage to Hicaz*, Thacker, Spink and Co, Calcutta 1909.

Kelly Laurence, *Lermontov, Tragedy in the Caucasus*, Robin Clark, London, 1983.

Kinross Lord, *The Ottoman Centuries*, Morrow Quill, New York, 1977.

Latimer Elizabeth Wormeley, *Russia and Turkey in the 19th century*, A.C. McClurg Chicago, USA, 1903

Mansel Philip, *Constantinople*, John Murray, London, 1991.

Maclean Fitzroy, *To Caucasus, the End of the Earth*, Jonathan Cape, London, 1976.

Norwich John Julius, *The Middle Sea, A History of the Mediterranean*, Vintage Press, London, 2007.

Pears Sir Edwin, *Forty Years in Constantinople*, Herbert Jenkins Ltd, London, 1916

Rasim Rushdi, *Tragedy of a Nation, the Commercial Press, Jerusalem*,1939.

Ryan Sir Andrew, *The Last of the Dragomans*, Hazell Watson & Viney Ltd for Geoffrey Bles Ltd, London, 1951.

Presenting an Image, from the Royal Collection, Merrell Holberton, London, 1995.

Smith Sebastian, *Allah's Mountains*, I. B. Tauris, London, 1998.

Strang Lord, *Britain in World Affairs, Faber and Faber Ltd, London, 1961*

Şhaplı Zubeydet, Abrek, Kuzey Kafkasyalılar Kültür ve Yardım Derneği Yayını Istanbul, 1977

The Near East from Within, author's name undisclosed, Cassell and Company Ltd, London, 1915

Journals, Encyclopedia, Papers, Documents from historical archives,

Illustrated London News, July, 1867.

Ibrahim Alaettin, *Türk Meşhurari (Turkish 'Who's Who')*, Istanbul, 1941.

Ibrahim Alaettin, *Meşhur Adamlar (Famous People)*, Istanbul, 1933-35

Berzag Sefer, *Gurbetteki Kafkasya'dan Belgeler (Documents from a Circassian in Excile)*, Ankara, 1985.

Iskit Server, *R Mufassal Osmanli Tarihi (Comprehensive Ottoman History) vol 6*, Istanbul.

Larousse (Meydan) Ansiklopedisi (Encyclopedia) vol 9, Istanbul, 1985.

Mümtaz Semih, *Evvel Zaman İçinde Arabistan (Once upon a time in Arabia)*, Tarih Kitapları Serisi, S. Hilmi Kitabevi, Istanbul, !948.

Nedim, Mahmud Paşa, (Last Ottoman Governor of Yeman) *Arabistanda Osmanli İmparatorluğu Nasıldı? (The Fall of Ottoman Rule in Arabia)*, Tarih Kitaplari Serisi, Istanbul, 1935.

Qhuaze, *Circassian Newspaper no 42, Istanbul, August 8*, 1912, .

Salname-i Deveti Aliye, *(Grand Imperial Registry of State) Istanbul*, 1905.

S. N. Yıldız'dan Ordu Köşküne (Yıldız Army Kösk) Milliyet Daily, serial no, 59, Istanbul, July 16, 1933.

Tahsin Pasha, *Yıldız ve Meşrutiyet, (Yıldız Palace and Constitutional Monarchy) Milliyet Daily, serial*, Istanbul March 26, 1931.

Orders and Decorations awarded to Osman Ferid Pasha

      1864 – Medal of Achievement

      1867 – German Cross of Merit -2nd degree

      1869 – Medjidye Order – 4th-degree

      1876 – Osmaniye Order – 4th degree

      1878 – Russo-Turkish War Medal and Medal of Merit

      1882 – Medjideye Order raised to 2nd degree

      1883 – Osmaniye Order raised to 2nd degree

      1884 – Medjidye Order raised to 1st degree

      1884 – Silver Medal of Imtiyaz (Distinction)

      1885 – Osmaniye Order raised to 1st degree

      1886 – Gold Medal of Imtiyaz (Distintion)

      1886 - Shiri-Hurshit (Lion and Sun) Gold Medal of Persia-diamond studded

      1893 – Gold Medal of Merit – Liyakat

      1901 – Grand Order of the Medjidye- diamond studded

The Shapli Family

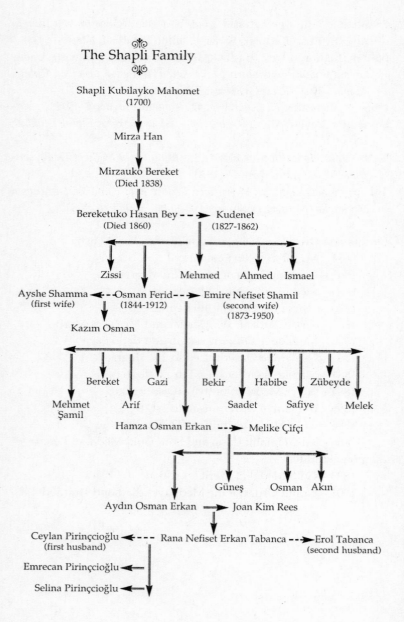

Shapli Kubilayko Mahomet
(1700)

Mirza Han

Mirzauko Bereket
(Died 1838)

Bereketuko Hasan Bey - - → Kudenet
(Died 1860)   (1827-1862)

Zissi   Mehmed   Ahmed   Ismael

Ayshe Shamma ← - -Osman Ferid - - → Emire Nefiset Shamil
(first wife)   (1844-1912)   (second wife)
                                     (1873-1950)

Kazım Osman

Bereket   Gazi   Bekir   Habibe   Zübeyde

Mehmet   Arif   Saadet   Safiye   Melek
Şamil

Hamza Osman Erkan - - → Melike Çifçi

Güneş   Osman   Akın

Aydın Osman Erkan → Joan Kim Rees

Ceylan Pirinçcioğlu ← - - - Rana Nefiset Erkan Tabanca - - → Erol Tabanca
(first husband)   (second husband)

Emrecan Pirinçcioğlu ←

Selina Pirinçcioğlu ←

The Shamil Family

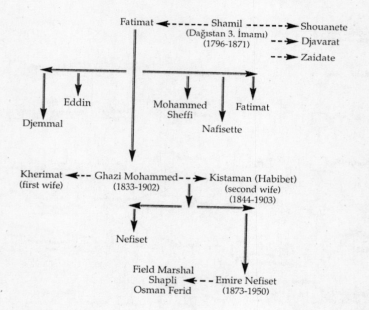

Dengau an Avar - - ➤ Bahou-Messadou

Fatimat ◄- - - - - - - Shamil - - - - - - - ➤ Shouanete
(Dağıstan 3. İmamı)   - - ➤ Djavarat
(1796-1871)   - - ➤ Zaidate

Djemmal   Eddin   Mohammed   Fatimat
                        Sheffi
                              Nafisette

Kherimat ◄- - - Ghazi Mohammed - - ➤ Kistaman (Habibet)
(first wife)   (1833-1902)   (second wife)
                              (1844-1903)

Nefiset

Field Marshal
Shapli ◄ - - Emire Nefiset
Osman Ferid   (1873-1950)

——➤ Children
- - ➤ Marriage

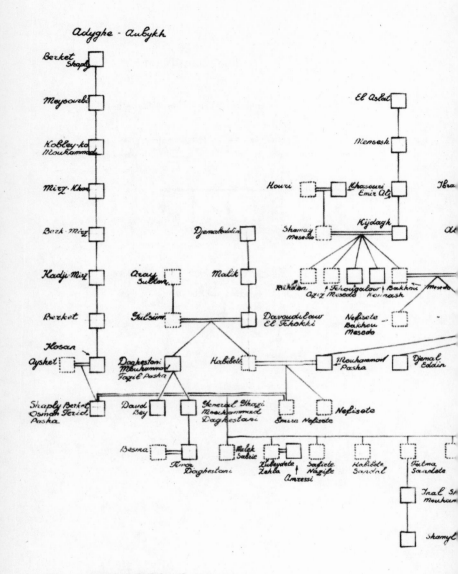

The original detailed family tree was
recently found amongst the belongings of
Osman Erkan, who dead in February 2009.

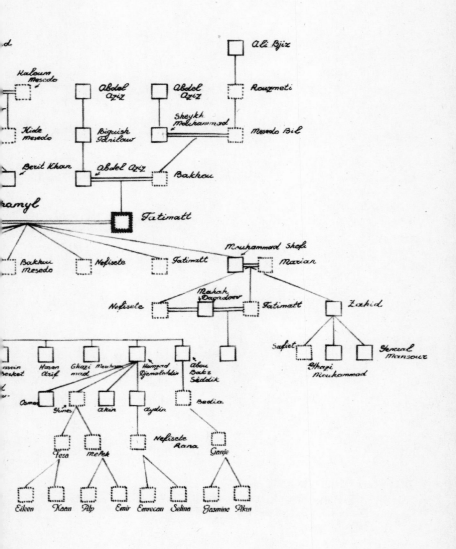